D1397884

TECHNICAL
COMMUNICATION

STRATEGY AND PROCESS

162911938

HUMBER COLLEGE
LAKESHORE CAMPUS
LEARNING RESOURCE CENTRE
3199 LAKESHORE BLVD. WEST
TORONTO, ONTARIO M8V 1K8

LILITA RODMAN

THE UNIVERSITY OF BRITISH COLUMBIA

HARCOURT BRACE JOVANOVICH, CANADA
Toronto   Montreal   Orlando   San Diego
London   Sydney   Tokyo

Copyright © 1991
Harcourt Brace Jovanovich Canada Inc.
All rights reserved

It is illegal to reproduce any portion of this book except by special arrangement with
the publishers. Reproduction of this material without authorization by any duplication
process whatsoever is a violation of copyright. Every effort has been made to
determine and locate copyright owners. In the case of any omissions, the publisher
will be pleased to make suitable acknowledgements in future editions.

Canadian Cataloguing in Publication Data

Rodman, Lilita
 Technical communication

Includes bibliographical references.
ISBN 0-7747-3135-4

1. Technical writing.   I. Title.

T11.R63 1991   808'.0666   C90-095109-5

Acquisitions Editor: Heather McWhinney
Developmental Editor: Deborah Adamczyk
Editorial Co-ordinator: Marcel Chiera
Editorial Assistant: Sandy Walker
Copy Editor: Jim Leahy
Cover and Interior Design: Landgraff Design Associates
Typesetting and Assembly: Computer Composition of Canada Inc.
Printing and Binding: John Deyell Company

⊖ This book was printed in Canada on acid-free paper.

1 2 3 4 5   95 94 93 92 91

for my mother
and
for Andris and Jānis

PREFACE

This technical writing textbook is designed to prepare Canadian students in colleges and universities for the writing requirements of entry-level positions in Canadian organizations and to provide technical writing principles to guide these students as they advance in their careers. It is informed by technical writing scholarship in Canada and the United States and by the experience of teaching technical writing in Canada since 1969. The traditional topics and assignments (definition, description, instruction, summary, job application, memo, letter, report) are placed within a context of more recent emphases such as the writing requirements of the professional, writing as a process, concern for audience and purpose, strategies for increasing readability, and the effective use of graphics.

This book is not distinguished from similar books by any single feature; rather, it is the particular combination of characteristics that distinguishes it. Its greatest strengths are the following:

- a process approach, with strong chapters on defining the task, gathering evidence, organizing, and revising.
- an approach to the writing of a formal report that includes the writing of a proposal, outline, and progress reports.
- an approach to the writing of a formal report that is integrated with the discussion of the writing process.
- examples of student work in the chapters on defining, describing a mechanism, writing about processes and procedures, summarizing, writing the formal report, and preparing the job application. These examples show the quality of work to which a student using the book can aspire. Class discussion can centre on the strengths, as well as the weaknesses, in these examples. Further examples of student work are provided in exercises.
- extensive exercises that have been tested in the classroom. Some of these are designed for collaborative work.
- strong chapters on style, on defining, and on job applications.

The book is organized into seven semi-autonomous parts whose sequence can be altered to suit the particular course, instructor, and class. In other words, I expect that instructors will choose a path through the material in the book that defines their particular course. For less experienced instructors, the Instructor's Manual suggests some proven paths.

PART ONE: INTRODUCTION

Part One begins with a general introduction to technical writing. The chapters on style and graphics, designed to be referred to throughout the course, are placed early because their principles apply to all the writing discussed in the book.

PART TWO: THE TECHNICAL WRITING PROCESS

The six chapters of Part Two present a linear, sequential discussion of what is, in fact, a recursive and individual process. Although this section can be studied on its own, it should be applied to the preparation of all documents. This section is meant in particular to be integrated with the preparation of a formal report.

PART THREE: BASIC TECHNICAL WRITING STRATEGIES

Part Three provides a traditional introduction to defining, describing a mechanism, writing about processes and procedures, and summarizing.

PART FOUR: REPORTS

Part Four provides an overview of report writing and includes an extensive chapter on gathering evidence for reports. Chapter 16, the pivotal chapter of the book, leads the student through the process of preparing a formal report. It is integrated with the chapters on the technical writing process. Instructors can, of course, apply this approach as closely as it suits their philosophy and curriculum.

PART FIVE: BUSINESS CORRESPONDENCE

Part Five is a traditional introduction to memoranda and business letters. It includes professional examples and extensive exercises that have been tested in the classroom.

PART SIX: OTHER DOCUMENTS

Part Six includes an extensive discussion of job applications and a more brief introduction to the writing of proposals. These chapters are placed together because both are concerned with the writing of persuasive offers of services or products.

PART SEVEN: TECHNICAL SPEAKING

The chapter on technical speaking focuses on how the characteristics of the oral medium have to be accommodated in oral discourses.

This book assumes that the student has access to a handbook and a dictionary and has reached the level of general writing competence usually achieved at the end of a first postsecondary course in English. The selected bibliography lists authoritative, more exhaustive treatments of topics whose full discussion is beyond the scope of this introductory text.

ACKNOWLEDGEMENTS

This book would not have been possible without the help and encouragement of many people. My sense of the writing requirements in the Canadian professional context owes much to the following friends in both the public and private sectors who discussed their writing and illustrating tasks with me and who very generously showed me documents they had prepared: Andy, Arvid, Carol, Cathy, John, Laurel, Mary, Maryette, Mike, Myrna, Reynold, Rob, Robert, Roger, Steve, and Stew. I am also grateful to my colleagues at UBC who have tested some of my materials with their classes and who encouraged me to prepare this book. The most important contribution, though, has been made by my own students, whose responses over the years have moulded both the general thrust and the details of my approach. I am particularly grateful to those students who agreed to include examples of their work in this book. I also wish to thank TobyAnn Mayes, who so conscientiously and cheerfully typed the manuscript and solved the problems of several changes in hardware and software: without her co-operation I would have been lost.

All the staff at Harcourt Brace Jovanovich have helped, but particularly, Heather McWhinney, whose enthusiasm and encouragement have been vital from the beginning of the project, and Marcel Chiera, whose patience and expertise were critical at the end. Finally, I want to thank my reviewers, whose thoughtful assessments and many useful suggestions improved the book:

Joanne Buckley
University of Western Ontario

Mary Finlay
Seneca College

John A. Gillies
University of Saskatchewan

Anne Parker
University of Manitoba

Dave Parsons
Lakehead University

Judy Z. Segal
University of Waterloo

Dixie Stockmayer
British Columbia
Institute of Technology

CONTENTS IN BRIEF

PART SEVEN: TECHNICAL SPEAKING

CONTENTS

PART TWO: THE TECHNICAL WRITING PROCESS

CHAPTER 6   ORGANIZING AND OUTLINING

CHAPTER 7   WRITING THE INITIAL DRAFT

CHAPTER 8   REVISING

CHAPTER 9   PREPARING THE PRESENTATION COPY

PART THREE: BASIC TECHNICAL WRITING STRATEGIES

CHAPTER 10   DEFINING

CHAPTER 11   DESCRIBING A MECHANISM (TECHNICAL DESCRIPTION)

CHAPTER 12   WRITING ABOUT PROCESSES AND PROCEDURES:
               INSTRUCTIONS, DESCRIPTIONS, AND EXPLANATIONS

PART FIVE: BUSINESS CORRESPONDENCE

PART SIX: OTHER DOCUMENTS

CHAPTER 22 **PROPOSALS**

PART SEVEN: TECHNICAL SPEAKING

PART ONE

INTRODUCTION

CHAPTER 1

INTRODUCTION TO TECHNICAL WRITING

INTRODUCTION

The kind of writing this book discusses has been called by a variety of names: technical, business, practical, transactional, professional. It includes a very wide range of types of documents, such as letters, résumés, memoranda, formal reports, proposals, instructions. Perhaps the most useful approach is to think of it as the kind of writing a professional does *as* a professional. In this book you will examine the kind of writing you can expect to do as an engineer, nurse, chemist, dietitian, forester, accountant, social worker, architect, museum curator, technologist, urban planner, geologist, or almost any other professional. You will not study how to write essays in college or university.

In this chapter you will be introduced to the usual writing requirements in the professions, the usual writing conditions in the professional context, the characteristics of a good document, and some special features of technical writing.

WRITING REQUIREMENTS IN THE PROFESSIONS

Good writing skills are a prerequisite to success in almost every profession. Although writing ability alone won't guarantee success, weaknesses in writing skill will normally guarantee limited advancement. In most professions you can expect to spend at least 20 percent of your time writing, and in some jobs more than 50 percent of the time is spent writing.[1] When you write as a professional, you will be writing as a member of an organization, whether this organization is your own business, a private company, a government agency, a non-profit organization, or an academic institution. You will be paid to write and paid to read, and your professional success will depend in part on how well you do both. Often the only opportunity you have to establish your professional reputation is through the documents you write. Both you and your organization are judged by them; they may be the only visible products for judging your skill in your profession.

You will probably find that writing will be part of the following professional activities:

- *Technical.* You may have to write technical specifications or explain how to solve a technical problem.
- *Business.* You may have to write persuasive documents related to getting and spending money to conduct a research project, to buy equipment, or to promote a new product.

- *Administrative.* As a member of an organization you may have to write reports to account for your activities.
- *Educational.* You may have to prepare educational materials, such as user manuals, pamphlets for the public, or handbooks for new employees.
- *Academic.* You may write articles for professional or academic publications or research reports that will become part of the literature of your discipline.

The kinds and amount of writing you do will depend on the size and type of organization you work for and on your particular role within it. The size of the organization may determine the amount of written internal communication needed. Private, public, and academic institutions may require different kinds of documents, as will the specific type of business, be it consulting, construction, production, or sales. As you change jobs, even within an organization, you can expect your writing tasks to change as well. In an entry-level position, your writing will probably be supervised quite closely, but as you advance in the organization, you can expect to supervise the writing of others and to do more administrative work.

WRITING CONDITIONS IN THE PROFESSIONAL CONTEXT

The writing conditions on the job will differ from those in college. The following are the more obvious differences you can expect:

- *Topic.* When you write as a professional, you will not be free to choose your topic, unless you are writing an article for a journal. Rather, your writing tasks will be assigned by a supervisor, or you will have to write in order to make something happen or to respond to a communication. There will always be a very specific purpose, audience, and context for writing.
- *Independence.* As a student, you are solely responsible for your work. On the job, you will seldom have the opportunity to write only as an individual. Instead, you will normally be writing as a representative of your organization or of your department. As a representative, you cannot act independently; you always have to remember how much authority you have and to whom you are accountable. In your first jobs, you probably will not be writing over your own signature but, rather, over someone else's, usually your supervisor's. Your supervisor will make the assignment and take final responsibility for it, but you will do the actual writing. It will be as though your college instructors were going to send out your assignments over their signatures. In addition to having to work with your supervisor, you will often complete documents with a team of other workers and you will have to learn to write collaboratively, to work as part of a writing team.

- *Deadlines.* Deadlines are generally firm and tight. The document is needed by a specific date; business can't wait for your convenience or inspiration. You will have to work quickly and efficiently and arrange your schedule to meet these deadlines. If the company loses a contract because your report was late, you could lose your job. One consequence of tight deadlines may be that you will seldom be able to polish a document to the same extent as you would as a student, and you will often have to settle for acceptability rather than perfection.
- *Interruptions.* You will probably have to write in your office while other work is going on around you and while your telephone is ringing.
- *Resources.* You can expect resources such as a dictating machine, a word processor, and secretarial help. You may have to learn to allow time for the secretaries to process your work.
- *Costs.* Your writing will be expensive. Not only will you be paid for your time, but so will your supervisor for the time he or she spends correcting what you have written, and the resource staff for the time they spend reprocessing your work. For this reason, the efficient writer will be valued more highly than the inefficient writer.
- *Consequences.* Your professional writing will usually have consequences, and so you will have to be much more careful than you might be in preparing student work. Your writing could lead to damage to equipment that far exceeds your annual salary, or it could offend a client and lead to ill will and loss of business, or it could even lead to litigation. On the other hand, your writing could also help to win contracts and increase your employer's profits.

CHARACTERISTICS OF A GOOD DOCUMENT

A good document must satisfy the needs of the source (the organization or department from which it originates) and the needs of the audience (the users). When we judge the quality of a document, we must consider its effect. For example, if a letter is meant to convince a client to agree to something, and the client does indeed agree, then we can conclude the letter is good, but if the client does not agree, then we will have to call the letter bad, or at least ineffective.

As a rule, a successful document has the following five qualities:

- *It is based on good research and analysis.* The quality of the writing is irrelevant if the information presented is inaccurate or unreliable. In technical writing your reader assumes that your claims are based on verifiable evidence. If you can't prove it, don't say it.
- *It is complete and concise.* The document presents all and only the information the audience needs, and it does so in as few words as are needed for clarity. To meet this goal, you must have an accurate estimate of what your audience already knows and of what it needs to know, and you must be able to make every word count.

- *It is readable.* A good document is comfortable for the intended audience to read. It is organized, and the organization is made explicit in headings and forecasting statements. The sentences are short enough to accommodate the reader, but complex enough to indicate the necessary logical relationships. Technical terms are defined where necessary. Graphics are used when they can present information more clearly and concisely than prose. Graphics are integrated with the text.
- *It observes the conventions of usage, grammar, spelling, punctuation, and form.* Although failure to observe conventions seldom interferes directly with communication, it does convey a negative social message that may very well interfere with the success of the document. A document that does not observe the above conventions may suggest that the writer – and the organization that employs the writer – is either ignorant or sloppy. Since a good professional image is critical, the effects of otherwise minor mistakes can be very serious.
- *It is attractive.* A carefully prepared document attractively presented creates an impression of care, responsibility, and professionalism.

SPECIAL FEATURES OF TECHNICAL WRITING

Because technical writing is usually done within the context of organizations, and because it is expensive to write and to read, various conventions have evolved to facilitate efficiency. The most important of these are headings, lists, and graphics. Headings break up the page, help the reader locate material, and indicate the organization of a document. Lists can make text clearer and more concise. Graphics (graphs, tables, photographs, drawings) show certain kinds of information and relationships more clearly, concisely, and emphatically than words alone can.

The format conventions for different types of documents have also evolved so that repetitive parts have become standardized. Some formats have become codified as forms. The memo form is a particularly good example, but most organizations also have a variety of other standard forms to use if the same kind of information is needed repeatedly.

NOTE
1. Lilita Rodman, "Advanced Technical Writing: The Student as Investigator," *Technostyle* 4.3 (Winter 1985): 7 – 15.

See also:

Paul V. Anderson, "What Survey Research Tells Us about Writing at Work," in *Writing in Nonacademic Settings*, ed. Lee Odell and Dixie Goswami (New York: Guildford Press, 1985), 3 – 85; Richard M. Davis, "How Important Is Technical Writing? – A Survey of the Opinions of Successful Engineers," *The Technical Writing Teacher* 4 (1977): 83 – 88. Reprinted in *Journal of Technical Writing and Communication* 8.3 (1978): 207 – 16; Harold P. Erickson, "English Skills among Technicians in Industry," *Technical Education News* 28 (Jan./Feb. 1969): 16 – 18; Jack Selzer, "The Composing Processes of an Engineer," *College Composition and Communication* 34 (1983): 178-87.

EXERCISES

1. Examine a chapter in a textbook for your most technical course. Prepare a brief oral report on how headings, lists, and graphics are used to enhance readability. What other devices are used to make the text more readable?

2. Write a memo to your instructor asking permission to enrol in this course. Explain what relevant background and skills you have, what you expect the course to be like, and why you have decided to take it. If you are uncertain about memo format, see Chapter 18 (Memoranda).

3. Prepare a brief oral report for your class on the kinds of writing you have already done as part of a job. Use the questions suggested in exercise 4 as a guide. Note to whom you submitted each document and what function the document had in the activities of the organization. Who used the document and for what purpose? What did you find most difficult about writing on the job?

4. Write a memo of 800 to 1000 words to your instructor reporting on the writing requirements in the profession you hope to enter. If you are uncertain about memo format, see Chapter 18 (Memoranda).

   To complete this assignment, you will have to find someone who has been working in your discipline for at least five years, interview that person about his or her professional writing and reading, and then report your findings to your instructor. You may also be required to give an oral report to the class.

   In your report, answer at least the following questions:

   INFORMANT INFORMATION
   - Whom did you interview?
   - What is the informant's position or job, and how long has he or she held it?
   - What education and previous work experience did your informant have?

   IMPORTANCE OF WRITING
   - What portion of working time does the informant spend writing?
   - To what extent does success in this profession depend on the ability to write well?
   - What advice does this informant have for students?

   KINDS OF WRITING
   - Which types of documents (letters, memos, manuals, proposals, reports, articles) does your informant write?
   - What is the usual length, frequency, purpose, audience of each type of document?

WRITING CONDITIONS

- How is writing initiated? Is it assigned, or can your informant decide to prepare a document?
- How much time is normally available for preparing a document?
- How firm are deadlines? Who sets them?
- How many drafts are usually needed?
- Is a word processor used?
- Is a dictaphone used?
- Is most of the writing done at work or at home?
- Is group writing done?
- Which aspects of the writing conditions does the informant find most problematic?

READING

- What kinds of documents does your informant have to read?

STYLE

INTRODUCTION

The primary aim of technical writing style is efficient communication. Good technical writing is adapted to the needs of its audience and directed to achieving the stated communication purpose. In this chapter you will examine the following qualities of technical writing:

- readability (being easy to read)
- clarity (being clear)
- conciseness (being economical with words)
- precision and specificity (being exact)

At the end of the chapter you will also review the use of four structures frequently debated in discussions of technical writing:

- the passive voice of the verb:
    The solution was heated to 45°C. (passive)
                    versus
    Joe heated the solution to 45°C. (active)
- anticipatory *it*
    It has been shown that this medication can prolong life.
- personal pronouns (*I, you, we*)
- nominalizations (comput*ation*, achieve*ment*, conclu*sion* versus compute, achieve, conclude)

Since style will concern *all* your writing, you should expect to consult this chapter throughout the course.

READABILITY

In its general sense, readability refers to how easy a text is to read. We should note, of course, that "reading" can cover a range of activities, and "easy" in this context can also have a variety of interpretations. Does "readability" refer to the time required to read a text, or to how much of it is remembered after a single reading, or to how well it is understood on first reading?

Two related questions about readability have occupied researchers and will be reviewed here:

1. How can the readability of a text be measured objectively?
2. Which features make a text more readable?

MEASURES OF READABILITY

There is no absolutely accurate and universally accepted index, or measure, of readability, but several can be used as rough measures, provided you keep in mind their limitations. Rudolf Flesch proposed what he called the reading ease index:[1]

$$RE \text{ (reading ease)} = 206.835 - 0.846wl - 1.015sl$$
$$\text{where } wl = \text{syllables per 100 words}$$
$$sl = \text{average number of}$$
$$\text{words per sentence}$$

The reading ease index is interpreted as follows:

100	very easy
50–60	fairly difficult (grade 10 to 12)
30–50	difficult (college or university)
0–30	very difficult (university graduate)

The two variables in the formula are word length (number of syllables) and sentence length, with the claim being that the shorter the words and the shorter the sentences, the easier the text is to read. All readability formulas are based on this claim, but differ in the weight they attach to the variables and the degree to which other factors are introduced.

It would be wrong, though, to conclude that simply by reducing word length and sentence length you will increase readability; although readability generally appears to correlate with shorter words and sentences, it is certainly not caused by them. Consider, for example, whether *marmalade* is three times as difficult as *jam*, or whether *quark* is easier than *television*. Shorter words tend to be easier to read because the most familiar words – the core of the common, everyday vocabulary – are the short ones, and the more unusual, technical words tend to be longer. However, provided the reader understands the word, readability is probably not affected by word length alone. What may be a very difficult passage for a nurse or forester to read may be very easy for a geologist, and vice versa.

In evaluating the effect of sentence length, we have to consider the structure of the sentence. Selzer in "What Constitutes a 'Readable' Technical Style?" notes that there is "no evidence that shortening sentences will make writing more comprehensible."[2] However, there is some evidence that clause length may be a factor because long clauses may be a burden to short-term memory. We must also remember that sometimes short sentences are less readable because they do not show the relationship between clauses and the reader must guess what that relationship is. Consider, for example, which of the following passages is easier to read:

1. Sociolinguistic studies of urban areas assume that language co-varies with socioeconomic status. This is clearly the case in highly stratified European cities such as Norwich and Berlin, and in large but compact North American cities, notably New York. It is more difficult to demonstrate in smaller Canadian cities, such as Ottawa. For such cities, again, there is a potential danger that the appearance of patterning revealed by a sociolinguistic study which builds

in very strong theoretical assumptions by taking over a methodology designed originally for a more stratified city, or for one stratified in a quite different way, may in fact be a purely coincidental product of the sampling procedure, and actually fail to reveal the real sociolinguistic patterns of the city. But even if the methodologies borrowed from highly stratified European and North American cities really can be applied to smaller Canadian cities, that still does not constitute a valid claim that they can be applied directly to rural areas in Canada. There is in fact no known basis for prestratifying a rural area such as the Ottawa Valley in advance of designing a sociolinguistically valid sampling procedure.[3]

2. Rangers are encouraged to set the culvert trap in locations where the public is less likely to see it. The rationale is that people will become frightened if a bear trap is set in close proximity to the campsite. The problem is that the bear is attracted to the campsite by the smells of cooking and garbage. It is not the trap which brings the bear. The most successful locations for the trap are those where the bear will likely be. Hiking trails leading into the park are utilized by the bear when it is attracted to the campground. Locating the trap along these trails and roadways will allow the public to see it. However, the probability of success is much greater than in more remote locations.

Both passages are difficult, but in very different ways. The first passage, which was written for specialists in the study of dialects, uses terms that you may not know (*sociolinguistic studies, co-varies, socioeconomic status,* and *stratified*) and has a rather high average sentence length (31.5 words). However, if you knew the meaning of the special terms, you would find the passage very clear because it is well organized and the relationships between ideas are indicated clearly. The second passage, which was written for an audience of park administrators, uses terms that you probably know, and its average sentence length is half that of the first passage (sixteen words). Its source of difficulty is the unclear organization and the failure to indicate relationships between ideas; it will not be clear to *any* audience.

In addition to avoiding a reading level that is too difficult for your audience, you should also avoid a level that is too easy. A reading level significantly lower than what the readers are used to could insult or bore them, and their emotional response could distract them from your message. The aim, then, must be to adjust the reading level to your audience.

CUES TO ORGANIZATION

It is obvious that a readable text must be well organized. What may be less obvious is that it must also *appear* to be well organized. The main cues that indicate organization in technical writing are headings; forecasting, transition, and summary statements; and topic sentences.

HEADINGS. Headings serve the following interrelated functions:

- *Forecast the topic* of the following section and thereby prepare the reader for it.
- *Locate topics* so the reader can skim or scan a document and see which topics are discussed and where.
- *Indicate the topical structure* by showing the hierarchical relationships among topics and subtopics. They show which topics are parallel in importance and which are subordinate, and in this way they make the organization of the document visible.

FORECASTING, TRANSITION, AND SUMMARY STATEMENTS. Forecasting statements prepare readers by helping them make a frame within which to place the material that follows. A forecasting statement such as "three factors affect how well this insulation functions" tells readers that they are about to read about these factors and that there are three of them. After they have read about two of these factors, they still expect one more; they are prepared for the structure of a part of the text. Forecasting statements should be used to introduce subheadings, to introduce lists, and to preview the structure of a long document. Transition statements indicate that one part or topic is finished, and another is about to begin. They underscore the shifts in the text. Summary statements indicate the end of a section or document and remind the reader of the main points.

You may object that these kinds of statements are inefficient because they repeat what is in the text or reiterate what you could supply yourself. The point is that these statements make explicit what the reader would otherwise have to provide, whether this be the fact that two variables are about to be discussed, that a section has ended and a new one is beginning, or what the main recommendations presented in a document are. Part of developing a good technical writing style is learning when to use these cues; overusing them may indeed annoy and even insult the reader. The length and difficulty of the document, as well as how the document will be used, will help determine how useful these devices are.

TOPIC SENTENCES. A topic sentence – usually the first sentence of a paragraph – states the main point of the paragraph. This main point is the generalization that is then explained or demonstrated in the rest of the paragraph. Topic sentences help the reader by announcing the subject of the paragraph and by providing a frame within which to place the details that follow.

LAYOUT AND TYPOGRAPHY

Layout refers to the placement of print and graphics on the page, and typography refers to the sizes and types of print. White space functions to separate blocks of print from each other and to make each block appear as a unit in the reader's mind. This separation and unification is, of course, the fundamental principle of the paragraph, which is signalled by indention and sometimes also by extra spacing. The main aspects of layout in technical writing are the following:

- *Placement of headings.* Headings are separated from text by white space, and their placement indicates which headings are parallel in importance and which are subordinate.
- *Placement of graphics.* Graphics are surrounded by white space to make them more emphatic and more readable.
- *Arrangement of lists.* Lists are a visual way of showing that points are parallel. Vertical lists are, of course, easier to read than horizontal ones. Numbering the items in a list can help the reader remember the points in the list. Because a long list may be difficult for a reader to process, you should consider breaking it into parts. Few readers are comfortable with lists of more than seven items.

Typography should complement the layout to make a readable and attractive page. The main function of typography is, of course, emphasis. The reader assumes that larger and darker letters signal more important messages and that underlining also adds importance. As a reader, you probably underline or highlight important points when you are studying. Good technical writing highlights the main points for you. However, the typographic features you can use in a document are limited by the printing resources available to you and by the conventions that govern the kind of document you are preparing. You have the least opportunity to manipulate typography in a letter, whose conventions have been most strongly influenced by the limitations of pen and ink. At the other extreme are pamphlets and advertising copy in which there are very few constraints.

COHESION

Cohesion is the linking of clauses and sentences to make a text.[4] A more cohesive document is easier to read than a less cohesive one because if the links are not explicit in the text, the reader has to supply them. The principal means of expressing cohesion are the following:

- repeated nouns
- pronouns
- transition words (conjunctions)

REPEATED NOUNS. Repeated nouns link sentences. Compare the following passages:

- I've taken several courses in geography and history and travelled in Asia and South America. Mrs. Smith used to grow cucumbers.
- I've taken several courses in geography and history and travelled in Asia and South America. The courses allowed me to understand more of what I saw.

Clearly, the second passage is more cohesive than the first, though most people can, if they try hard enough, make a link between any pair of sentences. In the first pair of sentences there is no common noun; the second pair share the noun *courses*. Often you will want to replace the common noun (*courses*) with a more abstract one (*academic preparation*) or a less abstract one (*Geography 201*). However, in technical writing, you should not use synonyms simply to vary your vocabulary; the technical audience will expect a change in term to indicate a change in meaning. The more difficult the concepts you are writing about, the more important this principle becomes.

PRONOUNS. Pronouns that refer to nouns earlier in the text serve the same function as repeated nouns. Make sure that the pronoun is not too far from the noun that is its antecedent, and make sure that there is no uncertainty about which noun is the antecedent.

TRANSITION WORDS. For a text to be cohesive, successive clauses must be related. To make these relationships explicit, and the text more cohesive and readable, you should use the appropriate transition words. The following are some of the more common transition words and phrases and the relationships they indicate:

- *addition*: and, also, as well, in addition
- *comparison*: similarly, likewise
- *example*: for example
- *explanation*: that is, in other words
- *contrast*: but, however, on the other hand, yet
- *concession*: although, even though
- *cause-effect*: if ... then, because, therefore, so

When you use transition words, make sure you use them correctly. If you don't, your writing may be cohesive, but wrong. Be particularly careful when using *because, therefore,* and *however*. When you use *because* or *therefore*, you are making a claim about causation. Consider the following example:

Next, the apparatus is plugged in <u>because</u> the solid is heated electrically in the heating block.

Does the fact that the solid is heated electrically in the heating block *cause* the apparatus to be plugged in? You could rephrase the sentence as follows:

Next, the apparatus is plugged in so that the solid can be heated electrically in the heating block.

When you use *however*, you are making a claim about contrast. The following example illustrates an inappropriate use of *however*:

The furnace has to be replaced next year; however, our budget has been reduced by $10 000.

You could express the relationships more clearly as follows:

> The furnace has to be replaced next year; however, it may be impossible to do so because our budget has been reduced by $10 000.

GIVEN-NEW CONTRACT

By the "given-new contract" we mean the assumption that at the beginning of the sentence – normally in the subject position – will be what is known, familiar, old, and that in the predicate will be what is unknown, unfamiliar, new. Usually the given information is familiar to the reader because it has been mentioned recently in the discourse, often in the previous sentence.

To see how this principle applies, let us look again at the first few sentences of the two passages whose readability we compared earlier in the chapter. In each sentence below, the given information – the information mentioned earlier in the discourse – is underlined.

1. Sociolinguistic studies of urban areas assume that language co-varies with socioeconomic status. This is clearly the case in highly stratified European cities such as Norwich and Berlin, and in large but compact North American cities, notably New York. It is more difficult to demonstrate in smaller Canadian cities, such as Ottawa. For such cities, again, there is a potential danger that the appearance of patterning ....

2. Rangers are encouraged to set the culvert trap in locations where the public is less likely to see it. The rationale is that people will become frightened if a bear trap is set in close proximity to the campsite. The problem is that the bear is attracted to the campsite by the smells of cooking and garbage. It is not the trap which brings the bear. The most successful locations for the trap are those where the bear will likely be. Hiking trails leading into the park are utilized by ....

In the first passage, the given information is at the beginning of each sentence. *This* in the second sentence and *it* in the third sentence refer to "that language co-varies with socioeconomic status." In the second passage, given information is found later in the sentences and the subject of most sentences contains new information (*the rationale, the problem, the most successful locations, hiking trails*).

Other factors remaining unchanged, maintaining the given-new contract will make a text more readable. In fact, the given-new contract can be extended to all levels of a discourse, making it a good rule to always work from what the reader knows to what the reader doesn't know. An introduction should establish this format by setting the document or section of the document within the context of what the reader already knows and by announcing what the new information will be. Subsequent

Date Due

OCT 15 1996		
NOV 04 1996	DEC 22 1999	
	DEC 15 1999	
NOV 28 1996		
NOV 29 1996	JUL 30 2001	
FEB 26 1997	JUL 30 2001	
FEB 19 1997		
MAR 13 1998		
MAR 16 1998		
SEP 30 1998		
OCT 16 1998		

JUN 03 2011

HUMBER COLLEGE L. R. C. (LAKESHORE)

sections and subsections should build on the introduction by systematically turning what was new information in one sentence into given information in another sentence, and so on.

CLARITY

DEFINITION

A passage is clear if and only if a competent reader who knows the meanings of any technical terms used will understand it on the first reading in the way the writer intended. Although a clear text would normally also be readable, clarity and readability are not synonymous. A clear text need not be particularly readable; it may take hard work to decipher it. On the other hand, a readable text may not be clear; the competent reader may understand something quite different from what the writer intended. Also, whereas we usually consider entire documents when we speak of readability, we are often concerned only with segments when we discuss lack of clarity; few documents lack clarity throughout, but many contain sentences that are not clear.

Clarity is very important in all technical writing. Not only will lack of clarity usually result in a waste of time for the reader, but it can also have more serious consequences. For example, if instructions are not clear, equipment could be damaged, and workers could be injured. Many of the documents you write could be used as evidence in court, and expert readers could then be called to testify about the meaning of a passage. Only if the passage is absolutely clear can you be certain that the meaning you intended will be the same as the meaning the expert finds.

Parts of a text can be clear, unclear, misleading, or ambiguous. Based on the relationship between the intended meaning and the meaning received by a competent reader, passages can be classified as follows:

Intended Meaning	Received Meaning	Classification of Text
X	X	clear
X	–	unclear
X	Y	misleading
X	X or Y	ambiguous

CLEAR. A competent reader will understand a clear text on first reading and various readers will agree about what it means. They will not say "Well, I think it means X," or "Maybe it means X," or "Common sense tells you it must mean X." Make sure that readers cannot argue about what your text means.

UNCLEAR. Unclear passages cannot be understood. Although they are, of course, inefficient, they are seldom dangerous, because a reader knows when a text is unclear and will usually either stop reading or consult the writer to find out what was intended.

MISLEADING. If a text is misleading, the message the reader receives is different from the message the writer intended, but the reader does not realize this. Although misleading passages are probably rare, they can be extremely hazardous, because even though the readers are not getting the meaning you intended, they are confident that they understand what you meant. If the document is a set of instructions, they will simply do what they *think* you have said.

AMBIGUOUS. If a passage is ambiguous, it has at least two possible interpretations. If the reader is not aware of the ambiguity, then the text could be misleading for that reader. If, however, the reader does recognize the ambiguity, he or she is likely to guess what the writer meant. Not only does this mean that the writer has lost control of the interpretation, but there is a good chance that the reader's guess will be incorrect.

COMMON SOURCES OF LACK OF CLARITY

There are many reasons why sentences may be unclear. To identify such sentences, you can try reading your documents aloud to see whether your ear will alert you to a problem, or you can ask a friend to read your document. Here we will discuss how the placement of modifiers and how pronoun reference can lead to unclear passages.

PLACEMENT OF MODIFIERS. In English, the position of a modifier determines what is modified. If the modifier refers to the wrong word, the sentence is misleading; if the modifier can refer to two words, the sentence is ambiguous. While any modifier – word, phrase, or clause – can be incorrectly placed, the more common sources of difficulty are the following:

- *Prepositional phrases.* Consider how the position of the prepositional phrase *with the knife* affects the meaning of the sentences below:

  - The criminal with the knife injured the lawyer.
  - The lawyer with the knife was injured by the criminal.
  - The criminal injured the lawyer with the knife.
  - With the knife the criminal injured the lawyer.

  Which sentence is ambiguous? What are the two possible interpretations of the third sentence? The third sentence is ambiguous because the prepositional phrase *with the knife* could modify either the noun *the lawyer* or the verb *injured*. The first two sentences are clear because the phrase can only modify the preceding noun, and the last sentence is clear because the phrase has no noun on its left to modify and so can only modify *injured*.
  To identify a misleading or ambiguous placement of a prepositional phrase, then, it is wise to double check whether it should modify the preceding noun. For example, does *Move the book to the right* mean that you are to move the book that is now on the right, or that you are to move the book to the right of where it is now?

- *Modifiers with "and."* The placement of modifiers can be particularly troublesome when two nouns are joined by *and* or *or.* Consider, for example, the following sentence:
  - The manager fired a systems analyst and the accountant in Toronto.

You can assume that both employees are in Toronto. If you want the modifier to apply only to one noun, make that noun and modifier the first element:

- The manager fired the accountant in Toronto and a systems analyst.

Consider now the following example:

- It consists essentially of a circular rack holding the receiving tubes and a photoelectric counter to count the number of drops emerging from the column.

Is the rack holding the photoelectric counter or not? To clarify, we can rewrite the passage as follows:

- It consists of a circular rack and a photoelectric counter. The rack holds the receiving tubes; the photoelectric counter counts the drops emerging from the column.

- *Adverbs and quantifiers.* The placement of some words, such as *only* and *even*, can lead to quite different interpretations. Consider, for example, how the position of *only* and *even* affects the meaning of the following sentences:
  - <u>Only</u> the mechanic should test the brakes on the bulldozer.
  - The mechanic should <u>only</u> test the brakes on the bulldozer.
  - The mechanic should test <u>only</u> the brakes on the bulldozer.
  - The mechanic should test the brakes <u>only</u> on the bulldozer.
  - <u>Even</u> yesterday the engineer did not notice the break.
  - Yesterday <u>even</u> the engineer did not notice the break.
  - Yesterday the engineer did not <u>even</u> notice the break.

- *Relative clauses.* A relative clause (beginning with *who, which, that*) will be interpreted as modifying the noun to its left. Consider, for example, the following sentence:
  - A chair is a piece of furniture that includes a seat that has a back on which usually only one person sits.

It includes the following three relative clauses:
- "that includes a seat"
- "that has a back"
- "on which usually only one person sits"

Two of these relative clauses are incorrectly placed. Can you identify them? Can you clarify the sentence? One solution would be the following:

- A chair is a piece of furniture on which only one person sits. It has a seat and a back.

Note that you were only able to spot the problems because you know what a chair is and how it is used. If you did not already know this, you would have been either confused or misled.

Also, avoid relative clauses that modify the entire main clause, as in the following example:

- This will result in the formation of "nonsense" DNA, which will mean that the organism will no longer be able to code for that protein.

The main clause is "This will result in the formation of 'nonsense' DNA," and the relative clause is "which will mean that the organism will no longer be able to code for that protein." You can clarify this sentence as follows:

- This will result in the formation of "nonsense" DNA <u>and mean</u> that the organism will no longer be able to code for that protein.

- *Participial phrases.* A present participle is a verb form that ends in *-ing*. A participial phrase may begin a sentence, as in the following example:

- Having inspected the brakes, the mechanic began to check the transmission.

The important point to note is that the phrase must modify the doer of the *-ing* action (in this case, *having inspected*); this noun must be the first noun after the comma (the *mechanic*). When this is not the case, the error is called a *dangling participle*. Sometimes a dangling participle makes a passage unclear, as in the following sentence:

- By planting different varieties of crops, the pests were unable to adapt.

The problem, of course, is that the pests seem to have planted the crops, and we know that is absurd. To clarify the sentence, we can change the participle to a verb and specify who planted the crops, as in the following sentence:

- When we planted different varieties of crops, the pests were unable to adapt.

A participial phrase may also be used to modify a noun that is immediately on its left, as in the following example:

- The tree growing next to the barn is a spruce.

If the participial phrase is not intended to modify the noun to its left, then we have a misplaced modifier and the sentence might be misleading, as is the following example:

- He experimented with guinea pigs measuring their oxygen intake, their food intake, and their heat production.

Again, we can clarify the sentence by changing the participle to a verb and specifying who did the measuring, as in the following passage:

- He experimented with guinea pigs. He measured their oxygen intake, their food intake, and their heat production.

Avoid using a participial phrase at the end of a sentence to comment on an earlier part, as in the following example:

- Sometimes a gene may undergo an actual physical change, resulting in a new gene being formed.

The problem is that such a phrase has nothing to modify. One way to correct this problem is to rewrite the sentence to focus on the result, as in the following example:

- Sometimes an actual physical change in a gene may result in a new gene being formed.

Another solution is to write two sentences, as follows:

- Sometimes a gene may undergo an actual physical change. This change may result in a new gene being formed.

UNCLEAR PRONOUN REFERENCE. A pronoun (*he, she, it, this, that*) should have one and only one antecedent. If it has more than one antecedent, the passage may be ambiguous, like the following sentence:

- If the solder is applied to the iron, it will melt even though the wires may not be hot enough to allow cohesion.

In this case, *it* has two potential antecedents, *solder* and *iron*, and only prior knowledge would allow the reader to know which was intended. We can clarify the sentence as follows:

- If the solder is applied to the iron, *the solder* will melt even though the wires may not be hot enough to allow cohesion.

If the pronoun has no antecedent, the passage will be vague. Consider, for example, the following sentence:

- Since I am presently working Saturdays in the stationery department, this will give me an opportunity to analyze the problems closely.

This has no clear antecedent. We can clarify the sentence as follows:

- My Saturday job in the stationery department will give me an opportunity to analyze the problems closely.

CONCISENESS

DEFINITION

Conciseness is a high information to words ratio in a text. The opposite of conciseness is wordiness. Conciseness is especially valued in technical writing because it reduces some production costs and because it reduces reading time. Since many documents are read by extremely well-paid managers, reducing their reading time by 20 or 30 percent can be an important saving. The following examples illustrate how easy it can be to make some passages more than one third shorter:

1. It is our view that the building, machinery, and equipment and stock at x should be marketed (at least initially) on an en bloc basis. It is our intention to prepare an Information Package regarding these assets and advertise them for sale on an offers basis as soon as possible. (50 words)

1a. The building, machinery, equipment, and stock at x should be marketed en bloc. As soon as possible, we will prepare an Information Package and advertise these assets for sale on an offers basis. (33 words)

2. The Company is involved in the manufacture and distribution of waterbed supplies including heaters, thermostat controls and mattresses. The bulk of the raw materials involved in the manufacture of the products was imported from the United States. (37 words)

2a. The Company manufactures and distributes waterbed supplies, including heaters, thermostat controls, and mattresses. Most of the raw materials are imported from the United States. (24 words)

STRATEGIES FOR INCREASING CONCISENESS

Make sure that as you try to make your text more concise by applying the strategies outlined below, you do not sacrifice clarity, tone, or emphasis. Try not to lose anything as you gain conciseness. The most common strategies for increasing conciseness are the following:

- Replace wordy phrases.
- Remove redundancy.
- Use nominalizations effectively.
- Combine sentences.
- Use lists and tables.

REPLACE WORDY PHRASES. Often a phrase can be replaced with a single word, as in the following examples:

a majority of	most
a number of	some
at the present time	now
at this (point in) time	now
at that time	then

due to the fact that	because
during the time that	while
in a careful manner	carefully
in a clear way	clearly
in order to	to
in the event that	if
on a weekly basis	weekly
subsequent to	after

REMOVE REDUNDANCY. Remove redundancy, the unnecessary repetition of an idea. In the following examples, the underlined words or phrases should be removed because they add no new information:

- This approach employs the use of modelling algorithms.
- The scheduled sailings are frequent in number.
- I will need a year to completely finish the work.
- The new algae are red in colour.
- I have been specializing in the area of adolescent psychology.
- My future plans include travel in Australia.
- My past experience with animals has increased my interest in the environment.
- That was the most useful course I took.
- The results were constant and stable.

USE NOMINALIZATIONS EFFECTIVELY. A nominalization is a noun form that is related to a verb or an adjective. Most verbs and adjectives in English can be nominalized.

Noun (Nominalization)	Verb	Adjective
assumption	assume	
conclusion	conclude	
description	describe	
development	develop	
fulfilment	fulfil	
statement	state	
acceptance	accept	
dependence	depend	
removal	remove	
clarity		clear
firmness		firm
precision		precise

Use a nominalization if you have a meaningful verb to use with it, as in the following example:

The ventilation of the greenhouse costs $10 000 annually.

Do not use a nominalization if you are forced to supply a verb, such as *do, occur, exist,* simply to fill the verb slot of the sentence. Unnecessary nominalization is a common source of wordiness, as in the following example:

The ventilation of greenhouses can be done either naturally or me-chanically.

The problem is that when *ventilate* is replaced with *ventilation*, a verb, *to do*, has to be added. The solution, of course, is to replace the nom-inalization with the related verb and to remove *do*:

The greenhouses can be ventilated either manually or mechanically.

Whether or not you retain *either* should depend on whether or not it is needed for emphasis.

Sometimes the nominalization is found in the predicate, and the verb and nominalization together can be replaced with the verb that is related to the nominalization. The following are some common examples:

Verb + Nominalization	*Verb*
make an assumption	assume
make a decision	decide
make a recommendation	recommend
give a description	describe
draw a conclusion	conclude
find a solution to	solve

COMBINE SENTENCES. Often a passage can be made more concise by combining related sentences. In the following example, three sentences have been combined to reduce the length of the passage by one third:

- The language C is a flexible computer language. It is a general-purpose programming language that is not tied to any particular hardware or system. C is good for major numerical, textprocessing, and database programs. (35 words)
- C, a general-purpose computer language not tied to any particular hardware or system, is good for major numerical, text/processing, and database programs. (23 words)

USE LISTS AND TABLES. Use lists and tables to make repetitive passages more concise. In this chapter, the informal table on page 19 replaces a passage like the following:

If the intended meaning is X and the received meaning is X, then the text is clear. If the intended meaning is X and a competent reader receives no meaning, then the text is unclear. If the intended meaning is X and the received meaning is Y, then the text is misleading. If the intended meaning is X and the received meaning could be both X and Y, then the text is ambiguous.

PRECISION AND SPECIFICITY

DEFINITION

Precision and specificity refer to being exact rather than vague, and individual rather than general. Although generalizations are certainly important in technical writing, they should also be supported with precise particulars. A common error made by beginning technical writers is not to be precise and specific enough.

COMMON SOURCES OF VAGUENESS

Usually, vagueness and generality are the result of word choice and can be easily corrected by substituting a more precise or specific word. The following are common sources of vagueness:

- abstract nouns
- *someone, something, somewhere, somehow*
- adjectives and adverbs
- quantifiers
- vague verbs

ABSTRACT NOUNS. Nouns differ in how abstract or concrete they are. More abstract nouns, such as *people, furniture,* or *equipment,* refer to larger classes of individuals than do less abstract nouns, such as *freshmen, chesterfields,* or *saws.* Use the more abstract nouns when you intend to generalize, and use more concrete nouns when you intend to be specific.

SOMEONE, SOMETHING, SOMEWHERE, SOMEHOW. The indefinites are, of course, very vague. Consider, for example, the difference between the following recommendations:

- Someone should clean the windows.
- The janitor should clean the windows.

Use the indefinites only when they are necessary, as, for example, when you do not have the authority to say who should be assigned to clean the windows.

ADJECTIVES AND ADVERBS. Most adjectives and adverbs, such as *big, old, expensive,* or *fast,* are useful for interpretations and evaluations, but are not precise. For example, *fast* may have quite different interpretations, depending both on the standards of the speaker and on the context. The sentence *John was driving fast* could apply to any of the following situations, among others:

- John was driving at 40 km/h in a 20 km/h zone.
- John was driving at 130 km/h in Manitoba.
- John was driving at 210 km/h in Germany.

To be more precise, replace these adjectives and adverbs with the appropriate measurements.

QUANTIFIERS. Most quantifiers, such as *many, most, some, few,* are vague. Usually you should replace or support them with precise numbers. Note how the second and third sentences are more precise than the first:

- Few students complained to the dean.
- Thirty students complained to the dean.
- Four students complained to the dean.

VAGUE VERBS. Many verbs are vague. *Damage,* for example, is more vague than *scratch, dent, crack, bend; change* is more vague than *increase,* or *decrease.* Consider the following sentences:

- X affected Y.
- X involves Y.
- X concerns Y.

What do these sentences mean?

SPECIAL PROBLEMS

The use of four structures – the passive voice of the verb, anticipatory *it,* personal pronouns, and nominalizations – are traditional, and sometimes controversial, subjects in discussions of technical writing.

PASSIVE VOICE OF THE VERB

You may have been warned against using the passive voice of the verb. Do you know what the differences between the active and the passive voice are? The differences are illustrated in the following sentences:

Active: The technician weighed the rats each morning.
Full Passive: The rats were weighed by the technician each morning.
Truncated Passive: The rats were weighed each morning.

There are three differences between the active and the passive:

1. The agent, or doer (*the technician*), is the subject in the active version, but the object of the preposition *by* in the full passive version. In the truncated passive, the agent is omitted. If you are writing about the agent, then use the active to place the agent in the subject position. In other words, use the active in the example above if the discourse is about the technician.
2. The recipient of the action (*the rats*) is the subject in the passive version, but the object in the active version. If you are writing about the recipient, then use the passive to place the recipient in subject position.
3. Different forms of the verb are used.

The truncated passive, which accounts for at least 70 percent of the cases of passive voice, is useful if you want to avoid naming the agent. Sometimes you may want to conceal the agent, for a variety of political reasons, as when you report a suggestion or decision: "It has been suggested that...." Of course, you could do the same with the active voice by using an indefinite agent: "Someone has suggested that...." Sometimes naming the agent is simply tedious and irrelevant, as in the example of the technician weighing the rats. The truncated passive is also useful in describing standard procedures (The DNA is broken into small pieces), in describing natural processes (The particles are dispersed throughout the medium), and in describing the state of knowledge (The reasons for this are well understood).

The key principle in using the passive is to do so deliberately. Regard the passive as a special resource you can use where the active is less effective.

ANTICIPATORY *it*

Anticipatory *it* is a structure that is used when the notional (or 'real') subject has been moved to a position following the verb, as in the following sentences:

- It is generally assumed that this is the case.
- It should be noted that *x* does not increase.
- It is possible that the solution became contaminated.
- It is difficult to balance these nutrients.
- It is clear that this is the correct solution.

Many authorities disapprove of the use of the anticipatory *it* on the grounds that it is wordy and delays the subject. The first objection is valid if no purpose is served by using the anticipatory *it*. The second objection is not valid because we know that delaying the notional subject actually adds emphasis.

Anticipatory *it*, like the passive, should also be used deliberately. A recent study has shown that in scientific writing there are only five or six cases of this structure per one thousand words.[5] What, then, are its uses? Its primary use is to allow author comment, usually about the reliability of knowledge or information, or about the source of knowledge. It can evaluate, it can mark your response, or it can mark validity. If your comment isn't necessary, then don't use the anticipatory *it*.

PERSONAL PRONOUNS

There is nothing inherently wrong with using the personal pronouns *I, you, we*. Two important factors that affect their use are how personal or impersonal the discourse is and the capacity in which you are writing. Generally speaking, letters and memos are more personal, and reports, articles, and proposals are less personal, and so the personal pronouns are more appropriate in the former than the latter. The capacity in which you are writing is linked to how personal the document is. If you are writing as an individual, then you can, and perhaps even should, use *I*. However, if you are writing as a representative of an organization, you may have to use *we* instead of *I*.

NOMINALIZATIONS

As indicated in the section on conciseness, a nominalization is a noun form that is related to a verb or an adjective. The only valid cautions about the use of nominalizations are that they are abstract and could contribute to vagueness and that they can lead to wordiness if they are used unnecessarily.

NOTES

1. Rudolf Flesch, "A New Readability Yardstick," *Journal of Applied Psychology*, 32 (1948): 221–33.
2. Jack Selzer, "What Constitutes a 'Readable' Technical Style?" in *New Essays in Technical and Scientific Communication: Research, Theory, Practice*, ed. Paul V. Anderson, R. John Brockmann, and Carolyn R. Miller (Farmingdale, NY: Baywood, 1983), 74.
3. Ian Pringle, Ian R.H. Dale, and Enoch Padolsky, "Procedures to Solve a Methodological Problem in the Ottawa Valley," in *Papers from the Fifth International Conference on Methods in Dialectology*, ed. H.J. Warkentyne (Victoria: Dept. of Linguistics, University of Victoria, 1985), 484–85.
4. M.A.K. Halliday and Ruquaiya Hasan, *Cohesion in English*, (London: Longman, 1976), 10.
5. Lilita Rodman, "Anticipatory *It* in Scientific Discourse," *Journal of Technical Writing and Communication*, 21.1 (1991): 17–27.

EXERCISES

1. Explain what is unclear in each passage below. Rewrite the passage to make it clear.
   a. Soak the chain in just enough kerosene to cover it and scrub it thoroughly with the toothbrush.
   b. Excess liquid should be drained from the raisins before adding into the batter.
   c. From this number of rolls, subtract one roll for every set of two ordinary-sized windows and one door.
   d. The benefit of the ballpoint pen is that the ink source is within the pen, dispensing with the former need to continuously dunk it in an ink well, and the feature of the ball itself.
   e. Unfortunately, the natural course of untreated bulimia is not unknown, making it impossible to determine if the drug therapy has had any positive influence.

2. Correct the errors in the following sentences:
   a. The information which this report is based upon is my experience in the British Columbia Packers salmon cannery in Prince Rupert.
   b. Upper Canada in 1820 contained 100 000 sparsely populated settlers.
   c. The purpose for the actual operation of the apparatus is so that a melting-point range can be determined.
   d. The importance of using the apparatus is so that one can determine the temperature at which a compound's solid and liquid phases are in equilibrium.
   e. The style is again very technical and often written in mathematical terms.
   f. When there is a change like the wind speed, the computer asks what the change is and then checks to see what the proper correction could be.
   g. The overall impression of the writing is a layman's approach, that is, the level of vocabulary used is relatively low.

3. Make the following passages more concise:
   a. After this is done, the process of applying grease is repeated.
   b. Before an antibiotic can be administered, it must be decided what organism is causing the infection. The reason for the importance of such a decision is that antibiotics have a specific effect on a very limited range of micro-organisms.
   c. The lack of training occurred in terms of improper introduction to the workplace and insufficient computer training. This combined with a lack of computer terminals and research documents inhibited the students' potential productivity and led to many wasted hours.
   d. Articles are consistently tending toward the formal in tone.
   e. Provision of jobs to an expanding labour force must be met.
   f. Footnotes are discouraged from being used.
   g. Solar heat is discussed only as to its initial cost.
   h. The report will be beneficial to aid in changing the present inefficient procedures, in order for new personnel to be trained efficiently.
   i. Projects of environmental concern are discussed as to their progress and significance.
   j. Suntan lotions are discussed regarding their effectiveness.
   k. The machine declined to a state of uselessness.
   l. The paper provides evidence that individual trout demonstrate differences in the food they eat.
   m. Milking the cow is ready to begin when the stool is in place.
   n. It is often advisable to work on a piece of newspaper as it is easy to remove when finished.
   o. Extraction of the chemical is done through activated charcoal and evaporation of the medium.
   p. The first recognition of inhibited bacterial growth was by Professor Fleming.
   q. At the Standard bred racetrack harnessing of horses is a daily occurrence designed to prepare the horses to be exercised or raced.
   r. Therefore, by using direct three-dimensional object data, it is possible to obtain a more general-purpose vision system in terms of the flexibility with respect to the environmental aspects of the object sensed and to the way in which the object is modelled.
   s. The importance of this technique is for the detection of abnormalities soon enough to allow selective abortion of abnormal fetuses.
   t. The whole procedure is relatively easy and will take between 35 and 45 minutes to complete.
   u. Previous experience I have had pertaining to English includes writing business letters.
   v. The whole set costs about twenty dollars.
   w. He will have access to all the necessary tools that will be required.

    x. The guitar sounded lifeless and dull.

    y. The table top is square in shape.

4. Identify and then correct the errors in the use of pronouns in the following passages:

    a. Along with my own experience at Continental Can, I will visit it and conduct interviews there when the need arises.

    b. Due to the amount of handling, the fish become stressed. This appears in their feeding habits immediately after sampling and a few days later.

    c. The capacity of the oil pan is three litres, so be sure no more than three litres and no less than two litres is put in. This would result in improper operation of the engine.

    d. This pamphlet gave good descriptions of physical fitness and why a person's fitness level should be of importance to them.

    e. The idea is to create a set of waves that cancel out the bow waves. To do this they must be similar in frequency and amplitude and out of phase by 180 degrees to the bow waves.

    f. The ski must be steady before beginning the waxing procedure. This is done by placing the centre of the ski in a vise.

    g. Each major motorcycle manufacturer promotes their version of the rising rate linkage by giving it a special name.

    h. The present application of optic fibres is in the telephone industry where it will replace existing copper cables and it will be for new installations.

    i. Indices are more widely used in the sheep and swine industry than with cattle because there are more traits involved in their successful production.

    j. By covering the metal tip a person can put the pen in their pocket without spilling any ink on their clothing.

    k. One liquid breaks up into droplets or globules and becomes completely surrounded by the second liquid. This liquid is said to be in the discontinuous phase. The other liquid which surrounds the droplets is said to be in the continuous phase.

    l. The brain will instantly make a person's arms move out to break their fall when they trip.

5. Identify the problem(s) in the following passages. Rewrite the passages to correct the problems.

    a. The transform boundary occurs when two plates slide past one another, creating topography features which are displaced along the fault. The San Andreas Fault is a member of this class.

    b. The future path of the space program will be influenced by politics. This book will provide a background in this area.

    c. The language in this article was not too technical which made it much easier to understand. I tried to stay away from journal articles for this reason.

6. Each of the following sentences contains an error in the use of a present participle (a verb form ending in -ing). Identify the errors and then correct the sentences.

   a. In 1941, penicillin was used to treat serious infections causing rapid and complete recoveries.

   b. The problem is outlined simply and concisely, creating a feeling of definiteness and a statement to be believed.

   c. Also, the lunch and coffee breaks are not set for each lab aide, resulting in arguments between the lab aides, in the cafeteria, about whose responsibility it is to respond to an emergency when one occurs.

   d. The pen is picked up off the table or desk on which it rests using the thumb and forefinger.

   e. Being such an appealing item, I would like to purchase the Krafty Kitchen.

   f. By using needle injections or consuming pills, common diseases such as the flu are easily controlled by antibiotic therapy.

   g. Having done this, the ligaments should be visible.

   h. Having loosened the lugnuts, the can should be raised.

   i. Although confusing I did understand the term you were defining.

   j. A shirt is a garment worn by people having a collar, sleeves, and buttons down the front.

   k. Be sure the engine is cool enough to be touched before starting.

   l. When not being used a cap is placed over the point to prevent the ink from marking your clothes or your skin.

   m. When plugged into an electrical outlet, the blender's power supply as regulated by the electrical switch, activates the motor causing the steel rod and the cutting blade to rotate at a high speed in a clockwise direction.

   n. When placed on a stove element set at the highest temperature, the resulting boiling water creates a vacuum causing the water to rise into the upper dome through the extended glass tube.

7. The following sentences contain various errors in modification. Identify the errors and then correct the sentence.

   a. The inner tube is now ready to be put back in place. Once correctly positioned in the metal rim, the rubber tire has to be carefully wiggled over it.

   b. Skips are filled with ore and hauled up the shaft to the surface. Once on the surface, conveyor belts transport the ore to the mill.

   c. As a pediatric nurse with a sense of adventure, your advertisement immediately caught my eye.

   d. As indicated in your advertisement, I drive my own car.

   e. A ballpoint pen is a cylindrical barrel containing an ink cartridge used as a writing instrument.

f. The working cubicles are located at the centre of the office enclosed by dividers.

g. The bacterial cell wall is a structure that forms a net around the cell composed of interconnecting molecular units.

h. The separatory funnel was gently shaken, followed by the opening of the stopcock to release pressure.

i. I have completed a course on financial institutions with a heavy emphasis on commercial banks.

j. When cool, lift the bag out of the saucepan.

k. Approximately every eight hours the IV bottle must be changed before the solution runs out completely.

l. The initials of the person making up the deposit are put on the slip to identify who made up the deposit if problems should arise.

m. Any financial institution, such as a bank or a trust company, will agree to sell foreign currency in the future at an exchange rate agreed upon today for a nominal service charge.

n. All the journal articles had a polished character making the reading much easier which is imperative due to the complexity of the material involved.

o. There are several types of jacks available from the different car makers which makes an overall description of a jack and its use difficult.

p. The necessary condition to benefit from digging up and replanting a live tree is the knowledge of the proper process which involves four steps.

q. A mutation is a chemical change in the hereditary material of a gene that may result in a change in the phenotype of the offspring.

r. F-stop is the number engraved on the lens barrel of a camera which relates to the size of the aperture.

s. Discussions and reviews are generally written by professionals at the same level of technicality as the works reviewed.

t. As mines find it necessary to dig deeper, they will have to remove larger volumes of overburden, thus requiring larger more efficient draglines.

u. His purpose is to objectively show how these laws have evolved from a legal standpoint.

v. In evaluating the desirability of the four forms, the least desirable forms are the Assimilationist and the Sovereignty Association forms.

w. Hence, the American Dream became a single family house on a single lot in a low-density environment all enthusiastically endorsed by the government.

x. Dampers, or shock absorbers, prevent the vehicle from bouncing after receiving a road input by converting the kinetic energy into heat in the damper fluid.

y. Furthermore, the relatively low elastic modulus of polypropylene means that concrete reinforced with polypropylene must deform much more than concrete using steel fibres in order to develop the same resistance from the fibres.

z. By using direct three-dimensional object range data, the library of models required per object will be smaller as fewer aspect angle views of the object will be needed to completely define the object.

GRAPHICS

INTRODUCTION

One of the characteristics of technical writing is that it does use graphics. Graphics – what may also be called visuals, illustrations, pictorials, or exhibits – include not only graphs (line graphs, bar graphs, pie charts, and so on), but also photographs, drawings, diagrams, maps, tables, schematics, and other devices that have been developed to show a variety of visual messages. Although you are used to seeing graphics in your textbooks, you may not yet have had much practice in using them in your own writing. The purpose of this chapter is to familiarize you with some of the general principles that govern the use of graphics in technical discourse. You will examine the functions of graphics in technical discourse, learn guidelines for designing graphics, and see how to integrate the graphics with the text.

FUNCTIONS OF GRAPHICS

Graphics can make a document or oral presentation more emphatic, clear, and concise.

EMPHASIS

Graphics attract attention and are easier to remember than text. Most readers will look at illustrations before they read the text, and almost no listener in an oral presentation can resist looking at a graphic. As well as attracting attention, graphics emphasize the relationships they show. Sometimes the graphic functions almost as underlining, as in Figure 3-1.

Figure 3-1
A Graphic Used for
Emphasis

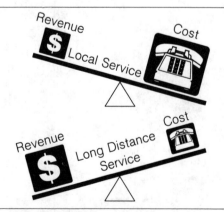

Source: *Dialogue* (Aug. 1984), p. 3. Printed by permission.

At other times, the graphic can also be used to persuade, as in the case of a graph that emphasizes the relationship of data (see Figure 3-2), or a photograph, such as one showing corrosion, or the results of a mudslide, or the effects of a disease on a tree.

Figure 3-2
Cost of Supplies in
1983 and 1984.

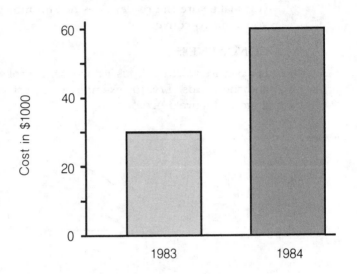

CLARITY

Graphics can communicate some messages more clearly and accurately than words, and these particular kinds of messages are frequent in technical writing. All but the most simple spatial relationships are very difficult to express in words alone because only a very few shapes have names in English. What would you call the shapes in Figure 3-3?

Figure 3-3
Irregular Shapes

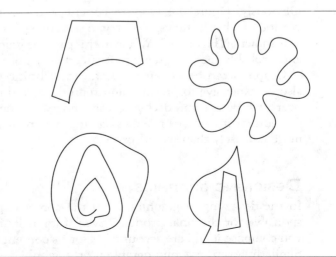

If you have any doubt about the limitations of words for describing appearance, consider what would happen if written descriptions replaced passport photographs. In fact, if you do use only words to describe or explain a more complex spatial arrangement, your reader will probably try to draw a sketch based on your words. By providing the sketch as part of your document, you make your document more readable and you make sure the reader does not misinterpret the spatial relationship you want to convey.

CONCISENESS

Is a picture worth a thousand words? It probably depends on the picture and the words. Try, for example, to describe the apparently simple diagram in Figure 3-4.

Figure 3-4
A Concise Figure

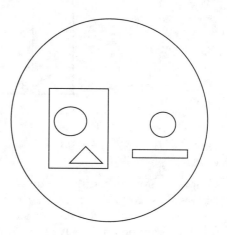

Obviously, Figure 3-4 is more concise and accurate than your prose version of what it shows. Now try to state in words the same information as is shown in Figure 3-2. While in this case the graphic is more emphatic, and probably more persuasive, it is certainly not more concise.

Graphics can be extremely useful in technical writing, but they can also be expensive to produce and reproduce, and they can definitely be overused. Before you decide to use a graphic, then, you should be convinced that it presents the message more emphatically, more clearly, or more concisely than would prose.

DESIGNING GRAPHICS

In the designing of graphics, as in the composing of text, you are responsible for the final product. Even if an assistant types a document, you compose it and are accountable for its content and final appearance. Similarly, even if a photographer or a graphics specialist prepares or executes your graphics, you are responsible for planning them. You provide the specifications, the graphic-resource person executes them, and you ensure that the finished graphic meets your specifications. You choose when to use a graphic, what kind to use, and what the details of its appearance must be.

ORGANIZATION OF THE GRAPHIC MODE

Different kinds of graphics have been developed to show different kinds of subjects—such as objects, spaces or areas, quantities, or processes—and there are many specific types of graphics available for illustrating each of these. One variable that can help us organize the graphic mode is the level of abstraction. Based on the subject of the graphic and its approximate level of abstraction, we can classify some common graphics as in Figure 3-5.

Figure 3-5
A Classification
Scheme for Graphics
on the Basis of
Subject and the Level
of Abstraction

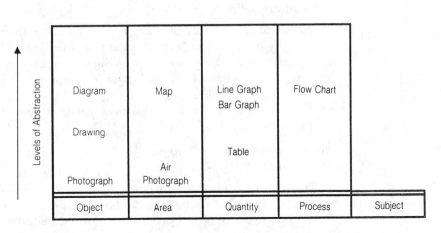

Source: Lilita Rodman, "Levels of Abstraction in the Graphic Mode" *Teaching Technical Writing: Graphics*, Anthology No. 5 ed. Dixie Elise Hickman, (ATTW, 1985), 2. © 1985, by the Association of Teachers of Technical Writing, and used by permission of ATTW.

Graphics that are at a relatively low level of abstraction tend to be realistic rather than symbolic; they show the particular rather than the generic; they show surface more than structure. At the other extreme, the most abstract graphics are symbolic rather than realistic in their method of representation; they show the generic, rather than the particular; they show structure, rather than surface. Between these extremes we can think of there being a continuum of level or degree of abstraction, with the continuity being more obvious in some columns of Figure 3-5 than in others.

GRAPHICS TO ILLUSTRATE OBJECTS

To illustrate objects, the main types of graphics available are photographs, drawings, and diagrams.

PHOTOGRAPHS. Photographs, which are at a low level of abstraction, are mimetic and they emphasize the particular and the surface. Obviously, photographs imitate what they show rather than representing it in some symbolic way; they are as close as we can come to "presenting" something on the page. Since they emphasize the particular, they can show what an individual person looks like, but not what people in general look like. Similarly, a photograph of a house can only be a photograph of that particular house, unless you use the caption to indicate that this house is typical of a class of houses, or the text to point out the "typical" elements. Photographs emphasize the particular because they show the surface in detail, and it is generally in these surface details that individuals or objects differ.

The main advantages and disadvantages of photographs are summarized below:

Advantages of Photographs:

• Accurate in showing surface. For this reason they are useful for identifying an object (as in a guide to edible mushrooms, or a guide to pharmaceuticals), or for showing damage (as in an automobile insurance claim or to show how a machine part has worn).
• Easy and relatively inexpensive to produce.
• Easy to read. Any audience that can read text can also "read" photographs.

Disadvantages of Photographs:

• Can be noisy. Photographs can show much that is not directly relevant, and the reader may need considerable help in the caption and in the text to interpret the photograph.
• Can be expensive to reproduce in printed material.

In preparing photographs, observe the following guidelines:

• *Minimize noise.* To remove distracting background detail, try to fill the frame with your subject. You can do this by moving the camera closer to your subject or by using a telephoto lens. In addition, you can use a smaller f-stop to decrease the depth of field and throw the background out of focus. To simplify the background for a small object, place the object on a cloth or a sheet of paper.
• *Increase clarity.* To make a photograph clear, position the camera close enough to the subject for the detail to be readily visible. The lens must be focused on the subject, the subject must be clearly lit, and the depth of field has to be large enough to include everything that you want to be in focus.
• *Indicate scale and orientation where appropriate.* To show size you can include a ruler in the photograph, or an object of known size,

such as a coin, a car, or a human figure. The caption can indicate orientation, and sometimes labelled arrows can direct the reader to particular parts or features that might be difficult to distinguish.

DRAWINGS. Drawings vary in abstraction. Some, like architectural renderings, obviously belong near the same level of abstraction as photographs, while some stylized drawings are only arbitrarily distinguishable from diagrams. Generally, the transition from photographs to drawings is characterized by the gradual removal of surface detail, the emphasis of structure, and the depiction of the more generic (see Figures 3-6a and 3-6b).

Figure 3-6a
Drawing of a
Particular House
with the Irrelevant
Detail Removed

Figure 3-6b
Generic Drawing of
a Type of House

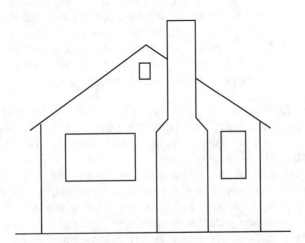

Source: Lilita Rodman, "Levels of Abstraction in the Graphic Mode," *Teaching Technical Writing: Graphics*, Anthology No. 5 ed. Dixie Elise Hickman, (ATTW, 1985), 4. © 1985, by the Association of Teachers of Technical Writing, and used by permission of ATTW.

When you design a drawing, you must decide how much detail to include, what kind of detail, and what purpose you want the detail to serve.

To show different views of an object, various kinds of drawings, each with its own specific conventions, have been developed. For a full discussion of the types of drawings and the conventions governing them, you should consult a book on drafting or mechanical drawing in your discipline. You should, in particular, be aware of the exploded view, which is designed to show the arrangement of parts. For a student example of an exploded view, see Figure 1 in the description of a calligraphy pen in Chapter 11.

The main advantages and disadvantages of drawings are summarized below:

Advantages of drawings:
- Can show what something will look like or should look like (useful in proposals).
- Permit control of details. Choice of detail and emphasis can be used to persuade.
- Are less noisy than photographs.
- Are relatively cheap to reproduce.

Disadvantages of drawings:
- Are less realistic than photographs. Cannot be used as evidence in the same way as a photograph can.
- Are less striking than photographs.
- Can be expensive to produce.

In preparing drawings, observe the following guidelines:
- Make sure the smallest significant detail is clearly visible.
- Draw to scale and indicate the scale. A drawing must maintain the same proportions as the original, and the reader must know what conversion factor you have used.
- Use drawing instruments to assure a professional appearance. Use a straight edge to make sure that all lines are straight.
- Label parts clearly and appropriately.

DIAGRAMS. Diagrams are at the highest level of abstraction, are frequently generic, emphasize structure, and use symbols and various graphic conventions. In a diagram, surface detail is removed so as to focus on the relationship of parts and on how components function. Most disciplines have evolved graphic languages that you master as part of learning the discipline. For example, a student of physiology knows how to interpret diagrams in physiology, while a student of geology knows how to interpret diagrams in geology. Remember, though, that these graphic languages can function as jargon and become a serious barrier to those outside your discipline.

The main advantages and disadvantages of diagrams are summarized below:

Advantages of diagrams:
- Show relationships, whether structural or functional.
- Present some messages efficiently because all irrelevant detail is removed and symbols are used to represent frequently shown parts, as in plumbing or electrical schematics, for example.

Disadvantages of diagrams:
- May require special training to execute.
- Are not accessible to some audiences, particularly if specialized symbols are used.

In preparing diagrams, observe the following guidelines:
- Do not use diagrams unless you can expect your audience to understand them.
- Use symbols and conventions accurately to assure your diagram is clear to experts.
- Make sure the smallest component is clearly legible.

GRAPHICS TO ILLUSTRATE SPACES OR AREAS

To illustrate spaces or areas, the main types of graphics are aerial photographs, maps, and floor plans.

AERIAL PHOTOGRAPHS. Aerial photographs, which are at a low level of abstraction, provide realistic images of an area. However, they would have limited use for someone trying to get from place to place on the ground because they do not show signs and because the point of view is completely different from that of the user. Aside from this, the main disadvantages of aerial photographs are high cost and great noisiness because all details visible from a particular altitude are included. It is possible, however, to get special satellite images that emphasize particular features such as type of crop or heat patterns.

MAPS. Maps are at a higher level of abstraction, though they vary in how much detail they show and the degree to which they rely on symbols.

Instead of simply including a map that is available, you should adapt it to meet the needs of your audience and the particular purpose of the map in the particular document. In preparing maps, observe the following guidelines:
- *Minimize noise.* Remove detail that the user does not need. To place "new" information in the context of "old" information, the readers will need some orienting features, such as street names on city maps, or city names on maps of larger regions. It is your job to judge how many of these features are necessary.
- *Increase clarity.* Make the map large enough for all important details to be distinguishable. Use highlighting techniques to focus attention on important features.
- *Indicate scale and orientation.* Make sure the map is to scale and indicate what the scale is. Indicate which direction is north and remember that it is customary to have north at the top of the page.
- *Use standard symbols.* Wherever possible, use standard symbols.

FLOOR PLANS. Floor plans can vary in abstraction from fairly mimetic ones that show the arrangement of furniture, to very symbolic schematics prepared to guide construction. If you use a floor plan to show the arrangement of a room, or the layout of a plant, observe the following guidelines:

- *Minimize noise.* Remove detail that the user does not need. If you are showing the relative position of rooms, for example, you may not need to include machinery or furniture, and if you are showing the arrangement of furniture, you may not need to include the relative position of other rooms.
- *Increase clarity.* Use labels and highlighting to make the floor plan easier to interpret.
- *Indicate scale and orientation.* Make sure the floor plan is to scale and indicate what that scale is. Indicate how the room or building is oriented to north or to the street or to some other reference point.
- *Use standard symbols.* Wherever possible, use standard symbols.

GRAPHICS TO ILLUSTRATE QUANTITIES

The graphics to illustrate quantities include tables and the various types of graphs. Unlike the graphics to illustrate objects, they are not continuous with respect to abstraction; there are clear distinctions between tables and graphs.

TABLES. The term *table* can be loosely applied to any matrix or grid. An informal table is simply a two-column list; it is not given a title or a table number. It usually shows simple relationships and displays relatively little data. The main advantage of a table over prose is conciseness and readability. If you find that you are repeating the same sentence structure with different numbers (or other similar variables), consider using a table to display this material. For example, the following excerpt should certainly be replaced by a table:

> In September, the average price of tomatoes was $0.60 per kilogram. In October, it was $0.80 per kilogram. By November, it had risen to $1.80 per kilogram, and in December, it was $3.20.

Tables are at the lowest level of abstraction because they show quantities as numbers, not as points or as lengths or areas. The main advantage of a table over a graph is that it shows the actual data, and so it is easy to read off the particular value of a variable accurately. This is often an important advantage when you are displaying experimental results. The main disadvantage of tables is that, unlike graphs, they do not show relationships among numbers. While the details are readily apparent, it is usually very difficult to see any pattern but the most trivial.

A formal table must have a title and a number. Tables are the only graphics that are not called *figures*, and they have a numbering system separate from the one you used for figures.

Formal tables are particularly useful if you must present a great deal of data or show the interrelationships of several variables. The simplest formal tables, like that shown in Table 3-1, have only two columns, one showing the values for the independent variable, and one showing the values for the dependent variable. More complex tables can show an independent variable and several dependent variables, some of which may be interrelated (see Table 3-2).

Table 3-1
Mean Daily
Maximum
Temperature by
Month in Little
Muddy River

Month	Mean Maximum Temp. (°C)
Jan.	3.7
Feb.	2.9
Mar.	5.3
Apr.	8.1
May	16.3
June	23.0
July	25.2
Aug.	20.6
Sept.	15.4
Oct.	12.1
Nov.	10.2
Dec.	3.6

Table 3-2
Relationship between
x, y, and z

x	y	z
1	2	0.7
2	4	1.7
3	6	3.1
4	8	5.9
5	10	12.1

In preparing formal tables, observe the following guidelines:

- Use one horizontal line at the top of the table and one at the bottom.
- Use one horizontal line below the column headings.
- Label each column clearly and concisely.
- Include units where appropriate.
- Use the first column for the independent variable, as in Table 3-1, or for the names of variables, as in Table 3-3.
- Align numbers at decimal points.

The table format can also be used as a reference grid for non-quantitative or only partially quantitative data. You may be familiar with troubleshooting tables that identify the causes of various car problems and their remedies, or with tables that compare the characteristics of various products. In these cases, the cells in the grid may contain numbers, words, or even symbols or diagrams. Tables that do not present quantitative data cannot be replaced by graphs.

BAR GRAPHS AND PIE CHARTS. Bar graphs and pie charts are somewhat more abstract than tables because they use symbols to represent quantities. Bar graphs use length (horizontal or vertical) to represent quantity, while pie charts use area to represent fractions (percentages). These graphic devices have the advantage of making some simple relationships readily

Table 3-3
Undergraduate and
Professional
Enrolment by Sex
and Program 1968-
69, 1974-75, and
1983-84

	1968-69		1974-75		1983-84	
	Female %	Total N	Female %	Total N	Female %	Total N
Engineering	1.5	19,564	3.2	15,333	8.4	35,475
Dentistry	4.5	1,756	16.4	1,974	24.8	1,890
Architecture	9.3	2,356	19.0	1,529	33.5	2,271
Agriculture	10.5	4,249	24.5	2,988	38.0	5,097
Commerce	7.3	17,427	19.5	22,174	40.3	48,575
Medicine	25.5	5,773	28.1	6,136	41.8	7,560
Law	6.9	4,726	22.0	8,162	43.7	8,178
Arts & Science	39.4	124,802	37.9	170,863	52.0	164,360
Education	58.8	22,565	63.1	34,864	67.5	35,414
Pharmacy	46.2	2,239	56.0	2,689	76.5	2,880
Nursing	95.5	4,037	97.9	5,190	97.7	7,447
Other	46.2	15,001	56.0	6,023	55.1	22,738

Source: Neil Guppy, "Accessibility to Higher Education — New Trend Data," *CAUT Bulletin ACPU*, 35.6 (1988): 15. Printed by permission.

visible. They are much more emphatic and persuasive than columns of numbers, and tend to be used when the audience is quite general and the purpose is to persuade. Their main disadvantage is that it is almost impossible to read off precise measurements. For this reason, the quantities are often also indicated numerically on the graphs.

In preparing a bar graph, observe the following guidelines:

- Choose between a vertical or horizontal graph on the basis of appearance and the nature of the variables. Favour horizontal graphs if there are too many bars to fit comfortably across a page, if the differences in the dependent variables are so great as to use up too much vertical space, or if the labels for the independent variables are too long to fit comfortably beneath them.
- In a vertical graph, show the dependent variable on the vertical axis; in a horizontal graph, show the dependent variable on the horizontal axis.
- Choose a scale for the dependent variable so that the shortest bar will be clearly visible, the graph will be only slightly longer than the longest bar, the differences between bars will be clearly visible, and the graph won't be smaller than one third of a page. It is best to begin the scale at zero, but if doing so obscures the differences between bars or makes the graph too large, use hash marks (parallel lines enclosing a break in the axis) to indicate a break in the scale; in this case, you must also use hash marks on all the bars.
- Label the scale on the axis for the dependent variable. Use natural intervals such as 2, 5, 10, 20, 50. Use tick marks between labelled intervals to increase readability. Identify the dependent variable and the units used.
- Arrange the bars in a logical order. If there is a bar showing a control value, place it at the left or at the top.
- Choose a bar width and a space width that will make the graph attractive and readable. Make the spaces between bars at least one half the width of the bars.
- Label each bar. Place the labels beneath vertical bars and to the left of horizontal bars.
- Use a title that states accurately what the bar graph shows.

In preparing a pie chart, observe the following guidelines:

- Do not try to include more than eight wedges in one chart. If you have more, combine the smaller ones.
- Use compasses or a template to draw the circle. The more wedges there are in the chart, the larger the circle should be to allow all wedges to be visible and to leave plenty of room for clear labels. In most cases, the radius will be between 30 mm and 50 mm.
- Use a protractor to measure the wedges. Calculate the size of each wedge in degrees. (If x is the quantity to be represented as a wedge, and y is the quantity represented by the entire circle, then the size of the wedge in degrees will be x/y x 360.) Draw a vertical line from the centre of the circle to the twelve o'clock position. Begin the

largest wedge with this line and measure clockwise. Place the other wedges in descending order clockwise.

- Label each wedge clearly. Keep all printing horizontal. If possible, place the label within the wedge; if not, place it outside. Include the percentage or the numerical quantity represented by the wedge.
- Use a title that states clearly what the pie chart shows.

LINE GRAPHS. Line graphs, which are even more abstract than bar graphs, represent quantities as points and variations in variables as a line. Their main advantage over tables is that they reveal the relationships between variables. Consider, for example, Table 3-2. Most readers would realize that Table 3-2 shows that $y = 2x$ and that this relationship can be represented by the curve in Figure 3-7.

Whether you present these data in a table, in a line graph, or as an equation will depend in part on your audience and in part on your purpose. Fewer readers would be able to visualize Figure 3-8, which graphs the relationship of x and z from Table 3-2. For this reason, as

Figure 3-7
Line Graph Showing the Relationship between x and y in Table 3-2

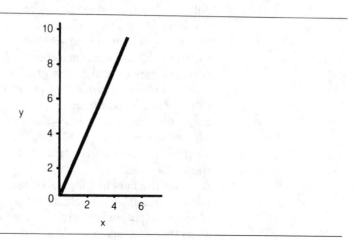

Figure 3-8
Line Graph Showing the Relationship between x and z in Table 3-2

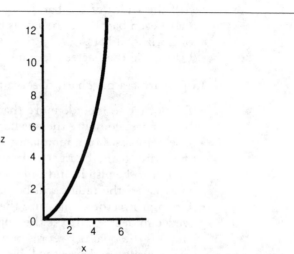

the relationships within data become more complex, the case for using line graphs becomes stronger. In fact, the making of line graphs is a standard discovery procedure in scientific research. The data are plotted to discover what the curve looks like. A skilled mathematician may then be able to find the equation that defines this curve and thereby expresses the relationship shown in the curve.

The main disadvantage of line graphs over tables is that they may obscure what the precise values of the points are. The other problem is that line graphs are difficult for some audiences to understand.

In preparing a line graph, observe the following guidelines:

- Use the vertical axis for the dependent variable and the horizontal axis for the independent variable.
- Make the vertical axis between two thirds and three quarters of the length of the horizontal axis. Make the graph no smaller than one third of a page.
- Decide whether or not the vertical axis will start at zero. In making this decision, consider the variable you are showing and the variation the graph shows. For example, if you were graphing a patient's temperature, it would not make sense to show 0°C. If the vertical axis does not begin at zero, you have to indicate this by leaving a space between the axes. Another solution is to begin at zero, but to use hash marks to indicate that the bottom portion of the graph is omitted.
- Choose a scale for the independent variable that allows you to plot your points comfortably.
- Choose a scale for the dependent variable that makes the vertical axis only slightly longer than the position of the point showing the largest value of the dependent variable and that will allow the important differences in values to be seen. Note that choice of scales will determine what the curve looks like and the impression it creates. If you want your readers to think a change is significant, you'll want to create a slope of at least 30°.
- Mark each axis in equidistant intervals, label main intervals, and use tick marks between main intervals. Use natural intervals such as 2, 5, 10, 20, 50.
- Label each axis clearly with the name of the variable and the unit of measure.
- Use very small circles, triangles, or squares to show points.
- Make the curve darker and thicker than the axis lines.

GRAPHICS TO ILLUSTRATE PROCESSES

To indicate the steps or stages in a process, and their sequence or interrelationship, various types of flow charts have been developed. Flow charts are abstract in the sense that they use symbols or words to represent the steps, and spatial relationships to represent time relationships, but they are still understood by most audiences. Figures 4-1b and 9-1 are examples of flow charts.

To indicate the planned schedule for a project, there are other types of graphics that show time as well as the steps in a process. The most common of these types of graphics is the Gantt chart. The activities or steps that are planned are listed in a column at the left of a Gantt chart. The rest of the chart consists of a series of labelled columns that represent specific time units (days, weeks, months) and a line or bar directly opposite each activity to indicate when and for how long that particular activity will be engaged in. See Figure 3-9 for an example of a simple Gantt chart for completing a survey.

COMPUTER-GENERATED GRAPHICS

The availability of graphics programs for personal computers has revolutionized the use of graphics in written communication. The main advantages of computer graphics are the speed and ease with which accurate and attractive graphics can be produced. These advantages have freed writers to control graphics as well as words. Graphics programs are tools that you can use to enhance your drawing skills and to remove the tedious work of plotting graphs.

Figure 3-9
A Gantt Chart for
Conducting a Survey

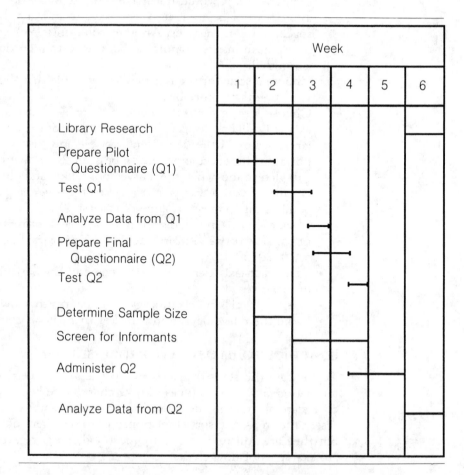

The principles outlined in this chapter should help you make sound decisions about the design of your graphics. The speed and ease with which your personal computer can produce a graphic should encourage you to experiment with design and to revise your graphics. Aim to produce the *best* graphics you can. Perhaps the most important guideline to follow in using computer-generated graphics is to *keep them simple.* Include only the information that is *necessary* and display it as *clearly* as possible.

CONVENTIONS GOVERNING THE USE OF GRAPHICS IN TEXT

When you use graphics in a text, you must observe conventions governing identification, labelling, and size. You can use the ones outlined here until you are given others by your employer or an editor.

IDENTIFICATION

Every graphic must be identified as a "Figure" or a "Table," followed by a number and then a title. Every graphic *except a table* is called a figure. The identification is centred on the page and placed above a table and below a figure. Both tables and figures are numbered using Arabic numbers, but have separate number sequences, so that you could have the following order:

Figure 1
Figure 2
Table 1
Figure 3
Table 2
Figure 4

The title should be as clear and revealing as possible because it is a major factor in telling the reader what to look for and how to interpret the graphic. It should provide a synopsis of what the graphic shows. To see how important titles are, consider what Figure 3-10 shows. Note how your interpretation shifts as you use the following titles:

- four cows
- the Coast Mountains in British Columbia
- the Fraser Valley
- Jerseys grazing
- pasture protected by a dike

Giving your graphic a number allows you to refer to the graphic in the text.

If you have copied a graphic from a published source, you must indicate your source as part of the identification, as in Figure 3-1.

Figure 3-10
A Photograph Whose
Interpretation
Depends on Its Title

LABELLING

Words are an essential part of most graphics, though exactly how they are used will differ with the type of graphic (see Table 3-4).

Table 3-4
What the Words in
Various Types of
Graphics Identify

Graphic	What the Words Identify
Photograph	Parts (rare)
Drawing	Parts
Diagram	Symbols
Aerial Photograph	Locations or Features
Map	Locations
Table	Variables
Bar Graph	Variables
Line Graph	Variables
Flow Chart	Steps

Generally, labels answer the question "What's this?" In graphics showing objects, the labels will identify parts by naming them and showing their location. The purpose of the graphic and of the discourse in which it is used will, of course, determine what has to be identified and how. In instructions, for example, there is no need to identify parts you do not need to refer to. The labels *select* information for the reader's attention, and *direct* the reader's attention to the important features.

Observe the following guidelines for labels:

- Make the wording brief and accurate.
- Label all the parts that the user needs to identify. Some labels of the "known" are needed as reference points for the reader. However, too much labelling of the obvious can insult the reader.
- Make the labels neat. Print the labels carefully, using a ruler to make sure the words are straight. If there are too many parts to label neatly, use a number code and a key.
- Use neat, straight lines or arrows to point to parts.

SIZE

In deciding on the size of a graphic, consider the subject you are showing, the appearance of the page, and any editorial constraints.

SUBJECT. First decide what you want to show in the graphic, and then make the graphic large enough to show this clearly and to make labelling easy. Sometimes you need several graphics to show one object. One graphic can show the shape of the object and the location of the main components. Other graphics can show the detail of the components. Consider also the complexity of what you are showing; the same size of illustration could be used to show the general shape of an elephant or the details of the eye of a spider. The simpler the illustration, the smaller it can be. Note, though, that we seem to have a psychological need for a size symbolism. This size symbolism will be offended, in particular, if large objects, such as bulldozers or airplanes, are presented in overly small illustrations.

APPEARANCE OF THE PAGE. Make illustrations no smaller than one third of the page; the most common size is half a page. Place each illustration as close as possible to the text reference. Try to have text both above and below an illustration, though this is not mandatory. In student work, avoid placing graphics beside text, even though in professional work this can be quite acceptable. The most common student errors are to make illustrations too small and to insist on placing them at the bottom of a page when placing them on the next page would be better.

EDITORIAL CONSTRAINTS. In professional manuscripts, it is customary simply to indicate where an illustration is to appear and then to submit it on separate paper for the editors to place where it is convenient in printing. Make the labels and the small details of the graphic large enough so that they will be legible after they are reduced in the printing process.

INTEGRATING GRAPHICS AND TEXT

In technical discourse, the text and graphics must be integrated to form a single unit. Three special functions the text must perform are the following:

1. *Direct the reader to the graphic.* It is the text that must tell the reader when it is time to look at the graphic; the text cues the reader. For the text to do this, you can use phrases like the following:

   - "Figure 3 shows the current arrangement of the workroom."
   - "See Table 2 for a comparison of this year's sales with last year's."
   - "Costs have increased by a third (see Figure 5)."

   You must observe two rules:

   - In the text you must refer to *each* graphic.
   - You must place this reference to precede the graphic.

2. *Help the reader read the graphic.* The degree and kind of help needed in reading the graphic will depend on the kind of graphic it is and on the audience's experience in reading graphics. The two main sources of reading problems are the noisiness of the graphic and the audience's unfamiliarity with the graphic conventions used. Graphics at the lower levels of abstraction tend to contain material that may not be directly relevant, and the audience may need to be guided in selecting the relevant information. Labels will help the reader, of course, but the text may need to point out explicitly what to note in the graphic. Sometimes, noise can also be reduced by preparing a graphic with a higher level of abstraction. Graphics at high levels of abstraction, however, may use graphic symbols and graphic conventions with which the audience may not be familiar. Obviously, you should use graphics that are understood by the audience; however, if you cannot avoid difficult graphic conventions, then you must use the text to help the reader interpret the graphic.

3. *Discuss the graphic.* Think of the graphic as providing the *what* and the text as providing the *so what*. It is rare for a graphic to require no comment. In reports, in particular, you will probably need to discuss the significance of what is shown in a graphic.

EXERCISES

1. How many graphics do you think you see in one day? Which types are they? Keep a record for one day of both the number and types you see and the context in which you find them (newspaper, TV, bulletin board). Display these data in appropriate graphics for class discussion.

2. Find and photocopy at least three examples of each of the following types of graphics:

- photos
- drawings
- diagrams
- maps
- tables
- bar graphs
- pie charts
- line graphs

a. Comment on the strengths and weaknesses of each.

b. Suggest how each could be improved.

c. Comment on how each has or has not been adapted to its purpose and audience.

3. Identify two physical plan problems either in the classroom or building in which you take this course. How could you use graphics to show these problems? Give instructions that a graphic artist could follow to produce these graphics.

4. Photocopy a map of your campus. Suggest how you would modify this map for the following purposes:

a. To show visiting high school students how to get from the gymnasium to the library and then to the classroom for this course.

b. To show visitors where they may park.

c. To show where a proposed statue should be placed.

5. Photocopy the portion of a map of your city that includes your home. Simplify the map to show your home, public transportation routes, and those places you visit regularly (bank, grocery store, doctor's office). How will you label the features on this map?

6. See exercise 3 in Chapter 15. How would you present the results for each question in the questionnaire?

7. Design a table that would show the following for your college or university:

- the total student population for the last five years
- the total faculty population for the last five years
- the distribution of the student population by faculty and/or major
- the male/female distribution of the students, faculty, and staff.

It is not necessary for you to know what the actual numbers are.

8. Propose a different design for the table in exercise 7 and note the strengths and weaknesses of each arrangement.

9. Explain how you could use bar graphs, pie charts, and line graphs to display the data in the tables you designed in exercises 7 and 8.

10. Get the data needed for exercise 7, or estimate the numbers. Then prepare either a bar graph, a pie chart, or a line graph to show some of these data. Prepare the figure exactly as you would in a report.

11. Consider Table 3-3:

    a. Suggest three bases on which you could arrange the nominal variables (Engineering, Dentistry, and so on).

    b. Suggest how you could use pie charts to present some of these data effectively. Prepare two pie charts.

    c. Suggest how you could use bar graphs to present some of these data effectively. Prepare two bar graphs.

    d. Suggest how you could use line graphs to present some of these data effectively. Prepare two line graphs.

PART TWO

THE TECHNICAL WRITING PROCESS

CHAPTER 4

INTRODUCTION TO THE TECHNICAL WRITING PROCESS

INTRODUCTION

The writing process refers to what takes place between the point at which a writer is given an assignment or decides to write something and the point at which the assignment is finished. If the assignment is one in technical writing, then we can speak of this process as "the technical writing process." In the professional context, this process is most likely to begin with your supervisor saying something like "Will you look into this and give me a report by Friday?" and end with your submitting the final, or presentation, copy of the report. The question this part of the book pursues is how best to proceed between these two points, how best to produce a document. The purpose of this chapter is to give you an overview of the writing process by introducing the main subprocesses and discussing how they are related. Each subprocess is discussed in more detail in a separate chapter.

Let us begin by looking more closely at the term *the writing process*. That we are talking about a process is indisputable. However, what about the word *writing*? Does one produce a document simply by writing? The answer, of course, is no. Consider what you do, besides writing, to get from an initial assignment to the finished copy. Do you worry? Do you think about what you should write? Do you plan what you will write? Do you get materials from the library? Do you discuss the assignment with anyone? None of these activities is what one could call "writing." The point, then, is that the actual writing is only one part of the writing process. A more accurate term for the process might be *the document generation process*.

SUBPROCESSES

We must recognize that it is impossible to write a simple algorithm or set of instructions for the writing process. Not only do scholars simply not know very much about exactly how people write, but they know very little about how thinking is related to speaking or writing. Further, it appears that people vary a great deal in how they write, and even the same person does not write all documents using the same strategies. The best we can do at this time is claim that the following subprocesses appear to be necessary to the production of a good document:

- *Defining the task.* The writer must determine the purpose and audience of the document, as well as the constraints on its preparation.
- *Gathering evidence.* The writer must determine what the document will contain. This subprocess may include designing and conducting research.

- *Organizing and outlining.* The writer must determine the structure of the document.
- *Writing the initial draft, including graphics.* The writer must prepare a first prose version of the document.
- *Revising.* The writer must improve the initial draft.
- *Preparing the presentation copy.* The writer must prepare a copy of the document that can be submitted. This preparation includes deciding matters of layout, preparing illustrations, and typing or printing the text in the appropriate format.

These subprocesses are discussed in detail in Chapters 5 to 9. Chapter 15 discusses gathering evidence.

RELATIONSHIP AMONG SUBPROCESSES

Although these subprocesses are listed here as though they are distinct and sequential, the relationship among them is complex. It appears that writers tend to apply the subprocesses recursively, and sometimes concurrently. In other words, the sequence is *least* likely to be as shown in Figure 4-1a, and more likely to be as shown in Figure 4-1b.

Figure 4-1a (left) Sequential View of the Writing Process

Figure 4-1b (right) Cyclical View of the Writing Process

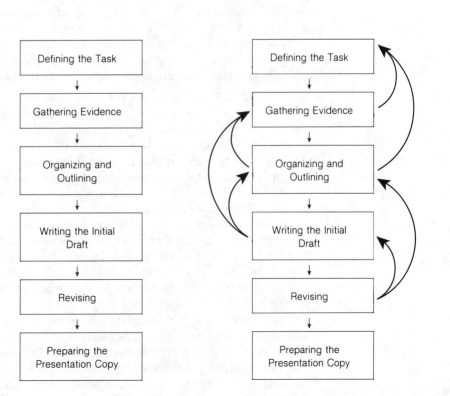

Few people can prepare any but the most routine documents by going directly to writing the initial draft (step 4) and then directly to preparing the final copy (step 6). In fact, writing the initial draft may be the least important step, and organizing (step 3) and revising (step 5) may have the greatest impact on the quality of the final document. Many students make the mistake of spending most of the total available time on writing the initial draft; experienced writers suggest spending as little as ten percent on this step.

The following chapters present a "maximal" view of the writing process; you will discover which specific strategies work best for you and which steps require special attention in preparing a particular document. But why, you might ask, don't we all write the same way? There is no simple answer to this question, but we can observe that, generally, people differ in how they process information. Not all students take notes the same way, or solve calculus problems the same way either. Some people find that a sketch will help them "see" a problem better, while others do not. In other words, there may be as many differences in how people write as there are in how people learn. As well, differences in temperament will affect how individuals write. Your attention span, your response to the "permanence" of writing, your tolerance of mess and uncertainty, your flexibility, your reaction to pressure, and even your energy level can affect how you write. The implications for you are that you should be aware of what you are doing, of what seems to work for you, and try to adapt suggested strategies so that they do help you.

It is most unlikely that any practising professional uses the maximal writing process for all documents. Factors that affect how completely and carefully you should apply these subprocesses include the following:

- *The availability of resources.* You will have to balance what you would like to do to produce a good document against the time, energy, and materials available. For example, if you have to prepare a proposal or report in only a day or two, you may have to curtail research and revise only the most serious flaws.
- *The uniqueness of the document.* Many of your writing assignments on the job will be fairly routine and you will be able to write these using an abbreviated process, often even copying sections from previous documents. However, when you are faced with a unique assignment, you will need to proceed much more deliberately.
- *The length of the document.* The longer the document, the more important it is that you plan it carefully before attempting a draft, first because it is impossible to hold a long document in mind, and second because false starts are costly.
- *The complexity or sensitivity of the document.* Some documents are inherently more difficult to write because of the number of variables you have to consider or the complexity of the issues you have to deal with. Others are difficult because you have to try to overcome the reader's resistance, or because you have to advocate an unpopular position, or because you must accommodate legal considera-

tions. Whenever you encounter one of these difficult assignments, you are more likely to need to follow the suggested strategies for the writing process; the simpler and more neutral the writing task, the more likely you are to use an abbreviated procedure.

- *The importance of the document.* Obviously, the more important you perceive a document to be, the greater the care you will take in preparing it, and the more deliberate you are likely to be with the writing subprocesses.
- *The degree to which the document will be judged as writing.* While you must always meet a standard of adequacy, in many documents you will want to aim for excellence. It is when a document is likely to be judged explicitly as writing that it becomes particularly important to follow the subprocesses of the writing process fully.
- *The permanence of the document.* A memo that will be discarded before you go home for the day normally does not deserve the attention you might give to a report that will be consulted for months or years to come.

Even though we have been talking about "*the* writing process," we do not pretend that there is only one writing process; rather, there are many writing processes, most of which will include the subprocesses discussed in the following chapters.

EXERCISES

1. Describe your own writing process. What exactly do you do when you write? What portion of the total time do you typically devote to each subprocess?

2. Describe how your procedure varies from assignment to assignment.

3. Order the subprocesses according to how difficult you usually find them to be.

CHAPTER 5

DEFINING THE TASK: AUDIENCE, PURPOSE, AND GENRE

Introduction

Why Is This Document Being Written?

Who Is the Audience?

How Will the Document Be Used?

How Will the Document's Success Be Judged?

What Genre (Letter, Memo, Formal Report, Manual) Is Required?

What Are the Constraints within which You Must Work?

Checklist for Defining the Task

Notes

Introduction

The first step in preparing any document, like the first step in most activities, is to determine as much as you can about what it is you are trying to do. This chapter discusses the following questions that you should answer in defining a writing task:

- Why is this document being written?
- Who is the audience?
- How will the document be used?
- How will the document's success be judged?
- What genre (letter, memo, formal report, manual) is required?
- What are the constraints within which you must work?

The chapter includes a checklist for defining a writing task.

Why is this document being written?

Almost all of the documents you will write as a professional will be written because someone needs them; documents will typically have specific audiences and purposes. In determining why you are writing a particular document, then, you will want to find out exactly who needs or wants it and why. Even though many of your writing tasks will be assigned to you by your supervisors, you should not assume that the document is needed to fill only their needs. In fact, most documents have several purposes. The situation is complicated by the fact that at work you will not write and read only as an individual. You will also write and read as one in your particular role in the organization, such as supervisor of sales; as a representative of your department; or as a representative of the entire organization. For this reason, we will use the term *source* to mean the writer in the role or capacity from which he or she is writing, and *audience* to mean the reader(s) in their roles or capacities. If you are working in the design department of O.K. Engines Ltd., for example, you could write documents for which you as an individual are the source, documents for which the design department is the source, and documents for which O.K. Engines is the source. Similarly, your audience could be an individual, a department, or another organization. Some documents arise primarily from the needs of the source, some from the needs of the audience, and some from the needs of both.

You should also consider the background or context from which the need to write the document arises. What prompted the need or want that you are responding to? Most documents are related to events or to other documents, and an important part of defining the task is to find out as much as you can about this history.

On the basis of who initiates the document, who needs or wants it, and what for, we can sketch a partial taxonomy, or classification scheme of technical writing.

SOURCE- (WRITER-) INITIATED DOCUMENTS

Source-initiated documents may be written in response to the following situations:

- The source wants money, work, action, or information. In this case, your purpose is to make clear exactly what you want and to persuade your audience to give it. Some important examples of this class of documents are the following:
  - A job application. (You, as an individual, want a job.)
  - A proposal. (Your organization wants to win a contract for a job.)
  - A letter or memo of inquiry. (You want information.)
  - A letter or memo of complaint. (You want a settlement or a change in behaviour.)
  - Advertising. (Your organization wants to sell something, such as goods or services.)

- The audience needs information, but you, the source, initiate the document. In this case your purpose is to inform, but it may also be to persuade. Some important examples of this kind of document are educational materials such as pamphlets and instructions, particularly user manuals.

- You, often as an individual, want to sell an idea in order to gain in reputation. Scholarly articles fall into this class, and again your purpose is persuasive as well as informative.

Whether or not your audience expects the document will affect how much background you have to provide and how much interest in your document you can assume. In the worst case, you may have an audience that does not want to read your document and you may even have to persuade it to consider your message at all.

AUDIENCE-INITIATED DOCUMENTS

Often the audience needs a document, asks the source for it, and pays for it. Usually it wants information, but it may also want advice. This category of document includes the various kinds of reports, both in-house and out-of-house, as well as replies to letters of inquiry. In this case, you must determine what the information needs of the audience are. The purpose of the document is to supply the needed information, and sometimes to persuade the audience that the information you are presenting is valid and reliable.

WHO IS THE AUDIENCE?

By audience we mean the person or people who will encounter the document. You may be surprised at the use of the verb *encounter* in this context. However, it has been chosen on purpose to convey the fact that a professional document may be submitted to one person who, without necessarily reading it, may forward it to someone else, who may read it and then pass it to someone else again to read and act upon. In other words, the audience is often a larger class than the reader(s), and the encounter does not always entail reading, particularly not in the ordinary sense.

Although there is little conclusive scholarly evidence about how audience variables and text variables do or should interact, it appears that audience characteristics are relevant to choices about form, content, organization, graphics, tone, and diction. The following questions will help you define your audience:

- How large is your audience?
- What is the relationship between you and your audience?
- What are your audience's responsibilities, interests, and attitudes?
- What information does your audience need or want in the document?
- What does your audience know?

SIZE AND MEMBERSHIP

Consider the person to whom the document is addressed and whether or not others have to be included in the audience. There are at least four possibilities:

- The document is addressed to *one* reader who will be the *only* reader. This situation is the easiest to deal with because it probably comes closest to the kind you have already experienced in writing personal letters and, to a lesser extent, in preparing assignments for your instructors. At work, this situation is likely to apply only for the less important and shorter documents, such as some letters and memos.
- The document is addressed to *several* readers. In this situation you will usually be writing to readers in their roles as members of a group. Because of their differences as individuals, this can be a more complex situation than that described above. Examples of this kind of writing assignment would be announcements or directives, such as those addressed to all the staff in a department, or reports to groups such as a board of directors. This situation is quite a common one in professional communication.
- The document is addressed to *one* reader who will direct it to other readers in an organization. This situation is much more difficult to accommodate, but it is probably the most common one you will encounter. Not only do you have to design the document to meet

what may be conflicting demands, but it may be difficult to determine exactly who is included in the audience. To do so you will have to find out the complete path that the document will take after you submit it. Typically, your supervisor will ask you to prepare a document, but will pass it to others who may, in turn, pass it further.

- The document is not addressed to anyone specific, but will be read by many, who may or may not constitute a homogeneous group. Included in this category are documents such as operator's manuals, educational pamphlets, and press releases. The main difficulty in this case is that since you cannot determine exactly who the audience is, you can only try to estimate the general characteristics its members are likely to share.

The questions or variables discussed below apply to individuals; if your audience is greater than one, you should try to apply each variable to each member.

RELATIONSHIP BETWEEN WRITER AND AUDIENCE

Obviously, there are many variables in the relationship between writer and audience, but some of the critical ones are the following:

- Are the writer and audience members of the same organization?
- What is the relative status of writer and audience?
- How well does the audience know the writer?
- Does the audience like the writer?

ARE THE WRITER AND THE AUDIENCE MEMBERS OF THE SAME ORGANIZATION? Documents addressed to members of the same organization are called *in-house documents*, and those addressed outside the organization are called *out-of-house documents*. It is customary to use memos for in-house communications and letters for out-of-house communications. In out-of-house documents you will have to be especially careful how you represent the organization you work for. As far as the audience is concerned, you *are* your organization, and your documents will contribute to your organization's corporate image. Also, what you say may have legal consequences, and your care and skill in preparing documents could prevent lawsuits. Some business letters may form parts of a contract; others could be used as evidence to support a case in court.[1]

WHAT IS THE RELATIVE STATUS OF WRITER AND AUDIENCE? Status may be difficult to define, but it is roughly equivalent to rank or position in the organization. Relative status is likely to be more important for in-house than for out-of-house communications, although even there it should not be overlooked. The relative status of your audience will determine the tone and the level of formality of your writing, as well as what you can do within the document. For example, if you are writing to someone with less status, you *can* tell him or her what to do, but if you are writing to someone with more status, you can't. On the basis of relative rank we can speak of writing *up, down,* or *laterally* in the organization. Relative rank will also determine in part the kind of document you write. For example, you will normally write reports *up* in the organization, while you will write directives *down.* Status becomes especially important in memos, which could be written up, down, or laterally.

HOW WELL DOES THE AUDIENCE KNOW THE WRITER? Familiarity of writer and audience should be reflected in the tone and the level of formality of letters and memos. In writing a particular document, then, you will have to gauge how familiar you should be, for you may offend and alienate your audience by being either too distant or too friendly. You must also be careful, though, to separate personal familiarity from "official" familiarity; the fact that you are dating the loans manager at the bank should not affect the tone of your appeal for the rescheduling of a loan.

DOES THE AUDIENCE LIKE THE WRITER? While much professional writing is independent of personal relationships, your audience's opinion of you always has some potential to affect how your document is interpreted. If there is friction between you and your audience, you must be especially careful in how you design your document so as to overcome any resistance to your message that may result from this friction. You may have to focus especially on being persuasive and on phrasing your message in the most appealing terms.

AUDIENCE'S RESPONSIBILITIES, INTERESTS, AND ATTITUDES

To identify your audience fully, you must know your audience's job. What does your audience do? What are its main concerns? What are the pressures with which it has to deal? What are the limits of its authority? What are its legal responsibilities? What is it obliged to do and what is it prevented from doing? The above questions are particularly important when you are writing documents that suggest or request actions or decisions.

AUDIENCE'S INFORMATION NEEDS

What information does the audience need or want in the document? If possible, you should ask your audience what it wants you to include. If this is not possible, or if your audience doesn't or can't know what it needs, then you will have to try to put yourself in your audience's place and decide what it will need to know. What questions do you expect your audience to want answered? These, of course, will be related to the audience's responsibilities and to how the document will be used.

AUDIENCE'S KNOWLEDGE

Closely related to what the audience needs to know is what it already knows, because this will determine how much background and introductory information you should include. In addition to providing new information to your audience, you should also *remind* your audience about information that is not new, but whose details may have been forgotten. Also, you have to consider what your audience will understand, particularly with respect to technical terms, mathematics, scientific and other principles, and graphics. This will depend in part on the audience's formal education, but it is not always easy to determine exactly what kind of education your audience has, and even if you do, you must remember that no two people who have the same education know or understand exactly the same things. In other words, your audience's education can at best give you a very general sense of what you do and do not have to explain. Usually, it is safer to direct the document at a slightly lower level than you might think is necessary. Consider also how well your audience reads, particularly if you cannot assume it has a postsecondary education. Ultimately, you will have to find a balance between being unclear because you have assumed knowledge that the audience does not have, and being boring because you are repeating the obvious.

How will the document be used?

To determine how the document will be used, both in the short and long terms, you have to put yourself in your audience's place. You may even need to research how various types of in-house and out-of-house documents are usually used. In particular, you should determine how the document will be read initially and what the audience will do with the document after reading it.

HOW WILL THE DOCUMENT BE READ INITIALLY?

Part of learning to read effectively is learning to use different reading strategies when faced with different kinds of reading tasks. For example, consider how you read the user's manual for your car, a newspaper, a magazine at the dentist's office, a textbook, a library book, a dictionary. If you can anticipate how a particular document will be read, you can design it so that it is best suited to the kind of reading it will receive.

The following subcategories of reading have been proposed:[2]

- *skimming*: determining the drift
- *scanning*: looking for particular kinds of information
- *searching*: looking for the meaning of special items
- *critical reading*: reading for evaluation

In the writing you have done as a student, you have probably been able to assume a critical reading. In professional writing you certainly should not always assume this; much of what you write will only be skimmed, scanned, or searched. Of course, the special features of technical writing are available to assist in these kinds of reading. Both headings and lists, as well as typographic aids help in scanning and searching; summaries and abstracts help the reader who only wants to skim. Also, in professional writing, you are often faced with the problem of designing a document so that different audiences can read it in different ways.

WHAT WILL THE AUDIENCE DO WITH THE DOCUMENT?

Try to determine what the audience will do as a result of reading the document and what it will do to the document.

- *Read and discard.* Many routine announcements and memos are discarded after reading.
- *Read and file for the record.* Many routine documents must be kept for the record, but may not require any particular response from the audience. These documents constitute the history of a project, decision, or of doing business, and may have legal importance. Within this category are lab reports, trip reports, job and procedure descriptions, and many kinds of reports that are prepared on printed forms. Most of these reports are written to account for time or money spent, or decisions reached.

    Even though these documents may initially seem unimportant, they should be clearly written, because some of them may have to be consulted and understood many years later when the immediate context will have been forgotten. In addition to knowing what will happen to a document immediately, then, you should also consider whether that document will be consulted in the future, by whom, and for what purpose. The specifications and progress reports for a construction project, such as a bridge, for example, may be consulted years later when problems arise or modifications are needed, or when the company undertakes a similar project.
- *Read and answer and then file.* Letters and memos of inquiry will be answered and then filed.
- *Read and use as the basis of action.* Instructions, directives, and some kinds of letters will be used as the basis of action. In this case you have to make sure your audience understands what it is to do. Try to assess the kinds of questions that will occur to the audience and answer them.

    Will the audience resist what you tell it to do? Why? How can you overcome this resistance? One of the important problems in writing instructions, for example, is getting your audience to read and follow them carefully. Similarly, if you are trying to get your audience to modify its behaviour, you may have to overcome its resistance to change.
- *Read and use as the basis of a decision.* Many reports are used as the basis of decisions. Determine who will make the decision and when. What factors will influence the decision? What will its effects be? What is at stake for you, for your role, and for your organization as a result of this decision? Will your document become part of the data for another document? Will it be used to support another argument?

How will the document's success be judged?

Try to establish the criteria for judging the success of the document so that you have a clear idea of what your goal is. The simplest way of judging the success of a document is, of course, by the reaction it brings, by the impact or result it has. If you win the contract, or get the job, or get the settlement you want, your document has succeeded. Most of the time, though, the situation is more complex and you may have to do quite a bit of consulting and interpreting to determine the document's success.

Consider also who will judge the success. There are at least three possibilities: you, your supervisor, and your audience. Often the criteria used by these three will not coincide, and then you will have the difficult job of striking a balance between them, or at least a compromise within which you can work.

What genre (letter, memo, formal report, manual) is required?

Most of the time, the genre, or type of document, will be specified as part of the assignment. If it isn't, you will have to decide what is most suitable. As well, you will have to consider what verbal and visual resources are available for this kind of document and decide how to use them for greatest success.

What are the constraints within which you must work?

Again, you are likely to be told some of the constraints at the time you receive the assignment, but if you are not, you must determine how much time you have and what personnel, library and lab materials, and production facilities you can use.

Checklist for defining the task
WHY AM I WRITING THIS DOCUMENT?

- Who initiated this document? Why?
- Who needs this document? Why?

WHO IS THE AUDIENCE?

- How large is the audience?
- What is the relationship between me and the audience?
  - Is the audience part of my organization?
  - Is the status of the audience higher or lower than my status?
  - How well does the audience know me?
  - Does the audience like me?
- What are the audience's responsibilities, interests, and attitudes?

- What does the audience need to know?
- What does the audience know?

HOW WILL THE DOCUMENT BE USED?

- Will the audience skim, scan, search, or read the document critically?
- After reading the document, will the audience discard it, file it, answer it, use it as the basis of an action, or use it as the basis of a decision?

HOW WILL THE DOCUMENT'S SUCCESS BE JUDGED?

- Who will judge its success?
- What must the document do to be successful?
  - Should it change attitudes? Whose? How?
  - Should it precipitate action? Whose? How?

WHAT GENRE IS REQUIRED?

WHAT ARE THE CONSTRAINTS WITHIN WHICH I MUST WORK?

- What are my deadlines?
- What resources can I use?

NOTES

1. Christine Parkin, "Technical Writing Assignments and the Law," *Technostyle* 7.3 (Winter 1988): 26-31.
2. A.K. Pugh, *Silent Reading: An Introduction to Its Study and Teaching* (London: Heinemann, 1978).

CHAPTER 6

ORGANIZING AND OUTLINING

Introduction

Formal Outlines

Informal Outlines

Exercises

INTRODUCTION

Whether or not they realize it, all writers organize, usually throughout the writing process. You are organizing when you ask yourself any of the following questions: Where should I begin? What should I say next? Is this in the right place? Although organizing is not really an isolated step or process, it is wise and efficient to try to organize as much as you can *before* you begin to write the draft. Very few experienced writers in the professions try to start a draft without some preliminary organizing. They recognize that although organizing can be very hard and frustrating work, this work saves them a lot of time later in the writing process.

This chapter first reviews what it means for a document to be organized, what is involved in the process of organizing, and what an outline is. Then it examines the following:

- formal outlines
- some strategies for making formal outlines
- a checklist for formal outlines
- informal outlines

Organizing, like other aspects of thinking, is a very individual matter. How you organize best is probably related to how you look at the world, how you learn, and how you see and make patterns generally. Your class notes, for example, probably look quite different from those of your friends. Because of these differences, each of us has to find those organizing techniques that work best for us. Also, the techniques that are most useful will vary with the kind of document that is being planned. For these reasons, the suggestions presented in this chapter are meant to be adapted to your personal strategies and to the needs you encounter.

ORGANIZATION OF A DOCUMENT

We would all agree that a document or oral presentation must be organized. If it is not already organized for us, then as readers or listeners we must try to find its structure – to organize it – before we can really understand it. Problems in organization impede reading, and if the organization is faulty enough, the reader may just stop trying to read at all.

But what do we mean when we say that a document is organized? In the broadest sense, a document is organized if its content has a structure or pattern that we can discern. Information that is related will be found grouped together, so that the reader won't ask, "What is this doing here?" or "What has this to do with anything?" Also, the information will be arranged in an order that makes sense to the reader.

Organization extends through all levels of a document. In a book, for example, not only must the chapters be well organized, but also the sections within chapters, the paragraph blocks within sections, and the statements within paragraphs. In other words, preparing a tentative table of contents would only be the beginning of organizing.

ORGANIZATION AS PROCESS

The act of organizing is a very complex process that takes place in the writer's mind and is probably not understood fully even by cognitive psychologists. Part of organizing – but we must stress that it is only a part – is the making of an outline. Making an outline is *not* the same as organizing. Organizing can and does take place even when there is no outline, and an outline does not guarantee good organization. An outline is simply a device for recording the broad strokes of an organization plan. The outline is a product of the organization that takes place in the mind. It is usually modified as the writer continues to organize and reorganize while writing and revising.

Because there are limits to what your mind can hold and manipulate at one time, it is important to use paper or some other recording medium (blackboard, word processor) when you are organizing. There are at least three purposes for which you can use this medium:

- *To keep track of the organizing you do in your mind.* By writing down the patterns you are evolving, you are providing a record you can later manipulate. You are assisting your short-term memory.
- *To discover organization.* There are many techniques, a few of which we'll look at in this chapter, for "discovering" patterns.
- *To record the pattern that finally evolves – your outline.*

Organizing is the making of a structure or pattern. The two most important components of this structure are hierarchy and sequence. *Hierarchy* refers to one category or group dominating or including another, and *sequence* refers to what comes first, second, and so on. In making an outline, not only will you have to decide what content to include in the document, but also how that content should be ordered into groups and subgroups, and what order or sequence should be used.

OUTLINES

An outline is usually a record of the projected structure of a document. More rarely, one might outline something someone else has written in order to analyze the argument or to help in reading or preparing a summary. One might also outline a draft of one's own document to analyze its shape.

Whether or not you need an outline for a particular document will usually depend on its length, complexity, and importance. To outline a short, routine, and relatively unimportant memo or letter would be a waste of time; not only are the possible structures very simple, but they are probably also obvious to you. At the other extreme are long, unique, complex, and important documents such as major proposals or reports for which outlines are essential. The difference is rather like the difference between planning and building a doghouse or planning and building an apartment complex; you can do the one with no planning on paper, but not the other. Between these extremes fall documents that require some outlining. You are probably safest to begin by making at least a very informal outline for each document. Think of the outline as a map you need for the first few times you travel a route.

FORMAL OUTLINES

If a supervisor or instructor asks you for an outline, then usually what is required is a formal outline. The most likely situations in which you will have to prepare this kind of an outline are the following:

- A supervisor has to oversee a report you are preparing in the company's name, perhaps over your supervisor's signature. The supervisor will use your outline to check that you are on the right track before you begin to write.
- You are preparing a document together with other writers. Each of you wants to see what the shape of the entire document will be and how your section fits into the entire plan.
- You are preparing a document for a client and the client wants to see the plan before agreeing to the project.

Generally, it is a good idea to prepare a formal outline if you are writing a document longer than 2000 words, and certainly if that document will use a system of headings.

DEFINITION

A formal outline is a special display device governed by conventions. Figure 6-1 shows a student's formal outline for a formal report.

A formal outline should show the following:

- *The headings (or topics) and subheadings (or subtopics).*
- *The hierarchical relationships between headings and subheadings.* The formal outline must show which are the main divisions of the document and which subdivisions and sub-subdivisions each will have. There are various conventions for indicating these hierarchical relationships. In Figure 6-1, indention and numbering show that II dominates A, B, and C, and is at the same level of importance as III. In other words, II and III are co-ordinate, and II.A and II.B are co-ordinate, but II.A and II.B are subordinate to II. Co-ordinate headings should be grammatically parallel to each other when possible. In the actual document (and in its table of contents, if the document has one), layout and typography will show these hierarchical relationships among headings.
- *The sequence of headings and subheadings.* The vertical order in the outline indicates the sequence the document will follow.

Figure 6-1
A Student's Outline
for a Report

HOW TO INCREASE THE EFFECTIVENESS AND SAFETY OF THE WESTBANK FIRE DEPARTMENT'S EMERGENCY TELEPHONE LINE

I. Introduction

II. Organization of the Fire Telephone Response Team
   A. Establishment of a line command
     • present situation
     • persons responsible for proposed set-up
     • types of command positions
   B. Establishment of a duty roster
     • present situation
     • persons responsible for duty roster
     • roster criteria
   C. Improved methods of firefighter contact
     • present situation
     • persons responsible for contact improvement
     • suggested methods
       – update pager system
       – siren
       – telephone operator
       – ten-ten

III. Training of the Fire Response Team
   A. Establishment of a training team
     • present situation
     • persons responsible for training
     • duties of training personnel
   B. Establishment of detailed training program
     • present situation
     • program content
       – etiquette
       – information to obtain and dispatch
       – caller reaction
       – topography
       – methods of simple fire extinguishing
     • program teaching tools

IV. Community Education
   A. Education program for Westbank residents
      • present situation
      • persons responsible
      • program targets and frequency
      • program content
      • education update
   B. Education program for emergency personnel
      • present situation
      • persons responsible
      • program targets
      • types of programs
      • ongoing education
V. Conclusion

Source: Gwen McClellan, "Outline of 'How to Increase the Effectiveness and Safety of the Westbank Fire Department's Emergency Telephone Line'." Printed by permission.

In addition to the numbering system discussed here, there are several others that are equally acceptable; all of them allow you to indicate hierarchy and sequence.

Some formal outlines also indicate which particular points will appear under which heading. How full an outline you make will depend on your needs, but it is a good idea to remember that the more you include in your outline, the easier it will be to write your draft.

ADVANTAGES

A formal outline can be a very powerful tool. It has the following advantages:

• It allows you to experiment with adding, subtracting, and moving content before you actually write anything. In other words, an outline allows you to *revise* before you write a draft. Most of us suffer from a very strong psychological attachment to every word we have written; we resist changing what we have written and find it particularly difficult to throw out paragraphs or even sections. However, few people feel the same degree of attachment to a line or two in an outline. And even if we are willing to make major revisions to what we have already written, it becomes more difficult to do so because, as we write, we must introduce various cohesive ties (transition words and phrases such as *also, on the other hand*, and pronouns such as *they*) that make it more difficult to move sections of text.

- If other people have to approve or agree with how a document will be written, then the outline allows the document to be discussed before it is actually written.
- It makes writing the draft much easier and the result more *fluent* because, instead of worrying about the larger aspects of organization, you'll be able to concentrate on the content and organization within paragraphs. Also, if you do not have to interrupt your writing to find added material or to make major decisions about organization, then you are much more likely to achieve a natural flow in your writing.
- It makes it easier to use *headings* because, before you begin to write, you have already determined what the headings will be and what their relationships are. Without an outline, it would be very difficult to develop a complex heading structure.
- It makes it easier to *balance* the length of the sections of a document because you can estimate from the outline how long each section will be. In fact, an experienced writer can often envision a document from an outline just as an experienced architect can envision a building from a plan. If you are doing collaborative writing, this feature can also help you divide the writing task into more equal parts.
- It allows *segmented writing.* If you know what the sections of a long document will be and in what order they will appear, you can begin writing with any section you please. If you already have the needed information for one segment, you can write it while you wait for the material for another section to become available. Also, if for some reason you don't feel like writing about a particular subtopic, you can begin to write about one you feel more comfortable with. If there are several writers, each of you can work on sections independently.

MAKING A FORMAL OUTLINE

Although the procedure of making a formal outline is presented here as a linear process, you must remember that in fact it is recursive and that you should expect to go back and forth between steps. Also you must remember that the procedure described here is not the only possible one. As we noted earlier, organizing is a very individual matter, and as you gain experience you will discover what works best for you. Note the following hints:

- Keep your outline *flexible* as long as you can. Expect to try at least three or four versions before you find the best one. Use scrap paper so you will be free to add, subtract, or move material. Do not let the outline *look* final until it *is* final.
- Work in *short bursts.* Because outlining is a very demanding intellectual activity and cannot be engaged in for much more than 20 minutes at a time, don't expect to be able to prepare the outline of

a complex document in one sitting. Try to allow your mind to work on the problems of organizing while you are doing something else.

We can isolate the following phases to the outlining procedure:

- brainstorming
- determining hierarchy
- determining sequence
- integrating brainstorming into a tree diagram
- making the formal outline from the tree diagram

BRAINSTORMING. The purpose of brainstorming is to get down on paper the points you plan to make so that you can evaluate and arrange them. Basically, it is an aid to memory. After all, you simply cannot hold very much information in short-term memory, and brainstorming allows you to record some of what you are thinking and to provide a visible trace of your thoughts. To brainstorm, you simply write down everything that comes into your mind related to the document you are planning to write. Brainstorming is like dumping a drawer to see what is inside before you start arranging it. Figure 6-2 shows a student's brainstorming.

When you brainstorm, observe the following guidelines:

- Since the brainstorming is for you, use whatever form makes you comfortable.
- Use the kind of paper you don't mind messing up.
- Use large pieces of paper to avoid feeling cramped.
- Write as rapidly as you can so you can keep up with the flow of ideas.
- Write words and phrases, not sentences. Avoid sentences because they are slow to write, and so will discourage or interrupt the flow of thoughts. They also tend to lock you in psychologically to a particular phrasing.
- Work in short bursts. Since thinking is such a tiring activity, you are unlikely to be able to brainstorm productively for more than 15 or 20 minutes. In fact, you may be better off trying ten-minute bursts at first.
- Avoid stopping too early. Use whatever aids you can to keep going. Go back to earlier points you have noted and expand on them when appropriate. Use the following questions: who? what? when? where? why? how? so what?

Although you will normally use brainstorming early in the outlining procedure, it is a very powerful idea-generating device you can use at every stage of the writing process. Brainstorming is also a very useful technique if a group of writers has to plan a document. In this case, a blackboard will probably be used to record the brainstorming. As you gain experience in writing, you may find you want to use a word processor or a dictaphone for brainstorming.

Figure 6-2
A Student's
Brainstorming for a
Report

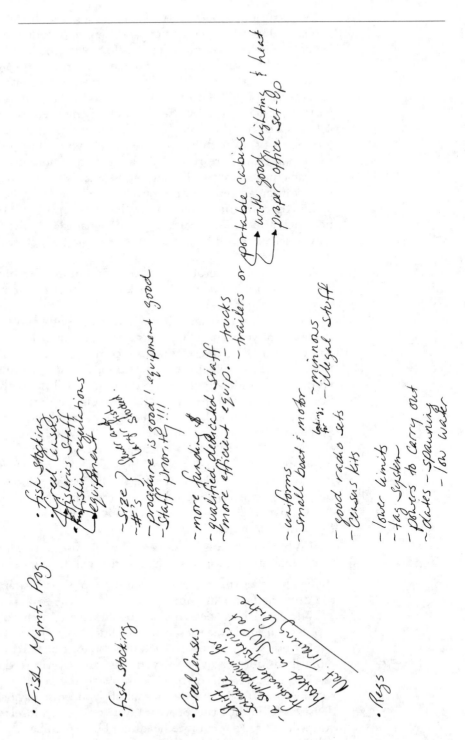

Source: Sherryl Yaciansky. Printed by permission.

DETERMINING HIERARCHY. Determining the hierarchy of topics is probably the most difficult step, and for complex documents you should expect to make several attempts before you find the best pattern. Determining hierarchy entails two cognitive processes – *partition* and *classification*. Partition is the dividing of something into its parts. In making an outline you will be dividing and subdividing the document into its parts. In other words, you will be identifying the subtopics and the sub-subtopics within the document. Classification, on the other hand, is the grouping of similar things. In the outline you will be grouping together those points that are related. In a sense, partition and classification are the same process viewed from opposite ends – the most general and the most particular. Since in a report you will be using headings, the hierarchy you construct when you outline the report will be a hierarchy of headings, and you will want to decide what exactly the headings will be, which headings will be at the same level, and which headings will dominate others.

A particularly useful device for determining the hierarchy is a tree diagram, a graphic device for making a model of hierarchical relationships. (See Figure 6-3.)

To make a tree diagram, you can begin with partition or with classification, or you can use classification together with partition recursively and construct the tree diagram by going up and down from particular to general. If you begin with partition, first decide what the major divisions or main headings of the document will be. If there are conventional divisions for the type of document you are preparing – such as introduction, method, results, discussion, conclusion – simply use these. Similarly, there may be obvious, natural divisions you can use, such as the parts of a mechanism when you are preparing a description of a mechanism. In other situations, however, you may have to choose one basis of division over several others. The first division may be critical to the document because it will often determine the angle, or perspective, from which you view a topic. In making this first division, consider the following questions:

- What are the various aspects I could use to subdivide this topic?
- What are the aspects the audience will be concerned with?

Remember that the audience's needs are most important and should be the deciding factor in your choice.

When you have determined the first level of headings, repeat the process and subdivide each main heading. Normally you can expect from two to four subdivisions for each division (or node). If you find you have more than four subdivisions, you may have overlooked an intermediate level of subdivision. Also, make sure that you do not have a single subdivision; if you have division at all, you must have at least two subdivisions. Continue this process until you are at a level where you think you will not need any more headings, but remember that ultimately you will have to organize to the paragraph level. A very common problem with organization is to think that you have finished organizing when you have determined the main headings.

Figure 6-3
A Tree Diagram
Based on Figure 6-2

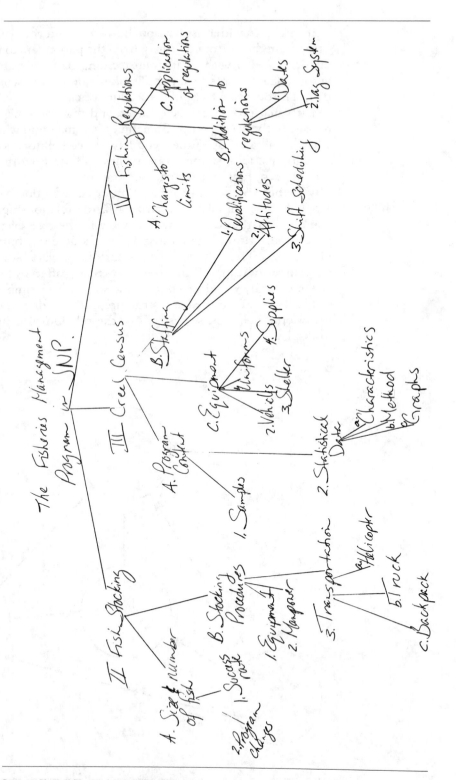

Figure 6-3
A Tree Diagram
Based on Figure 6-2

Source: Sherryl Yaciansky. Printed by permission.

If you begin with classification, however, then you will be constructing a tree from the bottom upwards, from the particulars to the more general divisions. Begin with your brainstorming or with notes on cards, and group related points together. The key question now is "What is this a part of?" Be aware that this procedure of classifying points as belonging to particular groups can be difficult, and that there may be several ways to classify the same points. Sometimes you may find it difficult to decide what to call a group. When you have placed all (or most of) the points into groups, look at the group names and see how these group names can, in turn, be grouped together, and so on.

Whether you begin with partition or classification, you may find that a bubble diagram (also known as a factor relationship chart) can help you discover the relationships to show in the tree diagram, particularly if you are writing about causality or about contributing factors. (See Figure 6-4.) The bubbles enclose factors or variables and the arrows indicate relationships. Figure 6-4 shows that y_3 affects y_2, y_1, and x, whereas y_1 is affected by y_3 and affects y_2 and x. Sometimes a simple bubble diagram can lead directly to the basic structure of a tree diagram, and sometimes it can only help you see aspects of the relationships the tree will have to display.

Figure 6-4
A Bubble Diagram
Showing the
Interactions of
Factors x, y_1, y_2,
and y_3.

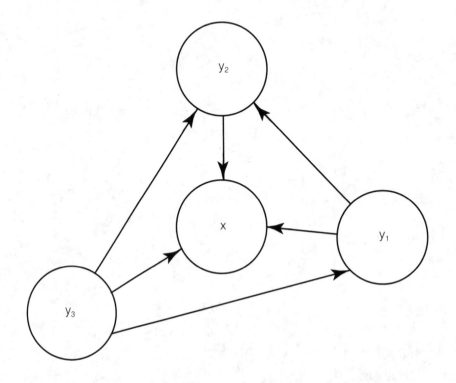

DETERMINING SEQUENCE. Because the tree diagram is not linear, and the document will have to be linear, you must decide on the sequence in which you will discuss the topics and subtopics. All your documents will begin with an introduction that prepares the reader by answering such questions as:

- What is this document a part of?
- What is the purpose of this document?
- Why am I reading this?

In arranging the other main headings in sequence, keep the reader's needs foremost. Ask yourself the following questions: What does the reader need to know first? What is most important to the reader? Should I use chronological order, spatial order, or order of importance?

Chronological order is a sequence based on time; whatever comes first in time is placed first in the document. Chronological order is particularly useful in writing about processes and procedures (descriptions of procedures, explanations of processes, instructions, analyses of procedures). For example, a report on how to improve the registration procedure at your college could be organized in the sequence of steps a student follows in registering. Similarly, a report on personnel procedures could be organized in the order of the procedures a new employee would experience: hiring, training, performance evaluation, and promotion. Spatial order is useful in writing about physical objects such as equipment or about various rooms, buildings, or sites. A spatial order leads the reader through space, usually in one direction only (top to bottom, left to right, north to south, front to back). An order of importance starts with the most important and moves to the less important and then to the least important.

After you have determined the sequence of your main headings, repeat the same strategies to work your way down the tree. Often a sequence decision at a lower level is quite arbitrary because the headings are equal in importance and there is no natural or logical reason for choosing one order over another.

INTEGRATING THE BRAINSTORMING INTO A TREE DIAGRAM. If you have not already done so, go through your brainstorming and transfer your points to the tree diagram. Decide where in the outline each point should go. Discard irrelevant points that don't fit.

MAKING THE FORMAL OUTLINE FROM THE TREE DIAGRAM. To make a formal outline from a tree diagram, remember that the top row of nodes in the diagram will become the first order headings, the next row will become the second order headings, and so on. As you prepare your headings, observe the following guidelines:

- Each heading should indicate *accurately* what the reader can expect in the section. If the heading is a single word, be sure that it is the correct word. Use modifiers or convert the word into a phrase or even a sentence if doing so will make a more accurate heading. For example, the heading "Checklist for Formal Outlines" is more precise and accurate for the next section than would be "Formal Outlines."

- Each heading should be *concise*. For example, "Checklist for Formal Outlines" is more concise than "Questions to Ask Yourself as You Check Your Formal Outlines."
- Co-ordinate headings (headings dominated by the same node) should be *grammatically parallel*. Particularly when you use phrases as headings, check that the headings are grammatically parallel. For example, the subheadings in this section all begin with an *-ing* form of a verb (gerund): brainstorming, determining, integrating, making. It would have been wrong to phrase the last subheading as "How to Make a Formal Outline from the Tree Diagram."

In a formal outline, the levels of headings are indicated by numbering and indenting. While many acceptable numbering systems are available, we will adopt the following:

I. First order heading
   A. Second order heading
      1. Third order heading
      2. Third order heading
         a. Fourth order heading
         b. Fourth order heading
   B. Second order heading
   C. Second order heading
II. First order heading
   A. Second order heading
   B. Second order heading

Figure 6-5 shows the formal outline that is equivalent to the tree diagram in Figure 6-3.

CHECKLIST FOR FORMAL OUTLINES

Since you will want to prepare the *best* outline possible, you should expect to prepare several versions of outlines, and work toward designing one that best reflects the nature of the material you are presenting and best meets the needs of the reader. When you have prepared your formal outline, use the following questions to check it:

- *Does the outline consider the reader's needs?* Make sure that what appears to be a logical arrangement from your point of view is also a useful arrangement for the reader. In a problem and solution document, for example, it may seem logical to you to separate the problems and solutions. However, such an organization may be very inconvenient for the reader, who may forget the details of a problem by the time your document explains the solution.
- *Are all the headings clearly and precisely worded?* Headings give direction both to you and to your reader. Ideally, the headings in

AN EXAMINATION OF THE FISHERIES MANAGEMENT PROGRAM IN JASPER NATIONAL PARK

I. Introduction

II. The Fish Stocking Program
   A. Size and number of fish stocked
      1. Examination of success rate of present program
      2. Necessary changes to program
   B. Procedures for stocking
      1. Human resources
      2. Equipment
      3. Transportation
         a. Helicopter
         b. Truck
         c. Backpack

III. The Creel Census Program
   A. Program content
      1. Statistical data
         a. Characteristics of data
         b. Sampling method
         c. Graphs
      2. Otolith Samples
   B. Creel Census Staff
      1. Qualifications
      2. Attitudes
      3. Shift scheduling
   C. Creel Census Equipment
      1. Uniforms
      2. Vehicles
      3. Shelter
      4. Supplies

IV. Fishing Regulations
   A. Changes to limits
   B. Additions to regulations
      1. Localization of opening and closing dates
      2. Tag system
   C. Application of regulations

V. Conclusion

Source: Sherryl Yaciansky. Printed by permission.

your outline and the points under them should be so clear that even someone else could follow the outline and write the document.

- *Do the headings reflect logical relationships?* Are there at least two subdivisions at each node? In our scheme, whenever you have an A, you must have a B, and whenever you have a 1, you must have a 2. If two subheadings are immediately dominated by a heading, are they related logically? Also, are they grammatically parallel?
- *Does the outline indicate there will be some text under each heading?* After each heading the reader expects the comments that apply to that entire section and a forecasting statement that introduces any subheadings.
- *Are sections of the document balanced?* While sections certainly do not have to be the same length, re-examine unusually long and unusually short sections. Subdivide the unusually long ones and amalgamate the unusually short ones.
- *Are there too many points under any headings?* If there are too many points to be included in two or three paragraphs, you probably need another level of subdivision.
- *Are there too few points under any headings?* There should be enough points at the lowest level of subdivision to make a well-developed paragraph. Do not confuse points and headings. If a subdivision heading is really only a point, move it under the higher level of heading.
- *Does each point appear only once?* If the same point appears in more than one place in the outline, the subdivisions need to be rearranged. The recurring point may need to be made into a heading.

After trying to write a draft from the outline shown in Figure 6-5, the student submitted the following note:

> "I found that the outline was far too detailed and tended to muddle the main points. The problem, I found, was that I examined every aspect of the Fisheries Management Program in JNP instead of simply examining the deficiencies of the program. I think that my title should be revised to 'An Examination of the Deficiencies of the Fisheries Management Program in Jasper National Park.' "

Her revised outline is shown in Figure 6-6.

INFORMAL OUTLINES

For most documents you will not prepare a formal outline. Instead, you will prepare an informal outline that gives you as much direction about organization as you need. However, even the most sketchy aids to organization are based on the principles we discussed above. The sections of this text devoted to particular kinds of documents indicate, where applicable, either what kinds of headings you are likely to use or the more common patterns of organization.

AN EXAMINATION OF THE DEFICIENCIES OF THE FISHERIES MANAGEMENT PROGRAM IN JASPER NATIONAL PARK

I. Introduction
II. The Fish Stocking Program
    A. Examination of the success rate of the present program
    B. Necessary changes to the program
III. The Creel Census Program
    A. Program content
    B. Creel census staff
    C. Creel census equipment
        1. Uniforms
        2. Office space and accommodation
        3. Transportation
IV. Fishing Regulations
    A. Changes to the regulations
    B. Additions to regulations
    C. Application of the fishing regulations
V. Conclusion

Source: Sherryl Yaciansky. Printed by permission.

EXERCISES

1. You have asked your peers to prepare a list of qualities that a good instructor must have. Now you must arrange this list into an outline for a description that will appear in the faculty newsletter. Arrange the qualities into related groups and then prepare the outline.

- Makes material intelligibly meaningful.
- Maintains continuity in the course.
- Is constructive and helpful with criticisms.
- Shows an expert knowledge of subject matter.
- Adopts an appropriate pace during the lecture.
- Includes material that is not readily accessible in textbooks.
- Is concise.
- Illustrates the practical applications of the theory of the subject.
- Tries to link lecture material to laboratory/practical work.
- Avoids trivial, time-filling material.
- Stimulates students to think independently.
- Does not ridicule wrong answers.

- Evenly spaces requirements of written work.
- Imparts enthusiasm for subject.
- Refers to the latest developments in the subject.
- Sets clear objectives for the student.
- Readily considers students' viewpoints.
- Presents material clearly and logically.
- Enables the student to understand the basic principles of the subject.
- Can be clearly heard.
- Has a good sense of humour.
- Writes legibly.
- Appears confident and at ease.
- Allows questions.
- Gets students to work willingly.
- Points out the links between various subjects.
- Is well informed in fields other than, but related to, own special subjects.
- Avoids an excess of factual details.
- Provides full references to books, papers, etc.
- Has a sympathetic attitude toward students.
- Avoids forcing own point of view.
- Is spontaneously friendly.
- Appreciates students' own accomplishments.
- Appears to enjoy teaching.
- Uses appropriate illustrative teaching aids (slides, films, programs, models, charts, etc.).
- Has a pleasantly modulated voice.
- Has a good vocabulary.
- Avoids distracting personal mannerisms.
- Has a democratic approach.

Source: Edwin F. Rosinski, "Some Characteristics of a Good Lecturer." Printed by permission.

2. Listed below are a number of defects in a car.

   a. How would you categorize these if you were evaluating the car for an aunt who is planning to buy it?

   b. How would you categorize these if you were preparing a repair plan for the car?

   c. How would you categorize these if you were preparing a repair guide for cars in general?

      - leaking radiator
      - broken windshield
      - flat tire
      - broken trunk lock
      - burned out brake light
      - plugged fuel filter
      - dirty spark plugs
      - ripped upholstery
      - broken thermostat

- dead battery
- worn brakes
- rust
- leaking head gasket
- broken alternator

3. Suggest at least two distinct classification schemes for each of the following:

   a. the vehicles on campus

   b. the student population on campus

   c. your possessions

   Note the basis of each classification scheme and suggest circumstances in which each one might be useful.

4. Critique and then revise the following outline for a student's formal report on how to improve the physical plant at a large farm:

FORMAL OUTLINE (I)

I. Introduction
II. Auxiliary Animal Barn
   A. Cleanliness improvements
      1. Reconstruction and maintenance
         a. ventilation installation
         b. painting
         c. entrances sealed
      2. Work schedule
         a. disinfect pens
         b. pens and alleys cleaned
   B. Efficiency improvements
      1. Reconstruction and maintenance
         a. loading entrance constructed
         b. calf pens
         c. drainage improvements
III. Milk House
   A. Cleanliness improvements
      1. Reconstruction and maintenance
         a. painting
         b. doors made self-closing
         c. ventilation
      2. Work schedule
         a. follow health regulations

    i. keep unnecessary items out
    ii. wash floors

IV. Dairy Barn
  A. Cleanliness improvements
    1. Reconstruction and maintenance
     a. gutters installed
     b. painting
    2. Work schedule
     a. milking parlour entrances cleaned
  B. Efficiency improvements
    1. Reconstruction and maintenance
     a. automatic feeding system
      i. dairy-tronic
     b. gates
     c. insulation
     d. ventilation
    2. Work schedule
     a. rakes used for stall maintenance
     b. gutters will decrease time to clean the barn

V. Conclusion

5. Examine the following revision of the outline you critiqued in exercise 4. How has the organizing principle changed? What are the advantages of this revision over the original? Which report is likely to be easier to use? Why? What further changes would you suggest?

FORMAL OUTLINE (II)

I. Introduction
II. Dairy Barn
  A. Construction
    1. gutter installation
    2. automatic feeding system
     a. dairy-tronic
    3. gates
    4. insulation
    5. ventilation

    B. Maintenance
       1. painting
    C. Cleaning
       1. milking parlour entrances
       2. the use of rakes for stall cleaning
III. Milk House
    A. Construction
       1. doors made self-closing
       2. ventilation
    B. Maintenance
       1. painting
    C. Cleaning
       1. regulate types of items in the room
       2. wash floors and walls
IV. Auxiliary Animal Barn
    A. Construction
       1. ventilation
       2. entrance sealed
       3. loading entrance
    B. Reconstruction
       1. calf pens
       2. maternity pens
       3. drainage
    C. Maintenance
       1. painting
    D. Cleaning
       1. pens and alleys
       2. pens disinfected
V. Conclusion

6. Prepare an outline of Chapter 6.

CHAPTER 7

WRITING THE INITIAL DRAFT

Introduction

Guidelines

Using Headings

Writing Introductions, Transitions, and Summaries

Integrating Graphics with the Text

Writing Paragraphs

Note

INTRODUCTION

The initial draft – sometimes called the *rough draft* or *first draft* – is the first prose version of your document. Note that the initial draft should never be the draft on which you are judged. If your supervisor asks to see a draft of a document, don't show the initial draft; show a draft in which the most obvious flaws have been corrected. The reason for this is that your reputation as a writer can be affected by every sample of writing a reader sees. This chapter presents some general guidelines for writing initial drafts and then examines the following special considerations:

- using headings
- writing introductions, transitions, and summaries
- integrating graphics with the text
- writing paragraphs

Although these considerations are separated for discussion here, you will not, of course, separate them when you write. Rather, the writing will be a continuous process in which you will pay attention to these considerations as they arise.

GUIDELINES

If you already have an outline and a plan for the placement of graphics, then in writing the initial draft you will be concentrating on converting the points in your outline into sentences and paragraphs. In particular, you should focus on organization, completeness of content and discussion, fluency, and uniformity of tone. Although you should also consider clarity, you can expect the initial draft to have rough spots that you can improve in the revision stage (Chapter 8).

When you choose the physical form of the draft, try to choose one that will allow you to revise without recopying; recopying is wasteful. If you handwrite or type, use one side of the paper only so that when you revise you can cut and paste. Leave ample space between lines so you can insert words and phrases easily. If you use a pencil to write, you can make many corrections simply by erasing. If you use a word processor, you will probably compose on screen. Remember, though, that a very rough initial draft may require time-consuming revision; you may want to write some complicated initial drafts by hand and enter them in your word processor after some revision. When you are making minor changes directly on screen, space your draft widely enough to allow room for further handwritten corrections on your printed copy. If you dictate your draft, ask the typist to prepare the draft so there is ample room for revision.

Because individuals compose differently, it is difficult to generalize about how you should write the initial draft. Use whatever method works for you. If at all possible, do try to write your draft in one sitting, though, because that will help you improve the flow and maintain a uniform tone. Try to avoid interruptions of any kind. Do not even interrupt yourself to check or correct grammatical errors, diction, spelling, or punctuation. You may, however, want to mark places in the draft where you think there are such problems so you can find them easily in the revision and editing stage. For longer documents you will need several sittings, but try to make each one substantial and try to take breaks at natural divisions in the text.

Using headings

You will be using headings in most of the documents you write, and you should integrate them as you write your initial draft. When using headings, observe the following guidelines:

- *Use typography and indention to show the hierarchy of headings.* This hierarchy should have been worked out when you prepared the outline.
- *Phrase the headings so that co-ordinate headings (headings at the same level) are grammatically parallel and so that each heading reflects what follows it.* Again, this should have been worked out in your outline.
- *Use forecasting statements to prepare the reader for the headings.* Prepare the reader for a new level of headings by naming the headings you will use at this new level. (See how the heading "Using Headings" was introduced in the first paragraph of this chapter.)
- *Check that each main heading is followed by at least one paragraph; do not simply list a series of headings.*

Writing introductions, transitions, and summaries

Introductions, transitions, and summaries function together to lead your reader through a document; they make your document more readable by providing important cues about how it is organized. The main purpose of an introduction is to prepare the reader for what is to follow, the main purpose of a transition is to indicate a change in direction and to lead the reader through that change, and the main purpose of a summary is to recapitulate what has been said. Note that your outline will normally only indicate the introduction that comes at the beginning of the document and the summary that comes at the end of the document; it will not indicate where you need additional introductions, transitions, and summaries within the text.

INTRODUCTIONS

You are no doubt aware that the beginning of anything is very important. It attracts the most attention and probably has the most to do with how something is judged. This means that the opening sentences of any document may have a disproportionate effect on how that document is perceived. In addition to the introduction that comes at the beginning of the document, you will also need introductions at the beginning of the sections and subsections of longer documents; you can even think of topic sentences as being introductions to paragraphs. Earlier we said that the function of introductions is to prepare the reader. How, then, do introductions prepare the reader? Most simply put, they provide a context for the document or section and a preview of what is to follow. Introductions answer the question, "What is this a part of?" They set the document or section in a framework of what the reader is familiar with. They show how the document relates to something the reader already knows, such as an event or transaction or other document. Introductions also answer the questions, "What is the main point of this?" and "What are the parts of this?" They may state explicitly what the purpose of the document or section is, and they may also state the generalization that the rest of the section will support or provide evidence for. If the document or section is long enough to require further subdivisions, the introduction will prepare the reader for these by including forecasting statements. The introduction gives the reader a frame in which to place the new information that is to follow. If you have planned a document carefully, you should be able to preview sections without difficulty; however, if you do get stuck, you can write the introduction *after* you have written the section. In fact, this book recommends that you prepare the introduction of your formal report after you have written the body.

TRANSITIONS

Transitions indicate shifts in the direction of a discourse and guide the reader through them; they are like a combination of signal and bridge. Transition words or phrases such as *on the other hand, however,* and *next* connect sentences within paragraphs and so achieve cohesion.

Transitions may also be needed between paragraphs, between paragraph blocks, or between sections of a document. The transition between paragraphs is often incorporated into the topic sentence of the second paragraph, which both indicates that there is a shift and introduces or previews the following paragraph. For example, *also* in the opening sentence of this paragraph indicates that we have shifted to another topic. Obviously, the longer the document, the more likely you are to need transitions between larger segments; however, if you are using a system of headings, you may find that the simple appearance of a new heading is a sufficient signal of the beginning of a new section. In addition to transition words and phrases, you may need transition sentences such as the following: "*Let us turn now* to massive 'close' binary systems, where the transfer of matter influences the evolution of the two companions." The above sentence is both a topic sentence and a transition sentence between sections of an article.

From George W. Clark, "X-Ray Stars in Globular Clusters." Copyright © 1977 by *Scientific American*, Inc. All rights reserved.

SUMMARIES

Summaries are normally found at the end of a document and often at the end of sections of a long document. They both signal an ending and provide a synopsis of what has gone before. Their form depends on the context; in a short document, such as a letter, a sentence will suffice, whereas in a longer document the end summary could be a separate section, and intermediate summaries could be paragraphs.

Summaries, transitions, and introductions are sometimes found together, as in the following transitional paragraph that joins two sections of an article:

This, then, is the general scheme of stellar evolution that can lead to the formation of isolated white dwarfs, neutron stars and possibly black holes. Before considering how such objects are implicated in the formation of X-ray stars, we must consider two important questions. How old are the stars in clusters? What is the range of masses for main-sequence stars that evolve into neutron stars?

From George W. Clark, "X-Ray Stars in Globular Clusters." Copyright © 1977 by *Scientific American*, Inc. All rights reserved.

Note how the first sentence looks back to the preceding section and indicates that it is completed, and how the second sentence announces the following topic, indicates that a digression is needed, and introduces the subdivisions of that digression. The two questions preview the topics of this digression and give the reader a frame within which to organize the paragraph that follows. Note also how the topic sentence of the next paragraph includes a transition (*the first question*) that links the two paragraphs:

Answers to the first question began to emerge in the 1950's, when advances in electronic computers made feasible the numerical modeling of stellar structure. Since one cannot directly observe the interior of a star (except perhaps the sun, whose internal processes are being studied through attempts to measure the flux of solar neutrinos), one must extract from such a model a prediction of external appearances that can be checked against the observable properties of stars: mass, luminosity, surface temperature, surface composition and age. The ideal places to check such predictions are in star clusters, both the ancient globular clusters found primarily in the galactic halo and the younger, smaller and rather amorphous clusters found in the region of active star formation in the galactic disk.

From George W. Clark, "X-Ray Stars in Globular Clusters." Copyright © 1977 by *Scientific American*, Inc. All rights reserved.

INTEGRATING GRAPHICS WITH THE TEXT

Your outline should indicate the proposed location of graphics, but in your initial draft you will have to introduce each graphic and help the reader interpret it, if necessary. For this reason, you should prepare very rough sketches of your graphics before you begin your draft. As is explained in Chapter 3, each graphic should be referred to in the text before the reader encounters it. The text of the draft, together with the title of the graphic, should also indicate what the reader is to see in the graphic and the direction or order in which the reader is to read it.

WRITING PARAGRAPHS

The main job in writing the initial draft is converting your outline into paragraphs. Because paragraph structure is a common weakness of technical writers, we will look at it more closely here. What, exactly, is a paragraph? The simple answer would be that it is a group of sentences that begins with an indention. While we normally identify paragraphs by the indentions, it would be as wrong to assume that the indention is a sufficient condition for a paragraph as it would be to assume that beginning a group of words with a capital letter and ending with a period constitutes writing a sentence. However, whereas scholars and writers understand what constitutes a sentence very well, the same cannot be said of paragraphs. What this means for you as a writer is that there is, in fact, greater latitude for deciding where to begin a new paragraph, and perhaps how to construct it, but it also means that it is more difficult for you to get firm guidelines for writing paragraphs. You should recognize that a paragraph is both a spatial unit and a logical, or structural, unit.

PARAGRAPHS AS SPATIAL UNITS

You already know that one important function of paragraphing is to break up a page visually to make it more readable. Try to imagine how difficult and boring it would be to read a page that had no paragraph breaks. On the other hand, try to imagine how disorienting it would be to read a page on which each sentence was indented as though it were a paragraph.

How long should a paragraph be, and what are the variables that affect its length? A recent study of paragraphing of expository texts suggests that paragraphs should not be less than two sentences or less than 40 words long and that they should not be longer than six sentences.[1] While it would be silly to insist that you never write paragraphs shorter than 40 words or longer than six sentences, these are probably good guidelines to keep in mind.

Paragraph length is affected by the length of the document as well as layout considerations. Paragraphs in longer documents such as reports can easily be six sentences long. Letters and memos, however, will normally have much briefer paragraphs, in part because the paragraph breaks will be used to divide a text that is short to begin with, and in part because the content structure will not demand the kinds of development that lead to longer paragraphs.

Another factor that will affect paragraph length is the function of the paragraph. The guidelines noted above apply to the normal paragraph that develops the argument in a longer document. If, however, the paragraph serves as a transition or forecast, as many paragraphs in reports and other longer technical writing documents do, then it is perfectly acceptable to have a single-sentence paragraph.

PARAGRAPHS AS STRUCTURAL UNITS

More important than their function as spatial units is the function of paragraphs as structural units. As you will recall from your earlier studies, paragraphs tend to be about or to develop a subject or topic that may be stated explicitly in a topic sentence, which will usually be the first sentence of a paragraph. When you change topics, you normally also begin a new paragraph and indicate the shift by some transition device. In addition to being concerned with a single topic – a quality that is often referred to as *unity* – a paragraph, as part of the text, should also be *cohesive*, or "flow" from sentence to sentence.

Although there certainly are paragraphs that do not have explicit topic sentences, it is advisable for you to have them because they act as cues to your reader and because they help you to focus your paragraphs and stay on the topic. If the topic sentence is the first sentence of a paragraph, as it usually will be, it should act as both an introduction and a transition, for it will also have to link the paragraph to the previous one. Note how in the paragraph below "*these* higher functions" in the opening sentence of the second paragraph and "*another* distinctive characteristic" in the opening sentence of the third one serve as links:

> The nervous systems of all animals have a number of basic functions in common, most notably the control of movement and the analysis of sensation. What distinguishes the human brain is the variety of more specialized activities it is capable of learning. The preeminent example is language: no one is born knowing a language, but virtually everyone learns to speak and to understand the spoken word, and people of all cultures can be taught to write and to read. Music is also universal in man: people with no formal training are able to recognize

and to reproduce dozens of melodies. Similarly, almost everyone can draw simple figures, and the ability to make accurate renderings is not rare.

At least some of these higher functions of the human brain are governed by dedicated networks of neurons. It has been known for more than 100 years, for example, that at least two delimited regions of the cerebral cortex are essential to linguistic competence; they seem to be organized explicitly for the processing of verbal information. Certain structures on the inner surface of the underside of the temporal lobe, including the hippocampus, are apparently necessary for the long-term retention of memories. In some cases the functional specialization of a neural system seems to be quite narrowly defined: hence one area on both sides of the human cerebral cortex is concerned primarily with the recognition of faces. It is likely that other mental activities are also associated with particular neural networks. Musical and artistic abilities, for example, appear to depend on specialized systems in the brain, although the circuitry has not yet been worked out.

Another distinctive characteristic of the human brain is the allocation of functions to the two cerebral hemispheres. That the human brain is not fully symmetrical in its functioning could be guessed from at least one observation of daily experience: most of the human population favors the right hand, which is controlled by the left side of the brain. Linguistic abilities also reside mainly on the left side. For these reasons the left cerebral hemisphere was once said to be the dominant one and the right side of the brain was thought to be subservient. In recent years this concept has been revised as it has become apparent that each hemisphere has its own specialized talents. Those for which the right cortex is dominant include some features of aptitudes for music and for the recognition of complex visual patterns. The right hemisphere is also the more important one for the expression and recognition of emotion. In the past few years these functional asymmetries have been matched with anatomical ones, and a start has been made on exploring their prevalence in species other than man.

From Norman Geschwind, "Specializations of the Human Brain." Copyright © 1979 by *Scientific American*, Inc. All rights reserved.

While the unity of topic will normally define the paragraph as a structural unit, the sentences within it should also be linked by cohesive devices. As we saw in Chapter 2, these include repeated nouns, pronouns, and transition words and phrases. The repetition of the same word or of words with closely related meanings serves to link sentences and also to maintain unity. (In the first paragraph in the example above, *specialized activities* is a topic that is sustained in the subsequent sentences in the words *language, music,* and *draw simple figures.*) Another common cohesive device is the use of personal pronouns (*he, she, it, they*) and demonstrative pronouns (*this, that*). Finally, transition words and phrases (*and, therefore, because, or, although, but*) are particularly important because they indicate explicitly the logical relationship between clauses and between sentences.

Because of the overlap between unity and cohesion, it is most unlikely that you could write a paragraph that had absolutely no cohesive ties. However, it is quite possible, if not probable, that you write paragraphs that could be made more cohesive, particularly by using more transition words.

NOTE

1. Sandra J. Bond and John R. Hayes, "Cues People Use to Paragraph Text," *Research in the Teaching of English* 18.2 (May 1984): 159.

REVISING

INTRODUCTION

Skills and care in revising are major factors in distinguishing good writers from poor writers. Some students don't revise at all; their initial draft is their presentation draft. Skilled writers, however, revise all but the very brief, unimportant, and routine documents. You should, then, accept the fact that you *must* revise.

This chapter defines revision and then explains some guidelines you can follow in revising content, organization, graphics, paragraph structure, sentence structure, diction, and mechanics.

DEFINITION

What is revision? The word *revision* has developed from words that mean "to look at again" or "to see again." Essentially, revision is change. Perhaps the most common error inexperienced writers make is to confuse revision with recopying. Instead, if you are not composing on screen, you should write the initial draft so that you can minimize the copying you have to do to revise. The key question to ask while revising, or "looking at the text again," is "How can I change this to *improve* it?"

The changes you make will be one or more of the following operations:

- addition
- deletion
- movement
- modification

Some recent research suggests that inexperienced writers favour deletion (scratching out) and substitution (which is deletion followed by addition).[1] However, to revise effectively, you should develop skill in all four operations and use them as needed.

GUIDELINES

Although revision is a very individual process, and although you will of course have to use whatever strategies work best for you, the guidelines presented here should help you as you develop your own revision procedure. On the job, your supervisor will probably participate in the revision of your documents and may even insist on changes that you do not agree with.

- *Review the definition of the task.* Before you begin to revise a document, review how you defined the task (see Chapter 5). If the document you have written does not meet the specifications you started with, then no matter how elegantly it is phrased, or how free it is of error, it is an unsatisfactory document. At first it might help you to have your specifications in front of you before you revise.

- *View the document as the reader will.* A major difficulty in revising is being able to view your own writing as a reader will. Most writers become so attached to what they have written that they develop a block against changing anything. You may be able to overcome this problem by making your draft less familiar, either by letting time pass before you revise, or by having your handwritten draft typed. Then try to approach the document as you think your audience will. Effective revision requires that you be able to recognize when you need to change something.
- *Make several passes.* To avoid wasting time and energy improving what you later have to discard, particularly if you are preparing a long document, revise by making several passes through the draft. Focus first on the larger considerations, such as organization, and on the larger components, and do not worry about the smaller units, such as sentences or words, until the larger questions have been settled. The number of passes you need will vary, but you should consider all of the following aspects of the document:

  - content
  - organization
  - graphics
  - paragraph structure
  - sentence structure
  - diction
  - mechanics (spelling, punctuation, capitalization)

In deciding how to group these aspects into passes, consider your own ability and personality, the length of the document, and the amount of change needed. A very skilled writer can revise a short document in one pass. For most students, the most efficient procedure for revising longer documents, such as a formal report, might be to consider content, organization, and graphics in one pass, paragraph and sentence structure in another, and diction and mechanics in a third.

While it is extremely important to revise, you must also realize that the revision process could, potentially, go on forever, for there is probably no text that could not be revised further. This means that you must balance the need to revise against the benefits that accrue from further revision. In other words, you should revise until you reach a point of diminishing returns. Your goal should be to produce the best document you can within the constraints governing the assignment.

CONTENT

The aim of revising for content should be to include all the information the audience needs, and *only* that. As you read through the document, ask yourself the following questions:

- Am I leaving questions in the audience's mind?
- Am I repeating myself?
- Am I supporting my claims adequately?

The first of these questions is perhaps the most difficult because it requires that you pretend to be your audience.

Let us now consider how the revising operations of addition, deletion, and modification apply to content. Since the fourth operation, moving content, is really a question of organization, we will discuss it in the organization section.

ADDITION

Adding content is a very important but often neglected revision strategy. You should add content if you have not answered your audience's questions adequately, or if you have not supported your claims. Have you indicated "who, what, when, where, why" wherever necessary? Have you used enough examples to illustrate generalizations?

DELETION

Most writers find some difficulty in discarding what they have written because they have formed an attachment to their words and because they hate to waste what has taken time and effort to write. If your writing is to improve, however, you must learn to overcome these feelings. Delete what is *redundant* or *irrelevant*. In deciding whether something is redundant, you have to distinguish between purposeless repetition and the kind of "repetition" that summarizes or that reminds the reader, and thereby makes the text more readable. Consider, first, whether or not you are repeating yourself, and then whether or not this repetition serves any function in the discourse. Deciding whether something is irrelevant requires you to consider the purpose and audience. Irrelevant content usually results from confusing information that is useful or interesting to you with information that is useful to the reader. Your discourse may be *Writer-Based* rather than *Reader-Based*; Writer-Based prose is directed at the writer, whereas Reader-Based prose is deliberately directed at the reader.[2]

MODIFICATION

The need to modify content is perhaps more rare than the need to add or delete, but it is also more difficult to judge. The main reason for needing to modify content is inaccuracy. Are your data accurate? Are your interpretations accurate? Does your evidence warrant the claims you are making? To modify content, then, you must review your investigative procedure, check information, and rethink your conclusions. A document that presents incorrect information is worse than useless; it can be harmful.

ORGANIZATION

In checking organization, your aim is to determine whether the sequence of content will meet the audience's needs and whether the hierarchy is logical. You will also want to check whether the cues to organization are appropriate. In other words, you will check the appropriateness of headings and the adequacy of introductions, transitions, and summaries.

SEQUENCE

Try to approach the document as your reader will. Check that the reader is given enough direction about the organization of the document and that you present information as it is needed. The main revision operation you will use in changing sequence is *moving content*. The segments moved will normally be sections or paragraphs. Of course, the more carefully the document was organized before you wrote the initial draft, the less you will need to move sections at this time. Nevertheless, you should be open to the possibility that the sequence can be improved.

HEADINGS

In revising headings, you have to check your hierarchy and the quality of fit between headings and the segments of text they apply to. You may need to add, delete, or modify headings.

ADDITION. Add subheadings if a section is insufficiently divided.

DELETION. Delete a subheading if the section it heads is too brief, or if you have a single subdivision. A subheading is usually not needed if there isn't a well-developed paragraph to follow it.

MODIFICATION. Modify the wording of a heading if it does not accurately reflect the text that follows. Make sure that headings at the same level are grammatically parallel and semantically related. If there is material under a heading that does not fit the heading, either move it to where it does fit, or delete it.

INTRODUCTIONS, TRANSITIONS, AND SUMMARIES

Remember that not only do your documents have to *be* organized, but they also have to *appear* to be organized. The headings, introductions, transitions, and summaries provide the reader with the needed cues about organization. These cues make the organization explicit. Ask yourself the following questions:

- Is the document introduced adequately?
- Is each section introduced?

- Is each heading, subheading, and graphic introduced?
- Are shifts in topic indicated by transition statements?
- Are longer documents or sections of documents summarized adequately?

When you revise for introductions, transitions, and summaries, you will probably have to add, rather than delete or modify.

GRAPHICS

In revising the use of graphics, you should be concerned with the following questions:

- Have I used all and only the graphics that are needed?
- Is each graphic in the best place in the document?
- Is each graphic appropriately designed?
- Is each graphic integrated into the document?

Again, we can apply the four revision operations.

ADDITION

Identify sections of text that could be replaced or clarified with a graphic. In particular, look for long descriptions that could be replaced with a map, photograph, or drawing, and for repetitive comparisons that could be replaced with tables. Also note that some claims, such as "The lunch-room is very messy," can be supported most effectively by a photograph.

DELETION

Delete any illustration that is superfluous. If you have planned your illustrations carefully, though, you are unlikely to have to delete them.

MOVEMENT

If the illustration is needed, check that it is in the best location. The test is that the graphic should be where the reader needs it; this means, again, that you must approach the draft as a reader would and anticipate the reader's needs. Remember that graphics are very useful in providing a schema for the reader; for this reason they should appear as early as possible. If the illustration is not discussed, or if it is not directly relevant to the argument, then move it to an appendix.

MODIFICATION

When you are certain that you do need the illustration, and that it is in the appropriate place, check that it is as useful as possible. Reconsider what you want the graphic to show and then make sure that it does. In particular, check that it is as simple as it can be. A common weakness of student illustrations is irrelevant detail that may distract the reader. To simplify, remove this unnecessary detail.

Also, check that the reading cues are as clear as they can be. Does the title identify the illustration clearly? Are the columns and rows of a table named clearly and are the axes of graphs labelled? Are parts of illustrations labelled clearly?

INTEGRATION

Is each graphic referred to in the text before it appears? Does the text provide any help needed for reading the graphic?

PARAGRAPH STRUCTURE

The paragraph is at the core of the document; it is in the paragraph that content, organization, and sentence structure meet and merge. Because of this, you should not think of the revising of paragraph structure as a totally separable step. The following questions are most directly related to paragraph structure:

- Does the paragraph have a topic sentence?
- Is the paragraph adequately developed?
- Is the paragraph length optimal?
- Is the sequence of sentences optimal?
- Is the paragraph cohesive?

Note that these questions will not necessarily apply to introductory and transitional paragraphs, some of which may only be a single sentence.

TOPIC SENTENCE

Although it is not necessary for every paragraph to have an explicit topic sentence, every paragraph should have a central idea that *could* be made explicit. In revising, you may wish to add a topic sentence if there isn't one, or to change it if the stated one does not accurately capture the core idea of the paragraph. If there is no central idea, then you will probably have to rewrite the paragraph.

DEVELOPMENT

If you have revised carefully for content, you should not have to add any new material to develop paragraphs more fully. However, you may have several short paragraphs that should be combined into one longer one. Note that if you do combine paragraphs, you will probably need a new topic sentence.

LENGTH

If the paragraph is adequately developed, it is probably not too short. However, some paragraphs may be so long that their length interferes with readability. If this is the case, you should simply split them at a transition point and supply a topic sentence if necessary.

SENTENCE SEQUENCE

In checking sentence sequence, you are checking the internal organization of the paragraph, and again you must approach the text from the point of view of your audience. Have you presented information in the order that best suits your reader? If the sequence is *not* optimal, then move sentences.

COHESION

As was pointed out in Chapters 2 and 7, cohesion is a very important factor in readability. You should make a separate pass through the document, checking for adequate cohesion devices – repeated nouns, pronoun reference, and transition words. A particularly good test is the "sound" of a document; if it sounds choppy, it probably is choppy, and needs more links. (To check how the document sounds, read it aloud.) Make sure, also, that when you do use transition words, you are using them accurately. A word such as *because* has a very precise meaning and you must make sure that you can defend the logical relationship that you are claiming by its use. Because cohesion is so directly related to sentence structure and diction, you may need to check for cohesion once more after you have revised sentence structure and diction.

SENTENCE STRUCTURE

When you are certain that the larger units of your document are satisfactory, you should make a pass at the sentence structure level to check for clarity, conciseness, and correctness. You must recognize that changes at this level will often involve several sentences at a time.

CLARITY

Review the section on clarity in Chapter 2, and check the document for ambiguity. Treat your sentences as you might treat commands in a computer program. Be precise. Say exactly what you mean. Do *not* rely on your reader's common sense to understand what you mean. Remember that to remove ambiguities you will usually have to move elements or change them.

CONCISENESS

Review the section on conciseness in Chapter 2, and check the document for conciseness. Expect your initial draft to be wordy. In fact, it is not unusual to be able to reduce the length of a document by 20 to 30 percent by applying the most obvious strategies for increasing conciseness. At the same time, you must remember that by increasing conciseness you may be making your text sound too brusque. If this happens, you should value the appropriate tone more highly than conciseness, particularly in letters or memos. When you revise for conciseness, you will delete, but you may also need to modify or move text.

GRAMMATICAL CORRECTNESS

Everything you write must be grammatically correct. Although errors in grammar seldom lead to misunderstanding, they do reflect most seriously on you and on the organization on whose behalf you are writing, for they imply a lack of education or a lack of care and responsibility. By making errors in grammar, you make yourself vulnerable to ridicule from those who recognize them.

Check your draft in particular for the following errors common in student writing:

- lack of agreement in number between subject and verb
- lack of agreement in number between pronoun and antecedent
- dangling modifiers
- lack of parallelism
- fragments
- comma splices and fused sentences

If you are at all uncertain about what these errors are or how to correct them, consult any standard composition handbook.

When your instructor returns an assignment, make sure you understand each error and know how to recognize it and avoid it in the future. Keep a personal list of grammar errors and work on overcoming them.

DICTION

Diction is word choice. In checking your diction – whether or not you make this a separate pass – you focus on words, and most of your revisions will be replacements. Be aware that some of the most powerful emotional reactions to a document will stem from the particular words you choose. In checking diction, pay special attention to tone and precision, and to the use of technical terms and non-sexist language.

TONE

Tone is a quality of writing that is very difficult to define, but one to which audiences always react. Since, in some ways, it reflects the writer's personality, we might think of it as the "personality" of the document. Some documents have a formal tone, some an informal one; some are courteous, some brusque; some are timid, some forceful. Although there is certainly more to the creation of tone than just diction, diction is almost always at fault if the tone is inappropriate.

Read the section on tone in Chapter 18, and then check that you have created the tone you designated when you defined your task for the document and that you have not shifted the tone. Because tone can be especially difficult to judge in your own writing, ask someone else to review your tone.

PRECISION

Review the section on precision in Chapter 2 and check that any vagueness in your document is intentional. Pay particular attention to relative adjectives and adverbs, such as *expensive* and *quickly*; abstract nouns, such as *damage*; indefinites, such as *someone*; vague quantity specifications, such as *some, a lot*; vague verbs, such as *affect*.

TECHNICAL TERMS

Make sure that your audience will understand every technical term you use. If you cannot be sure that your audience will know the term, consider whether you need to use that particular word. Is there a more commonly known word that will do as well? If you must use the technical term, then define it in a way your audience will understand (see Chapter 10).

NON-SEXIST LANGUAGE

The central issue in the use of sexist or non-sexist language concerns the use of *he* as a generic pronoun. In other words, if you are referring to a person, irrespective of that person's sex, should you use *he*? Those who advocate the use of non-sexist language feel that it is offensive to use *he*, or any other word that implies maleness, such as *mailman*, in a situation that could include women. For example, they would object to the following on the grounds that it implies that all students are men: "The student should check his work carefully." Others reject attempts to achieve non-sexist language on the grounds that it is awkward.

Since this issue produces particularly heated reactions that could very well interfere with how your document is viewed, you must consider your audience's attitude, as well as the policy of your organization, if it has a stated one. In place of the sentence in the previous paragraph, you could write the following: "Students should check their work carefully," or "The student should check her work carefully," or "The student should check his or her work carefully." To use non-sexist language, you must check for masculine pronouns and try to replace them by plurals or by some feminine pronouns. For a detailed discussion of non-sexist language, see Appendix C ("Avoiding Sexist Pronouns").

MECHANICS

When you have checked all the other aspects of your document, check the mechanics (spelling, capitalization, punctuation, use of numbers and units, and use of abbreviations). Although errors in mechanics seldom interfere with understanding, you must avoid them because they can be perceived as evidence of ignorance or carelessness. Appendix A provides a brief review of mechanics.

CHECKLIST FOR REVISING

CONTENT

- Have I left questions in the audience's mind?
- Have I answered who, what, when, where, why, how?
- Have I supported my claims adequately?
- Does my evidence warrant these claims?
- Are all data accurate?
- Have I used enough examples to illustrate generalizations?
- Have I repeated myself?
- Is any of this irrelevant to the reader?

ORGANIZATION

- Is the sequence of topics logical?
- Is the number of subheadings optimal?
- Does each heading and subheading accurately reflect the text that follows?
- Are subheadings at the same level grammatically parallel and semantically related?
- Have I introduced the document adequately?
- Have I introduced each section and subsection?
- Have I introduced each heading, subheading, and graphic?
- Have I used transition statements to indicate shifts in topic?
- Have I summarized long sections adequately?

GRAPHICS

- Have I used all and only the graphics that are needed?
- Is each graphic in the best place in the document?
- Is each graphic appropriately designed?
- Is each graphic integrated into the document?

PARAGRAPH STRUCTURE

- Does each paragraph have a topic sentence?
- Is each paragraph adequately developed?
- Is the length of each paragraph optimal?
- Is each paragraph cohesive?

SENTENCE STRUCTURE

- Is each sentence clear?
- Is each sentence concise?
- Is each sentence grammatically correct?

DICTION

- Have I used the right words to create the tone I need?
- Have I said exactly what I mean?

- Have I used only the necessary technical terms?
- Have I defined the technical terms my audience may not know?
- Have I avoided sexist language?

MECHANICS

- Are all words spelled correctly?
- Is capitalization correct and consistent?
- Is the punctuation correct?
- Are numbers and units used correctly?
- Are abbreviations used correctly and consistently?

NOTES

1. Lester Faigley and Stephen Witte, "Analyzing Revision," CCC 32 (1981): 400 – 414.
2. Linda Flower, "Writer-Based Prose: A Cognitive Basis for Problems in Writing," CE 41 (Sept. 1979): 19 – 37.

EXERCISES

1. Look through the checklist for revising. Which of the questions do you always ask yourself when you revise? Which ones do you ask sometimes? Which ones do you never ask?

2. Reproduced below is a section of a student's report on some problems in the 1983 summer program of a geological exploration company. Read the section carefully to check the content and organization. What are the strengths? What are the weaknesses? Rewrite the section.

EQUIPMENT

The 1983 program used equipment that had not been used in previous programs. Therefore, costs arose because this equipment was not properly chosen, maintained, and used efficiently. Loss of production time and expensive repairs resulted from problems with the generator and the vehicles.

GENERATOR

The generator was the power source for the main camp deep freezer, and therefore, had to be kept in operating condition. The two sources of problems affecting this condition were maintenance and refuelling.

Maintenance

The generator was bought and put into service without any of the crew consulting the accompanying operating manual. No regular maintenance was performed, and this led to an expensive replacement.

The Honda generator came with a comprehensive operating and repair manual which outlined a maintenance schedule based on hours of operation. Appendix A lists the maintenance suggested after every twenty hours.

The generator was used sixteen hours daily when the main camp was in operation. The only maintenance performed on the generator was an irregular oil change at one hundred hour intervals. After sixty days of operation, carbon began to build up on the spark plugs, and in another fifteen days the generator quit running. The generator was flown to Williams Lake, the nearest service centre. The flight was necessary because to drive would have taken two days, in which time several hundred dollars worth of food in the freezer would have thawed. The mechanic who looked at the generator when it was brought in reported that the engine was damaged due to lack of oil changes, and use of contaminated fuel. Because there was not enough time to repair the engine, a new generator was bought for $600. The cost of the helicopter flight was $1000, bringing the cost of replacing the generator to $1600.

To avoid breakdowns in the future, the project geologist should assign one of the workers to the job of following a regular maintenance schedule as outlined in the generator manual. This job will require the worker to keep a record of the maintenance performed, total hours of operation, and the date. As well, this worker should be the only person to work on the generator so the maintenance is not overlooked due to confusion over what has and has not been done. The tools required for this work are listed in Appendix B.

Regular maintenance will allow the generator to run cleaner, and therefore, breakdowns due to engine wear will not occur.

Refuelling

Fuel for the generator became contaminated while being transferred from a forty-five gallon drum to the generator fuel tank. The contaminated fuel damaged the engine, and contributed to the expenses described under Maintenance.

To refuel the generator, fuel was pumped through a hand pump into a five gallon jerry-can, and then poured from the jerry-can into the generator fuel tank. Most of the fuel contamination occurred with the hand pump. The open ends of the intake pipe and outlet hose of the pump picked up dirt and water when placed on the ground or when not properly stored. Once the contaminants entered the generator fuel tank, they settled to the bottom, where they then drained into the fuel line leading to the engine. According to the mechanic who looked at the engine in Williams Lake, the continual use of this fuel caused extensive piston ring and sleeve damage.

To solve this problem of fuel contamination, a plastic five gallon jerry-can and filter should be set up as an alternate fuel tank, as shown in Figure 1. This could be done by a worker while the main camp is being set up. See Appendix C for set up description. This will solve the problem of fuel contamination because contaminants will settle to the bottom of the jerry-can where they cannot be picked up by the fuel inlet. Any contaminants that are picked up will be removed by the filter.

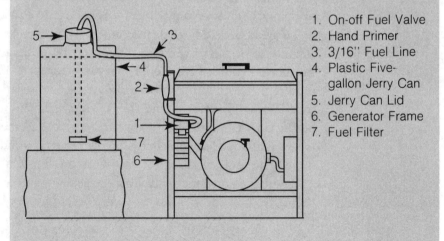

1. On-off Fuel Valve
2. Hand Primer
3. 3/16'' Fuel Line
4. Plastic Five-gallon Jerry Can
5. Jerry Can Lid
6. Generator Frame
7. Fuel Filter

Figure 1   Alternate Fuel Tank for the Generator

Source: Richard Haslinger, ''Equipment.'' Printed by permission.

3. Evaluate the paragraph structure in the text you examined in exercise 2.

4. Identify the main weaknesses in the following paragraph. Rewrite the paragraph to overcome these weaknesses.

> Software is basically comprised of code in a computer language. Computers can understand many different types of code. BASIC and FORTRAN are two common computer languages. These are known as high-level languages. Their syntax, the set of constructions of a computer language, are similar to English constructions. This enables the software designer to readily translate algorithms into a language that the computer understands. The languages listed above have some differences. FORTRAN, an acronym for formula translation, is used for scientific applications. It has complete numerical problem solving capability. BASIC is a language introduced for personal computers. Its syntax has only a small number of constructions. BASIC was initially developed for personal computers which had only a limited memory size.

5. Improve the following passages:

   a. In situations where the exchange of oxygen and carbon dioxide is inadequate, the concentration of carbon dioxide continues to increase in the lungs, and a chemical substance known as carbonic acid is formed. An example situation of this type is that of a drowning person. This new chemical substance, carbonic acid, increases the concentration of hydrogen ions, which results in a lowering of pH, and thus respiratory acidosis.

   b. The first real discovery of an antibiotic was by Alexander Fleming in 1929 who noticed that when he left cultures of the *Staphylococci* bacteria exposed to the air mold grew on them. He saw that the area of bacteria around the mold quickly disappeared and concluded something in the mold killed this bacteria.

   c. Owing to the high complexity of the bow-wave patterns, it is not yet possible to determine the amount of phase shift accurately for complete wave cancellation. Often, a macroscopic correction works satisfactorily on a simple hull to cancel the relatively simpler characteristic waves. As it turns out, in towing experiments the difference in wave patterns of the two scale models, one with and one without a bulbous-bow, are remarkable, particularly the simplicity of the former.

CHAPTER 9

PREPARING THE PRESENTATION COPY

INTRODUCTION

As we said earlier, the documents you prepare help to create your professional image. Not only must your work *be* good, but it must also *appear* to be good. If the document does not look good, it creates a negative impression that detracts from its content and from your professional image. This chapter explains how to schedule the preparation of the presentation copy, and then comments on format conventions, layout, and proofreading.

SCHEDULING

Preparing the presentation copy is a more complicated and time-consuming process than many beginning writers expect. Figure 9-1 presents an overview of the steps in preparing a presentation copy.

Figure 9-1
Steps in Preparing
the Presentation Copy

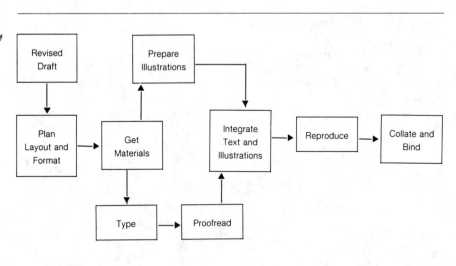

If you are using a word processor, the typing step will be replaced by a step for final adjustments in format and layout. If you are using desktop publishing, the proofreading step will come after the integration of text and illustrations.

The longer and the more important the document, the more crucial it becomes that you plan and schedule the steps for preparing the presentation copy. For each step, you need to know the following:

- *Who will do this step?* If other people are doing any of the steps, make your arrangements as early as possible to assure that these people will be available. Remember that typists and graphic artists have other commitments and that they also take vacations.
- *How long will this step take?* One estimate for typing and proof-reading a page is 0.6 hours.[1] This means that you would have to budget for 12 hours of work to type and proofread a 20-page document. If you use commercial facilities, such as a copying centre, include travelling time in your schedule. If you are using photographs, budget for processing time.

When you have the above information, you can prepare your detailed schedule. When you schedule your own time, do not overlook other commitments such as classes or preparation for exams at college, or meetings or other projects at work. Figure 9-2 is a student's schedule for a 15-page report.

Figure 9-2
A Student's Schedule
for Preparing the
Presentation Copy

Tuesday	
Plan layout and format	2 hrs.
Get paper, covers, labels	1 hr.
Wednesday	
Work in Wordprocessing Rm.	3 hrs.
(5-8)	
Thursday	
Take illustrations to Joe	1 hr.
Work in Wordprocessing Rm.	2 hrs.
(5-7)	
Friday	
Proofread	1 hr.
Work in Wordprocessing Rm.	2 hrs.
(5-7)	
Saturday	
Pick up illustrations from Joe	1 hr.
Integrate illustrations and text	1 hr.
Reproduce, collate, and bind at Speedy Copy	2 hrs.
	———
	16 hrs.

FORMAT CONVENTIONS

Each type of document has format conventions that you must observe. In this textbook you will find format conventions for the following types of documents:

- letter (Chapter 20)
- memorandum (Chapter 18)

- report (Chapters 16 and 17)
- proposal (Chapter 22)

On the job, you will learn how these formats have been adapted by your particular organization. Although typists will normally know your employer's preferences, you are still responsible for learning and following them.

LAYOUT

Layout is the arrangement of text and illustrations on the page. Layout can determine not only how attractive a page is, but also how readable the text is. The main variables in layout are the following:

- white space
- typeface
- size of illustration
- relative location of text and illustrations

One of the outstanding advantages of word processors, desktop publishing systems, and photocopying equipment is the ease with which the writer can alter layout. In preparing all but the most routine documents, you should get into the habit of trying several layouts to assure you choose the most effective one.

WHITE SPACE

Think of a page of technical writing as being made up of three elements: text, illustrations, and white space. Use the white space as a design component when you plan a page. In distributing white space, consider in particular the following aspects:

- margins
- vertical spacing of text
- indentions
- spacing around illustrations

MARGINS. Margins frame the text and illustrations. In choosing margin size, try to make the page look balanced, allow room for binding, and avoid lines so short or so long that their length will distract the reader; a well designed page does not call attention to itself. The following guidelines may help you:

- Avoid margins of less than 2.5 cm.
- Leave a left margin of between 3.5 cm and 4 cm if the document will be bound.
- Use a line length of between 14 cm and 16 cm.
- Use larger top and bottom margins to make a short document look more balanced on the page.
- Use wider margins if you expect your reader to want to make notes on the document.

VERTICAL SPACING. Your instructor may require you to submit all assignments double spaced so that there is room between lines for corrections and comments. At work, though, you will probably use single spacing within paragraphs and double spacing between paragraphs.

INDENTIONS. Use indentions to signal hierarchical relationships between headings and between sections of text. When you do indent, be careful that your indentions are not so wide that they waste space.

SPACING AROUND ILLUSTRATIONS. Use some white space to frame an illustration and to separate it from text. Normally a frame of 1 cm to 1.5 cm is sufficient.

TYPEFACE

Use capitalization, boldface, and underlining to emphasize headings and to show hierarchical relationships.

SIZE OF ILLUSTRATION

Review Chapter 3. You may want to use a photocopying machine to enlarge or reduce an illustration to make the page more attractive.

RELATIVE LOCATION OF TEXT AND ILLUSTRATIONS

For student assignments, this textbook has suggested that an illustration be placed so that there is no text running beside the illustration. Your only choices in this case concern how to arrange the illustrations vertically relative to text. At work, however, you may want to place text beside illustrations, particularly in instructional material.

PROOFREADING

Your responsibility does *not* end when you give the revised draft to a typist. You can expect a typist to be careful and to proofread, but you must never assume that anyone else's work is perfect. You must always check the presentation copy for errors. Any error that remains in your document is *your* error, no matter who actually made it.

You will be able to proofread most shorter documents simply by rereading them very carefully. If you assume that there are errors, you will be more likely to find them. Do whatever you can to overcome your familiarity with the text, because familiarity will make you see what you expect to see.

When you are proofreading longer documents, you must be systematic, and you may need to make several passes through the document. You may find the following checklist helpful:

- Are all headings correctly phrased and correctly placed?
- Are the formats of all sections and subsections consistent?
- Are the references accurate?
- Are the headings and page numbers in the table of contents accurate?

- Are the figure numbers and titles in the list of illustrations accurate?
- Are all numbers and mathematical expressions correct?
- Are all proper nouns (names) correctly spelled and consistently capitalized?
- Are hyphens used consistently?
- Are all abbreviations used consistently?
- Are all parentheses and brackets paired?
- Are all apostrophes used correctly?
- Are all words typed correctly? Spelling software is very useful for this check, but be very careful not to overlook typing errors that create legitimate words. Beware particularly of errors like the following:

  it for *if* or *in* or *is*
  not for *no* or *nor* or *now*
  fiction for *friction*
  to for *too* or *top*
  you for *your*
  for for *form*
  quite for *quiet*

NOTE

1. Rodney D. Stewart and Ann L. Stewart, *Proposal Preparation* (New York: Wiley, 1984), 169.

EXERCISES

1. Select a page from one of your assignments that uses headings, and use a word processor to present that page with three different layouts. Vary the margins, the vertical spacing, and the typeface. Comment on the different effects these layouts create.

2. Proofread the following passage:

   Layout is the arrangment of text and illustrations on hte page. In adition to determining how attractive page is, layout my also affect how readably the page is. The main variables in layout are the following:
   - white space
   - type face
   - side of illustration
   - relative location of tex tand illustrations

   One of the outstan ding advantages on word processors, desk top publishing and various types of photocopying equipement is the ease with which the writer can alter layout. In preparing all but hte most routine document's, you should get into the habit of tying several layouts to assure you chose the most effective on.

PART THREE

BASIC TECHNICAL WRITING STRATEGIES

DEFINING

INTRODUCTION

Defining is indicating what a term means. To remind yourself of how important it can be to know what technical terms mean, consider the following three passages:

- The Kolmogorov-Smirnov test can be used for any hypothesized contiguous CDF and is typically a very good approximate test if the population random variable is discrete.[1]
- Important though the rules which produce such focusing structures as Clefts, Pseudo-clefts, Passives, Object-frontings, Adverb-frontings, and Presentatives are, they are relatively insignificant in the extent to which they mutilate semantic structure for pragmatic surface purposes. The most important focusing rules in this respect are the Participant-raising rules and the Predicate-lowering rules.[2]
- For non-Newtonian fluids which are not time-dependent it is possible to convert capillary-viscometer measurements to the equivalent sliding-plate measurements, but this involves some mathematical manipulations. For time-dependent (e.g., thixotropic) fluids this does not seem to be possible.[3]

Even though these passages are written in English, you probably did not understand them because you do not know what some of the words mean. These words are technical terms that probably do not pose problems for senior students in statistics, linguistics, and fluid mechanics; they would have learned these technical terms as they studied their particular disciplines. Each course you take introduces you to a specialized vocabulary, and mastering any discipline, or subject area, includes mastering its technical terms. To get a rough measure of the number of terms you will learn this year, look at the entries in the indexes of all your textbooks. Audiences outside your field of expertise, though, will usually not share your knowledge of technical terms. To communicate with them, you will have to either define each special term in ways they can understand, or omit it entirely.

Definitions are very important in technical writing; in fact, it is difficult to find examples of technical writing that do not include definitions. After a brief overview of how words mean and the place of technical terms in language, this chapter discusses when to use a technical term, when to define it, and how to define it for various audiences and purposes.

HOW WORDS MEAN

The study of how words mean is called *semantics* and is part of philosophy and linguistics. A rather simplified way of looking at what a word or term means, particularly if it is a noun, is to consider the word as designating a set of specifics. To use set theory, we could say that *cat* refers to, or designates, all objects that are members of the set "cat." We can define a set either by listing its members or by specifying the characteristics the members share. Clearly, to list all cats would be impractical. To specify the characteristics that determine membership is to *define* the term *cat*. How to specify these characteristics is explored in more detail later in this chapter, particularly in the discussion of formal definitions.

The relationship between words and their meanings is arbitrary in the sense that there is no inherent dependency between a word and what it means. In other words, there is no particular reason why *cat* should mean a small, furry animal, for example. If you are not convinced, consider the fact that there are hundreds of different words in the world's languages that refer to what we call a cat. At the same time, within a language, or within a discipline, this arbitrary relationship becomes conventionalized, so that there is a consensus within the speech community about what a particular term means; then dictionaries usually record these conventionalized meanings. Once the relationship between word and meaning has been conventionalized, you are not, of course, at liberty to change it; you cannot, for example, use *cat* to refer to a cow. If you do for some reason need to use a word in an unconventional way, you must advise your audience explicitly, or communication will be impeded. The meanings of words may, however, change over time. Consider, for example, the following definitions from a dictionary published in 1899:

- *virus*: a slimy liquid; contagious or poisonous matter (as of ulcers, etc.): any foul, hurtful matter.[4]
- *atom*: a particle of matter so small that it cannot be cut or divided; anything very small.[5]
- *carburetor*: an apparatus of various forms by which coal gas, hydrogen, or air is passed through or over a liquid hydrocarbon, to confer or intensify illuminating power.[6]
- *bomb*: a hollow shell of iron filled with gunpowder, and discharged from a mortar, so as to explode when it falls.[7]

THE PLACE OF TECHNICAL TERMS IN LANGUAGE

We have already noted that each discipline has a specialized vocabulary that must be mastered as part of the discipline. Why do disciplines have these specialized vocabularies? The most obvious reason is that the general or common vocabulary lacks suitable terms to signify the special concepts in the discipline. In other words, new words are needed to refer to new things. As well, the technical terms allow more precise communication because they are defined precisely, often even mathematically, for use within the specialized speech community. When you graduate, you will join this speech community, and you will be expected to communicate with other members in it. You will be expected to use technical terms accurately when you speak or write to your peers. You will also be expected to understand those terms used by your peers, or in the books and journals in your discipline; you will be expected to be a technical audience in one or more disciplines.

At the same time, you will also be expected to adjust your use of technical terms when you communicate with audiences outside your special speech community. If you use unnecessary technical terms or ones your audience doesn't understand, you may be accused of using jargon. *Jargon* is simply a derogatory word for technical terms that are perceived as being used unnecessarily. No term in isolation is jargon; it only becomes jargon if your audience objects to your using it. In other words, whether or not a particular term is jargon depends first on the context in which it is used, and secondly on the audience's reaction to this use.

Because of the extremely rapid growth of scientific knowledge in the last century, there has been a tremendous growth in the number of scientific and technical terms. For example, the *McGraw-Hill Dictionary of Scientific and Technical Terms*, a comprehensive dictionary that includes terms from 100 fields, added 8000 entries between 1974 and 1978 and another 7500 between 1978 and 1984, for a total of about 115 500 definitions for about 98 500 terms in the 1984 edition. For comparison, you might note that *The Gage Canadian Dictionary* (1983) lists about 55 000 entries, the *American Heritage Dictionary* (1969) about 155 000, and *Webster's Third New International Dictionary* (1961) about 450 000.

How, then, are the specialized vocabularies related to the general vocabulary? We should note, first, that the distinctions between the two vocabularies are often arbitrary, for some technical terms are clearly also part of the general vocabulary. This is partly a consequence of terms from the specialized vocabularies entering the general vocabulary as a result of frequent use. For example, the following are probably part of the vocabularies of most educated people: *laser, virus, microwave,* UHF, *black hole,* RAM. Second, some words, such as *work, mass,* or *salt,* are part of the common vocabulary, but have special meanings as technical terms. Also, some terms have different meanings in different disciplines. Sometimes these are, of course, related, as in the meanings of *flutter,* which in acoustics refers to "rapid fluctuation of frequency or amplitude in radio reception," but in aeronautics to "sustained oscillation on a wing or tail of an airplane," in medicine to "an abnormality of cardiac rhythm," and in television to a "variation in brightness."[8]

THE PLACE OF DEFINITIONS IN TECHNICAL WRITING

A term must be defined if it is being introduced into a discipline for the first time, if it is used in a special sense in a particular document, or if a necessary term is new to the audience.

TERM NEW TO DISCIPLINE. Each time a new phenomenon, principle, or concept is discovered or proposed, it must be named and defined precisely to allow experts to communicate effectively about it. Periodically, these definitions are gathered in specialized dictionaries for particular disciplines and in more general dictionaries for related disciplines. As part of your preparation for your discipline you should become familiar with the main dictionaries in your field, normally housed in the reference section of the library.

SPECIAL MEANING IN A DOCUMENT. Sometimes a term is used in a particular sense in a document. To assure that the writer and audience agree on the particular meaning of the term, this meaning is stated explicitly in the document. You are probably familiar with this use of definitions in legal contracts such as insurance policies, where the definitions are usually gathered in a separate section. When such definitions are used in scholarly articles, they are likely to be part of the text and take a form such as "By X I mean ...." In either case, the definition does not become a part of the language; it is limited to the document in which it is found.

TERM NEW TO AUDIENCE. Whenever practical, use terms your audience already knows, unless the specific purpose of the document is to teach the audience new terms, as in a textbook. Using familiar terms will make your document more readable, and your audience will be able to focus on what you are saying without being distracted by the words you are using. If you use unnecessary technical terms, you are using jargon. Remember how you reacted to the passages at the beginning of this chapter.

As we noted in Chapter 5, you have to know what terms your audience understands, but even if you do know your audience quite well, and even if you do pay a lot of attention to this aspect of audience awareness, it is very easy to be wrong. Do you, for example, know which terms your friends or the members of your family would understand? Test them. You should also remember that we understand the meaning of different terms to varying degrees. Some words we don't even recognize; some we recognize, but don't know the meaning of; some we understand in a very general or vague way; some we think we understand, but can't define; and some we can even define. In addition to knowing whether or not your audience understands the term, then, you may need to be able to estimate the extent of this understanding and whether it is sufficient to understand your document.

If you have used a term that is necessary to your document and you are not certain that your audience has sufficient understanding of its meaning, then you must define it. But in choosing the means to define it, you must again be aware of the audience and the purpose of the definition. How precisely does your audience need to have the term defined? What other terms and which means of definition should you use in defining the term?

KINDS OF DEFINITIONS

As we noted at the beginning of this chapter, the purpose of a definition is to say what a term means; all definitions are about *words*, not things.

This is an important distinction between definitions and descriptions. Consider, for example, a definition of *cat* and a description of a cat. The definition refers to the word and must allow us to identify *all* cats and *only* cats as cats. If it does not apply to one particular cat, or if it includes one animal that is not a cat, then the definition is faulty. A description, though, can never apply to all cats; it can apply only to one cat, unless, of course, the cats are clones.

The three kinds of definitions discussed in this chapter – formal definitions, informal definitions, and expanded definitions – should together satisfy your definition-writing needs.

FORMAL DEFINITIONS

Formal definitions, which date at least from the time of Aristotle, are also known as sentence definitions, analytical definitions, or essential definitions. While formal definitions are seldom used by themselves, even in dictionaries, they are often a part of longer definitions. They are included here both because they are fundamental to understanding the process of defining and because writing formal definitions provides a particularly rigorous exercise in precise thinking and expression.

WHAT IS A FORMAL DEFINITION?

A formal definition is a sentence that takes the following form:

A *term* is a *genus* + *differentiae*

where

- *term* is the term being defined,
- *genus* is the class to which the referents of the term belong,
- *differentiae* are the characteristics that distinguish the referents of the term from all other members of the genus.

For example:

A *thermometer* is an *instrument for measuring temperature.*
Term   **Genus**   **Differentia**

Earlier in this chapter we said that we could consider a term as designating a set of specifics, so that *thermometer* would designate all thermometers. The formal definition indicates the larger set (the *genus*) to which the members of *term* belong and which characteristics (*differentiae*) only the members of *term* share. In our case, then, the definition indicates that all thermometers are instruments and that they are distinguished from all other instruments by having the function of measuring temperature. Figure 10-1 shows the relationship between genus and term and between instrument and thermometer.

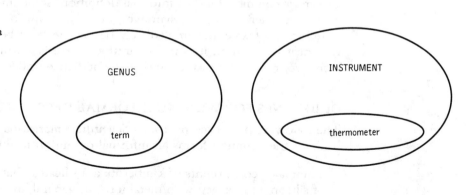

Figure 10-1
Venn Diagrams
Illustrating the
Relationship between
Genus and Term
and between
Instrument and
Thermometer

The following are other examples of formal definitions:

- A hexagon is a geometric figure that has six sides.
- Linguistics is the study of human language.

GUIDELINES FOR WRITING FORMAL DEFINITIONS

When writing a formal definition, observe the following guidelines:

- The *formal definition* should be only one sentence. The subject of this sentence should be the term you are defining, and the verb should be *is*.
- The *genus* should be as narrow, or specific, as possible. The larger the genus is, the more distinguishing features you will have to include to specify the membership of the term. Ideally, the genus should be a class just slightly more inclusive than that of the term. Note that it is illogical to repeat the term as the genus.
- The genus must be the same *part of speech* as the term. Do not write "X is where" or "X is when," unless X is indeed a time or a place.
- The *differentiae* must allow for the inclusion of all members of the term and exclude all non-members. It is the selection of correct differentiae that is the most difficult aspect of writing formal definitions. Check the accuracy of a formal definition by turning it around so that you are asking whether the term can be applied whenever the genus and differentiae fit.

INFORMAL DEFINITIONS

WHAT IS AN INFORMAL DEFINITION?

The term *informal definition* is used to refer to all the means of defining that do not take the structure of a formal definition and that are not as long as an expanded definition. The specific distinction between an informal definition and an expanded definition, however, is arbitrary. The most common kind of informal definition, sometimes also called a parenthetic definition, is a synonym, near synonym, or paraphrase inserted in the text either immediately beside the term being defined or very near to it. In an informal definition, there is usually less concern with rigour than with assuring that the audience understands the text.

GUIDELINES FOR WRITING INFORMAL DEFINITIONS

The following brief excerpt from a *Scientific American* article illustrates some of the common forms an informal definition may take:

> The major constituents of kimberlite are silicates, that is, compounds of silicon and oxygen with metal ions. In general, minerals cannot be defined as simple chemical compounds because their composition is not determined by a fixed ratio of atoms. Often two or more compounds are present and are said to be in solid solution with one another. As in a liquid solution, the component substances can be mixed in any ratio over a wide range. One important constituent of kimberlite is the mineral called olivine, which is a solid solution of magnesium silicate (Mg_2SiO_4) and iron silicate (Fe_2SiO_4). Another silicate present is phlogopite, a kind of mica rich in potassium and magnesium, and there are also various silicate minerals that are classified as serpentines. The serpentines are formed by the hydration of olivine, or in other words by chemically adding water to it. Kimberlite also contains the mineral calcite, which is not a silicate but consists of more or less pure calcium carbonate ($CaCO_3$).

From Keith G. Cox, "Kimberlite Pipes." Copyright © 1978 by *Scientific American*, Inc. All rights reserved.

Note particularly the definition of olivine, which uses a non-restrictive relative clause ("which is a solid solution...."); and the definition of phlogopite, which uses a phrase in apposition ("a kind of mica ... magnesium"); when you use either of these structures, remember to enclose it in commas.

To see how definitions may be adapted to audience and purpose, we can compare the above definitions of olivine with those in a scientific dictionary and a general dictionary. The *Chambers Science and Technology Dictionary* defines olivine as follows:

> Orthosilicate of iron and magnesium, crystallizing in the orthorhombic system, which occurs widely in the basic and ultramafic igneous rocks, including olivine-gobbro, olivine-dolerite, olivine-basalt, peridotites, etc.[9]

The American Heritage Dictionary of the English Language, on the other hand, has the following definition for olivine:

A mineral silicate of iron and magnesium, principally Fe_2SiO_4 and Mg_2SiO_4, found in igneous and metamorphic rocks and used as a structural material in refractories and in cements.[10]

EXPANDED, OR AMPLIFIED, DEFINITIONS
WHAT IS AN EXPANDED DEFINITION?

The term *expanded definition* refers to definitions that are more than one or two sentences long. Expanded definitions that stand alone take many forms, including encyclopedia entries, and sections of textbooks, review articles, or pamphlets. Often a one- or two-paragraph expanded definition will be part of a longer document. The main function of expanded definitions, whether they be separate documents, or parts of longer documents, is to educate; the audience may not understand the meaning of some term as well as it would like to, or as well as it needs to.

There is, of course, a gradation of amplification in definitions from very brief formal and parenthetic definitions to ones that are encyclopedic. In fact, an entire textbook could be considered an expanded definition of a term such as *thermodynamics* or *physiology*. The degree to which a definition will be expanded should depend on the needs of the audience and, if the definition is part of a larger document, the significance of the definition to the purposes of that document.

As a definition is amplified, it may also, depending on the term being defined, begin to merge with an explanation of a process or a description of an object. The distinction is that a definition tells what a *term* means, and in this sense it must be *generic*. In other words, if you are writing about what *all* snowmobiles are like, you are writing an expanded definition, but if you are writing about a particular model or even about an individual snowmobile, you are writing a description.

Expanded definitions can be particularly difficult to write well, mainly because they pose complex problems for audience adaptation, but also because they require a high degree of precision in thinking as well as expression. A good expanded definition must be accurate and it must be clear to the audience. Only someone who knows what the term means can test its accuracy; only someone who does *not* know what the term means can fully test its clarity.

AN EXAMPLE OF AN EXPANDED DEFINITION

The following expanded definition was prepared by a student for an audience of first-year students. While it is not perfect, it does have many strengths.

TEMPERED STEEL

If you have a favourite kitchen or pocket knife, it's probably one that is always sharp, a knife that "holds its edge" well. In contrast to this sharp knife, there may be one that is always dull. The difference may be that the "good" knife has a tempered steel blade. To understand what tempering is, it is necessary to look more closely at steel. When you see a building under construction, it is hard to imagine the steel girders as knife blades. Your instincts are correct. Structural steel used in buildings and bridges is very different from tempered steel used in tools and knife blades.

If a red hot steel slab is cooled slowly in air, the result will be structural steel, which is soft and ductile. This steel will stretch and bend without breaking. If the same slab is cooled rapidly (water quenched), the result will be hardened steel, which is brittle. This steel will break before it will stretch or bend. If the terms "ductile" and "brittle" are unfamiliar to you, imagine a coffee swizzle-stick and a piece of peanut brittle. The swizzle-stick is ductile, while the candy is brittle.

At this point you may well ask whether "hardened steel" is "tempered steel." The answer is no. A tempered steel knife blade will bend and we now know that hardened steel will not. What, then, is tempered steel? Tempered steel is hardened steel that has been baked in an oven designed for just that purpose. When hardened steel is reheated to a specific temperature and held there for a period of time, a marvelous transformation occurs in the steel. The results of this transformation can only be seen under a microscope. The microstructures of structural, hardened, and tempered steel are shown in Figure 1.

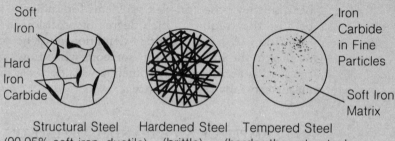

Figure 1   Microstructure of Three Steels

Tempered steel is more costly to produce than untempered steel because of the labour cost of the extra handling and because of the fuel cost of the reheating. These additional costs are reflected in the retail price of a knife or tool made from tempered steel.

Source: Michael Carriere, "Tempered Steel." Printed by permission.

ORGANIZATION

Expanded definitions should lead the audience from the familiar to the unfamiliar, from the *old* to the *new*. Beyond this, it is difficult to generalize about how they should be organized because there is a great variety of methods and combinations of methods that can be used to amplify a definition. A good way to begin is with a formal definition of the term.

METHODS OF EXPANSION

Many methods can be used to expand a definition, and usually several of these will be used in combination. In choosing which methods to use, you should consider which ones are most appropriate to the term, and which ones are most appropriate to your audience. Here we will discuss only the most commonly used methods:

- example
- comparison and analogy
- contrast and negation
- analysis into parts
- etymology
- graphics

EXAMPLE. Examples are a very useful and important means of bridging the gap with the audience, of using the *old* to explain the *new*. For example, you could note that hand lotion is an example of an emulsion, that aspirin is an example of an analgesic, or that the melting of ice when salt is added is an application of the depression of freezing point. Generally, concrete examples help the reader understand abstractions, but be careful not to choose examples with which the audience is unfamiliar, for then your reader will only become more confused.

In the expanded definition of tempered steel, the student begins by referring to the reader's favourite kitchen or pocket knife as an example of something that is probably made from tempered steel. Later he uses a coffee swizzle-stick as an example of a ductile object and peanut brittle as an example of a brittle substance.

COMPARISON AND ANALOGY. If your audience already knows something similar to what you are defining, you should use that knowledge. Compare the unfamiliar – the term – to something that is familiar. For example, in expanding a definition of a holograph, you can use a comparison to a photograph. A special kind of comparison is the *analogy*, in which the compared things are dissimilar, except for some critical feature they share. You are probably aware of the analogy that compares the flow of electricity to the flow of water. However, while analogies can be extremely useful for clarifying otherwise difficult concepts, there is a danger that the reader will extend the analogy in inappropriate ways and conclude, for example, that one can drink electricity or swim in it.

CONTRAST. Sometimes a term can be defined in part by showing what it does *not* refer to or what must be excluded. Often, comparison and contrast will be used closely together, with the comparison, rather like the genus, naming a class to which the term belongs, and the contrast indicating which members of that class are not members of the class designated by the term. How does a holograph differ from a photograph? The expanded definition of tempered steel contrasts tempered steel with structural steel and with hardened steel. To use contrast effectively, you must be able to imagine what sorts of things your audience might inappropriately include in the term.

ANALYSIS. Analysis means the breaking of something into its types, parts, or components. In defining *car*, for example, you could list and then discuss the various classes of cars. In classifying cars, you could use such criteria as origin (American, German, Japanese, Korean, Swedish, British), or type of fuel used (diesel, gasoline, natural gas, electricity), or capacity (sports, sedan, station wagon) to arrive at quite different subdivisions. Note, however, that when you do this, you must avoid mixing the criteria you use in establishing the classes. You could also, of course, expand a definition of *car* by discussing its main components.

Analysis can be used in expanding the definitions of most terms; objects can be separated into components, processes can be divided into steps or stages, disciplines can be divided into branches. When you use analysis, you can use the whole-parts organization in which you begin by listing the parts and then discuss each part in turn.

ETYMOLOGY. The etymology of a word is its original meaning and its history. It can be very useful in clarifying the meaning of a technical term that has been formed from Greek or Latin components. For example, to explain the meaning of *phlebography*, the radiological examination of veins, we can note that it is derived from the Greek *phleps*, meaning "vein," and *graphein*, "to write." Can you now guess the meaning of *phlebitis*, *phlebosclerosis*, or *phlebotomy*? A danger in using the etymology of a term is that the word may have changed its meaning so much that the original meaning may mislead. For example, the word *meat* is derived from the Old English *mete*, meaning "food," which is derived from the Indo-European *mad-*, meaning "wet." Clearly, then, this etymology would not help you understand *meat* better.

GRAPHICS. Graphics can be used in many ways to expand a definition. Photographs or drawings can illustrate the appearance of objects. Diagrams can show the structure of objects, or show how processes or scientific principles work. Most dictionaries, encyclopedias, and textbooks use graphics to expand definitions. If you use graphics, review the guidelines in Chapter 3. Note that many graphics that are used to explain concepts to you in your textbooks are not appropriate to a lay audience because they use graphic conventions the lay audience may not know. Remember also that since definitions are generic, and since photographs illustrate individuals, your caption and your reference in the text should indicate that the photograph illustrates a *typical* instance.

The graphic in the expanded definition of tempered steel shows differences among structural steel, hardened steel, and tempered steel that can only be seen at the microscopic level. While lay readers may not need to know the details of these differences, or even to know which type of steel is shown in each illustration, the graphic helps to convince that the differences in properties such as ductility and brittleness are the result of differences in structure.

AUDIENCE ADAPTATION

Adaptation to audience is critical to the success of an expanded definition. The kind of expanded definition through which you learned a technical term in your discipline will not usually be appropriate for most audiences. Two important causes of this inappropriateness are academic bias and technical diction.

ACADEMIC BIAS. Academic disciplines often emphasize aspects of a term that are not of primary concern to lay audiences. As a specialist you may be more concerned with causes, while a lay audience is more likely to be concerned with effects. This would apply particularly to terms designating diseases, geological formations, or economic phenomena, for example. Also, you are more likely to be concerned with the microscopic, or invisible, world of molecules, forces, and cells, while your audience will be more concerned with what it can experience directly. Finally, even though you have probably been taught to calculate various measures, such as standard deviation or the coefficient of friction, a lay audience will be more concerned with what this measure means and *why* one would calculate it.

To overcome the academic bias, you will have to examine the term from as wide a perspective as you can. Let us again consider standard deviation as our example. If you understand this term, you were probably taught how to calculate the standard deviation of a set of data. But does your audience need to learn how to do this? Why? In what kinds of situations is your audience most likely to encounter the term? Why are standard deviations calculated? What does knowing the standard deviation tell you? Consider now what kinds of audiences would want to learn to calculate standard deviations. What kinds would not? What aspects of standard deviation would you emphasize for a lay reader of a newspaper, a beginning teacher, a statistics student, a manager interpreting the results of a survey?

TECHNICAL DICTION. Remember that you are writing the expanded definition because your audience does not already know what the term means, but needs or wants to know. If your readers don't know what the term you are defining means, what other terms won't they know? They are also most unlikely to know the terms used in the definitions you have learned, and it would be a serious error to introduce such terms unless you also define them. You should try, then, to use only such technical terms as are essential, and you should define those that your audience may not understand. Informal definitions of the additional terms will usually be adequate to enable your audience to understand the expanded definition. At the same time, avoid getting caught in a chain of definitions that distract from developing the main definition. Note how the student who wrote the expanded definition of tempered steel defined *ductile*, *brittle*, and *water quenched*.

NOTES

1. Roger C. Pfaffenberger and James H. Patterson, *Statistical Methods for Business and Economics*, rev. ed. (Homewood, IL: Irwin, 1981), 678.
2. Robert P. Stockwell, *Foundations of Syntactic Theory* (Englewood Cliffs, NJ: Prentice-Hall, 1977), 161.
3. Noel de Nevers, *Fluid Mechanics* (Reading, MA: Addison, 1970), 424.
4. Daniel Lyons, *The American Dictionary of the English Language* (New York: Collier, 1899), 470.
5. Lyons, 23.
6. Lyons, 53.
7. Lyons, 91.
8. From Peter Walker, ed., *Chambers Science and Technology Dictionary* (Edinburgh: W. & R. Chambers Ltd., 1988), 355. Adapted and reprinted with permission of the publisher.
9. From Peter Walker, ed., *Chambers Science and Technology Dictionary* (Edinburgh: W. & R. Chambers Ltd., 1988), 626. Reprinted with permission of the publisher.
10. Copyright © 1981 by Houghton Mifflin Company. Adapted and reprinted by permission from *The American Heritage Dictionary of the English Language*.

EXERCISES

1. In the library find the main specialized dictionaries for your discipline or for one of the courses you are studying this year. Prepare a memo for your instructor (see Chapter 18) in which you do the following:

   a. List the title, editor(s), publication facts, and library call number for two or three specialized dictionaries.

   b. Explain briefly how these dictionaries differ in audience and purpose.

   c. Explain which one you would prefer to buy.

2. Select a term defined in one of your textbooks. Compare this definition with the definitions of the same term in at least two technical dictionaries. Finally, locate this term in an encyclopedia. In a memo report, explain how this entry differs from the dictionary definitions. Submit a photocopy of the textbook definition, the dictionary definitions, and the encyclopedia entry.

3. Select two terms in your discipline. The first one must be one that is known by everyone in your technical writing class. (In class you will check whether your choice was right and therefore whether or not you have an accurate sense of the terms your classmates know.) The second one must be one that only students in your discipline would know. Prepare an oral definition of the second term.

4. Indicate what is wrong with each of the following formal definitions:
   a. A library is where books are stored.
   b. A ruler is a device for measuring lengths.
   c. An equation is a statement used in mathematics.
   d. Interest is a payment that banks make to their depositors.

5. a. Write formal definitions for four of the terms listed below. Check that your definition applies to all and only the members of the set designated by the term.

   - pen
   - hammer
   - photograph
   - magazine
   - kite

   - shirt
   - chair
   - broom
   - office
   - lever

   b. Exchange your definitions with a classmate. Are your classmate's definitions accurate? Can you think of terms other than the one being defined that would be included by the definition? Can you think of referents that are not included?

6. The following expanded definition of dendrochronology was written by a student.
   a. Which of the methods of expansion discussed in this chapter are used in this definition?
   b. Which terms are defined informally within this expanded definition?
   c. What are the main strengths of this expanded definition?

DENDROCHRONOLOGY

Nearly everyone has taken a walk in the woods and paused to count the rings on the stump of a felled tree to learn the age of that particular tree when it was cut down. Such casual observations led to the study of dendrochronology. Dendrochronology is the science of dating events and objects as well as reconstructing environmental conditions by studying the annual growth rings of trees.

The growth of a tree by the formation of its annual rings is somewhat like the songs on a record that one plays on a stereo.

The needle starts on the outside and works its way inward, playing through each song until it reaches the centre of the record. Similarly, the growth of annual rings begins just underneath the bark in a layer called the cambium. Each completed ring, like songs on a record, is, in turn, surrounded by the next year's growth.

Each year, in the spring or early summer, the cambium produces large, thin-walled cells called earlywood. This is done by the process of cell division. Towards fall and winter, cell division in the cambium changes to produce small, dense wood cells with thicker walls. This dense wood on the outside of the annual ring is called latewood. Thus, each annual ring can be distinguished by the end of the dark latewood and the beginning of the light earlywood of the next year (Figure 1).

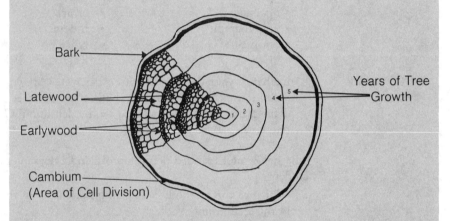

Figure 1   The Creation of Annual Rings by Cell Division

The growth of annual rings is influenced by factors such as the amount of sunshine, wind, rain, snow and ice. These climatic factors, along with other factors such as fire, are recorded in each annual ring. Thus, each ring pattern is unique to that time period and area. Specialists in the field of dendrochronology are able to read these environmental conditions in the past by studying the colours and widths of each ring. For example, tree rings are notably thicker in wet years and narrower in dry years.

Core samples can be attained from living trees by inserting a small round tube, called a borer, into the tree. The core samples can be compared in a master chronology of rings built up from many different trees in the area with overlapping sequences. The patterns of thick and thin rings are matched to the master chronology and are dated on the basis of their accurate fit to the master sequence. This process of comparison is called cross-dating (Figure 2).

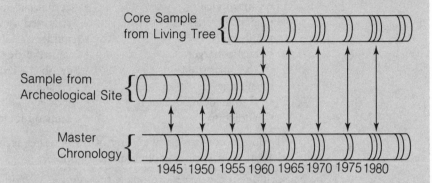

Core Sample
from Living Tree

Sample from
Archeological Site

Master
Chronology

1945 1950 1955 1960 1965 1970 1975 1980

Figure 2   Cross-dating Annual Rings

The most extensive master chronology in North America comes from the bristlecone pine in California. This master chronology has helped archaeologists date important archaeological sites such as Mesa Verde and Pueblo Bonito in the southwestern United States with extreme accuracy. This is achieved by crossdating the wooden beams that were used for housing in that area thousands of years ago.

As well as being able to date important archaeological sites, dendrochronology can be used to construct regional maps of past climatic conditions. Reconstructions such as these have improved knowledge of floods, droughts, unusually warm and cold periods, and other environmental conditions. Since some of these occur in cycles, dendrochronology may help scientists predict future environmental conditions.

To the dismay of many archaeologists, dendrochronology is only useful for dating objects and sites in the past 7000 years. Therefore, to establish dates beyond 7000 years archaeologists use radiocarbon dating. Dendrochronology is more accurate than radiocarbon dating because it is easier to count tree rings than to calculate the number of molecules per minute from the decay of carbon. Where possible, archaeologists combine the two techniques to accurately date early archaeological sites.

Source: Lori Stewart, "Dendrochronology." Printed by permission.

7. Write a 500-word expanded definition of *one* of the following terms for an audience of first-year students in another discipline:

- mutation
- fibre optics
- depreciation
- software
- antibiotic
- depth of field
- silviculture
- turbocharger
- marginal utility
- enzyme
- frequency modulation
- addiction

- motivation
- calculus
- surface tension
- emulsion
- commodity option
- stratified sampling
- modem
- gentrification
- aerobic exercise
- erosion
- motor
- semiconductor

If you are not familiar with any of these terms, write an expanded definition of your discipline or major subject.

8. Critique a classmate's response to exercise 7. Write a memo to this classmate evaluating the definition and explaining what you found clear and what you found confusing. Do you now understand what the defined term means? How useful did you find the methods of expansion?

CHAPTER 11

DESCRIBING A MECHANISM (TECHNICAL DESCRIPTION)

INTRODUCTION
WHAT IS A TECHNICAL DESCRIPTION?

A description of something tells what it is like, or specifies its qualities. In this chapter we will discuss the description of mechanical devices. A mechanism, or mechanical device, in this context includes anything made by people that has at least two components that interact in some mechanical way. Other subjects that can be described using the same principles include plants (botany), animals (zoology), or statues (art history). Chapter 12 will discuss how to describe processes and procedures; some of these include mechanisms in action, or the processes that allow a mechanism to work.

Describing differs from defining. A definition tells what a *term* (a word or phrase) means, while a description tells what a *thing* is like. A definition is *generic* and tells what all the individual things that bear the same name have in common, while a description is *particular* and tells what an individual thing is like. For example, consider the term *pen*. As you saw in Chapter 10, a definition of *pen* must indicate what *all* pens have in common – the features that make them all pens. A definition does not allow you to differentiate among the three or four pens you may own, but a description does. Also, while a definition of a mechanism may mention shape and size in very general terms, the physical characteristics need not be emphasized. In a description, though, these physical characteristics will receive the main emphasis.

MAIN FUNCTIONS OF TECHNICAL DESCRIPTIONS

Although technical descriptions can stand on their own, they are more likely to be parts of other documents that may have a variety of purposes, including the following:

- *To provide a record.* It is common in those disciplines that are concerned with natural forms (botany, zoology, geology, geography, archaeology) to describe new types and unusual cases. For example, a botanist who has discovered a new type of seaweed will describe it for other botanists.
- *To identify.* Descriptions of valuables, including descriptions of museum holdings, are written to identify individual items for legal purposes such as insurance claims.
- *To construct.* Patent applications have to include detailed descriptions of a product that is to be manufactured. Similarly, instructions

for making or assembling a mechanism should also include a description of what the finished product will be like.
- *To persuade.* Sales literature often includes detailed descriptions of a product.

Differences in the purpose of the description, as well as in the purpose of the document, together with differences in audience, will determine how extensive and/or precise and detailed a description should be. Here we will concentrate on how to write a full description of a simple mechanism.

AN EXAMPLE OF A TECHNICAL DESCRIPTION

The following technical description of a calligraphy pen was prepared by a student.

THE MODERN CALLIGRAPHY PEN

INTRODUCTION

The modern calligraphy pen is a writing instrument used to draw letters in the ancient styles of script. It has several advantages over its predecessor; it is portable, easier to use, and makes less of a mess. The pen is composed of four main parts: the cap, tip, ink cartridge, and barrel (see Figure 1). With the cap screwed on, the pen has an overall length of 130 mm.

CAP

The cylindrical cap is made of hardened plastic. It has a length of 61 mm, a radius of 7 mm, and a thickness of 1 mm. It is closed at one end. Located 5 mm from the closed end of the cap is a stainless steel clip 35 mm long, 4 mm wide, and 2 mm thick. At the end of the clip is a hollow stainless steel sphere used to hold the clip against surfaces like a shirt pocket. The sphere has a radius of about 1.5 mm. The purpose of the cap is to protect the writing tip, the nib, when it is not in use, and to help keep the ink from drying out.

TIP

The tip has an overall length of 52 mm and consists of three parts molded together: the nib, housing, and needle. The tip is also made of two kinds of materials: plastic and stainless steel (see Figure 2).

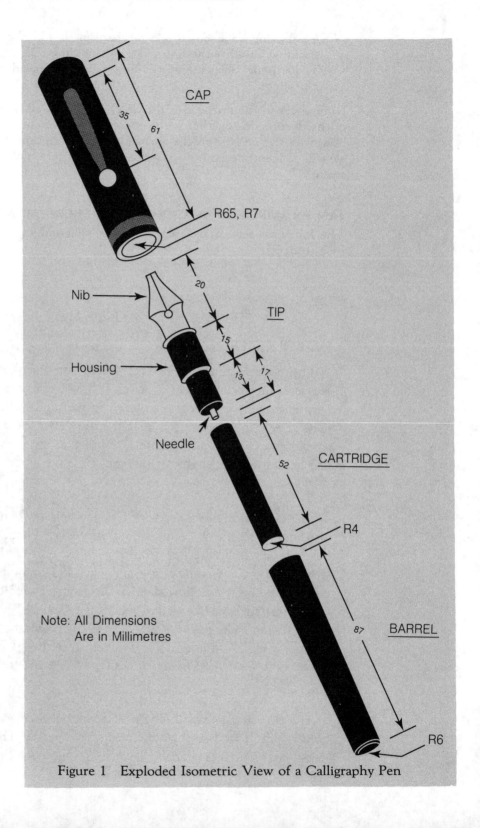

Figure 1   Exploded Isometric View of a Calligraphy Pen

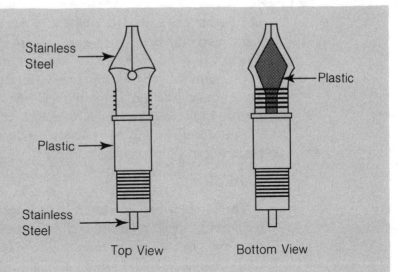

Figure 2   Nib Housing Materials

Nib

The nib, made of stainless steel, has a length of 20 mm, a thickness of 0.5 mm, and a width varying from 2 mm to 8 mm (see Figure 2 for shape). The nib is used to transfer the ink onto the paper.

Housing

The housing holds both the nib and the needle in place, and is made of molded plastic. The housing is a cylinder with a length of 28 mm and a radius of 4 mm. The housing also has a central hole, traversing its entire length, to hold the needle in place, and a 17-mm extension shaped like the nib, fitted under the nib, to hold it in place. Located 5 mm up from the needle-end of the housing are threads used to screw the tip into the barrel.

Needle

The needle is made of stainless steel and has an overall length of 40 mm, although only 4 mm are visible. The needle has a thickness of 0.2 mm and a central opening 0.5 mm in diameter. It is used to puncture the ink cartridge and draw the ink up to the nib.

INK CARTRIDGE

The ink cartridge, made of clear plastic, is a sealed cylinder with a length of 52 mm, a radius of 4 mm, and an approximate thickness of 0.5 mm. The cartridge, available in many different colours, fits easily inside the barrel. It is easy to store because it is sealed, and can only be punctured with the needle. Once punctured, it is held to the housing by the vacuum pressure created by the needle drawing ink up to the nib. Once emptied, the cartridge can simply be thrown away. The cartridge saves the writer from having to dip the nib into a tub of ink every few seconds, and makes for a truly portable pen.

BARREL

The barrel is made of plastic, has a length of 87 mm, a radius of 6 mm, and a thickness of 1 mm. It is used to hold the cartridge and the tip in place when one is writing. The barrel also keeps the ink cartridge in a dark place, so the sunlight will not affect the colour of the ink.

Source: Timothy K. Chia, "Calligraphy Pen." Printed by permission.

GUIDELINES FOR DESCRIBING A SIMPLE MECHANISM
THE VARIABLES

Objects are characterized by their shape, size, material, mass (weight), texture, and colour. A description specifies the values of these variables, and it does so as objectively as possible. It does not, as a rule, include aesthetic judgements such as *pretty* or *ugly*, and it avoids relative terms such as *long* and *little*, if more accurate measurements are possible. In writing your description, try to be complete (give all the needed details) and precise (give exact measurements and name shapes and materials accurately). Remember that, in practice, you would have to adjust the completeness and precision to the needs of the audience and the purpose of the document.

Each of the variables presents its own problems of description. To describe shape you may need both words and illustrations. See Figure 11-1 for the names of some of the most common three-dimensional shapes. Don't confuse these names with the ones that designate two-dimensional shapes, such as *circle, ellipse, rectangle, rhombus, trapezoid, hexagon, triangle*. Irregular shapes normally have to be illustrated. As part of describing shape you may have to use words such as *right, left, top, bottom, front, back*. Remember that the meaning of these words depends on the orientation of the writer or speaker.

When you specify the size of an object, include all *three* dimensions. In giving the size of a box, then, you would need to specify length, width,

Figure 11-1
Some Common
Three-Dimensional
Shapes

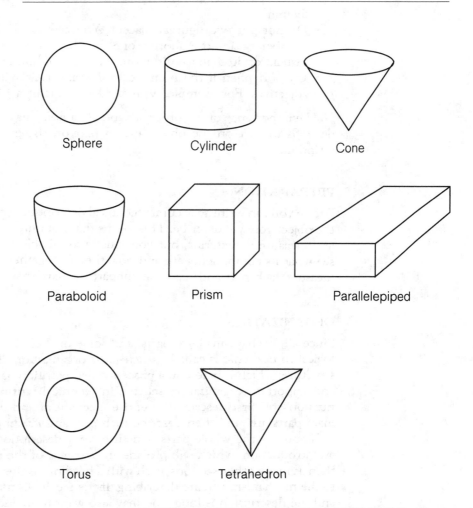

and height. However, the size of some shapes can be indicated by specifying fewer dimensions. A cylinder or cone, for example, requires radius and height, but a sphere only requires radius.

In writing about dimensions, observe the following guidelines:

- Use SI units (metre, centimetre, millimetre), not imperial units (yard, foot, inch).
- Use figures rather than words for dimensions, except when measurements are approximate, or when the number begins a sentence.
- Use decimals, not common fractions, and use a zero before the decimal marker for numbers less than 1. For example, write 0.75, *not* 3/4.
- Use the same symbol (m, cm, or mm) for the singular and the plural, and do *not* use a period at the end.

- Use a space between the figure and the symbol. For example, write 59 mm.
- Do not put two figures adjacent. You can use words for the first number or for the shorter one, but be consistent. For example, instead of *30 3-mm nails*, write *thirty 3-mm nails*.
- Use a hyphen if the numerical value and unit symbol are used as adjectives. For example, write a *30-mm pipe* or a *13-mm long bolt*.

The importance of the other variables (material, mass, texture, colour) depends in part on the object and in part on the purpose of the description.

PREPARATION

Before you can write an accurate technical description, you must examine the object you will describe. This means that not only must you examine and measure its exterior, but you must also be able to take it apart to see what its components are and how they fit together. Then you must measure each part and see what subparts it may have.

ORGANIZATION

Since all mechanisms have parts, and some of these have subparts, it is logical to use what is called a *whole-parts* organization. The whole-parts structure, which is based on a process called partition, is a very common and important organization scheme in technical writing. In this organization you first describe the entire mechanism and indicate what its main parts are, and then describe each part and its subparts, if any.

If you use the whole-parts structure, your description will consist of an introduction, which will provide an overview of the mechanism, and then as many other sections, each with a heading, as there are main parts to the mechanism you are describing. If the mechanism is fairly complex and the description is long, you may also want to include a conclusion.

The introduction should introduce the reader to the object, describe the entire object in relatively general terms, and provide the reader with a frame for the rest of the description. It should include the following:

- *Definition.* Name the object, define it briefly, and indicate where it is normally found or what it is normally used for. The audience and context should determine how much background you include.
- *Overview description.* Describe the shape, size, and material of the exterior of the entire mechanism. What is the overall shape? What are the overall dimensions? Does the mechanism have more than one position, such as "open" and "closed"?
- *Overview illustration.* Illustrate what the main parts are and how they are aligned. Avoid detail that could distract the reader.
- *Names of the main parts.* Name the main components of the mechanism in the order in which you will describe them in detail. If

possible, follow the order in which these parts are arranged spatially. Don't name the subparts yet.

Look again at the introduction in the student description of a calligraphy pen. The opening sentence defines the modern calligraphy pen. The second sentence notes its advantages over the traditional calligraphy pen. The third sentence names the main parts and directs the readers to the overview illustration. The introduction could have been improved by including a fuller overview description and by reversing the positions of the last two sentences.

After the introduction, use a separate heading for each main part. Begin the description of each main part by naming the part. Then describe its shape, size, material, and so on. Indicate the purpose of the part. Include a detailed illustration. If the main part has subparts, as the tip of the calligraphy pen did, first describe the general shape and dimensions of the main part, then name the subparts and describe them. Indicate how the subparts fit together.

USE OF ILLUSTRATIONS

Since words can be rather limited for describing the appearance of objects, expect to include several illustrations. The more complex the object, the more illustrations you will usually need. In the introduction you will need an illustration that orients the reader and prepares the reader for the description of parts. In choosing the particular illustration, ask yourself exactly what it is that the illustration must show the reader. Do you just want to show the external shape and the proportions of external parts? Is exact surface appearance important at this point? Do you need an exploded view to show the relationship of parts? Within the descriptions of the individual parts you will need an illustration of each part that hasn't been shown in enough detail in the overview illustration.

Review Chapter 3 before you decide exactly how to illustrate your description. Normally you will be choosing among photographs, drawings, or diagrams. Remember that photographs are the best choice for showing surfaces, and that diagrams are best for showing structure. If you do use photographs, try to remove distracting background material, move in close enough so the object dominates the photograph, use labels to indicate parts, and consider including a ruler to show size. If you use drawings or diagrams, make sure that they show only the relevant detail and that all the subparts are correctly labelled. Try not to include too much in one illustration.

Observe the following guidelines:

- Let the size and complexity of what is being shown determine the size of the illustration. The more detail you need to include, the larger the illustration should be.
- Don't overcrowd illustrations with detail. If too much detail would make an illustration difficult to read, then use a second illustration.

- Label parts clearly and carefully. Don't ruin a neat illustration with messy printing. Use a ruler to guarantee the printing is straight and uniform.
- Indicate scale and dimensions.
- Indicate the point of view, or perspective, from which the illustration was made, such as front, back, side, cross-section.

Exercises

1. Correct the following sentences:
   a. The handle is fifteen and a half centimetres long and has a one and a quarter centimetre diameter.
   b. I need a 2 centimetre wrench and 5 15 mm sockets.
   c. About 1/3 of the samples weighed less than .51 lb and 1/3 weighed more than .51 kg.

2. Partition the following objects into their main parts and subparts:
   a. a pair of eyeglasses
   b. a wallet
   c. a desk lamp
   d. a desk chair

3. Explain how your description of a pen might differ if you were writing it as part of assembly instructions, part of a patent application, part of a sales letter, or part of an insurance claim.

4. Prepare a brief oral critique of the following description of a retractable blade cutter.
   a. How effective is the introduction?
   b. How clear are the illustrations?
   c. How complete is the description of the main parts?

RETRACTABLE BLADE CUTTER

INTRODUCTION

A retractable blade cutter is a tool used to cut small objects precisely. The retractable cutter is 14 cm long, 0.5 cm deep, and 2.5 cm wide at the handle end, narrowing down to 1 cm at the blade end. The blade cutter is made of tin, aluminum, and plastic. When the cutter is extended, the sharp edge of the blade is exposed, whereas when the cutter is retracted, the blade is fully enclosed by the tin housing. The principal parts are the tin housing, the plastic snapper, the aluminum blade, and the plastic retractor (see Figures 1 and 2).

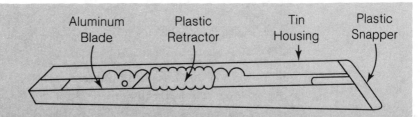

Figure 1   Overall Description (Retracted)

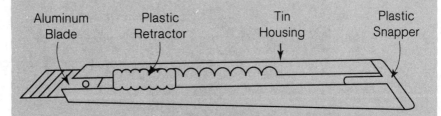

Figure 2   Overall Description (Fully Expanded)

TIN HOUSING

The tin housing is a long, flat box-shaped container which encloses all parts of the mechanism except for the snapper. The function of the housing is to hold the other parts in place and to protect the user from the sharp blade. The tin housing is about the size and shape of a pocket ruler. The housing is open at both ends, allowing the blade to retract at one end and providing a slot for the snapper at the other end.

PLASTIC SNAPPER

The plastic snapper is used to break off the worn blades and thus expose a new, sharp blade. It doubles as a clip so that the mechanism can hang on the breast pocket of a shirt (see Figure 3).

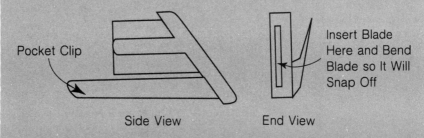

Figure 3   Side and End View of Plastic Snapper

ALUMINUM BLADE

The aluminum blade is a thin 10-cm long piece of metal, much like a razor blade, but with only one sharp edge and with narrower dimensions. Along the length of the blade are slight indentations which make snapping off the worn blades easier. The sharp edge of the blade is the part of the mechanism that comes in contact with the object to be cut (see Figure 4).

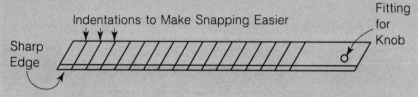

Figure 4   Aluminum Blade

The hole at one end of the blade fits over the knob on the retractor, thereby stabilizing the blade in the housing.

PLASTIC RETRACTOR

The plastic retractor is 3.5 cm long. A knob at one end provides an attachment for the blade. A slightly grooved top provides the retraction mechanism as it slides up and down the grooved tin housing. The function of the retractor is to move the blade from inside the housing to outside the housing, and vice versa (see Figure 5).

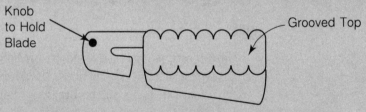

Figure 5   Side View of Plastic Retractor

CONCLUSION

All the parts, except the snapper, are contained by the tin housing. Together these parts provide a mechanism for cutting small objects. The plastic retractor enables the blade to move in and out of the housing, while the snapper breaks off the worn blades.

Source: Tammy Merritt, "Retractable Blade Cutter." Printed by permission.

5. Write a technical description of an object with which you are familiar. This object should consist of no fewer than three and no more than six principal parts. Kitchen utensils and simple tools are particularly well suited to this assignment. The description should include the following:

   a. formal definition of the object

   b. statement of the purpose of the object

   c. general description of the object, including an illustration

   d. division of the object into its principal parts

   e. description of each principal part

   Points a, b, c, and d will normally be included in one paragraph. The description of each principal part should be a separate paragraph. Include precise dimensions and identify the material from which each part is made. Number and title the illustrations.

   Remember that you are describing a *particular* object. If possible, specify its model name. Other students have described the following objects:

   - a turkey baster
   - a multihead screwdriver
   - a brass candle snuffer
   - the Stanley vise (model 277)
   - the Staedtler pencil sharpener
   - the Jones pocket tape measure
   - a garlic mincer
   - a cheese slicer
   - the tight-squeeze paint roller
   - the U-100 insulin syringe

WRITING ABOUT PROCESSES AND PROCEDURES: INSTRUCTIONS, DESCRIPTIONS, AND EXPLANATIONS

INTRODUCTION

A great deal of important technical writing is about processes and procedures. This chapter examines three types of writing about processes: instructions, descriptions, and explanations. Each type of writing is discussed in a separate section which begins with an introduction. Then in the instructions and descriptions sections student prepared examples are presented. The purpose of these examples is to show you the kind of writing assignment you may be asked to prepare. Each section also contains guidelines for doing the type of writing discussed in that section. Exercises for all three types of writing are presented at the end of the chapter.

INSTRUCTIONS

INTRODUCTION

Instructions may be one of the most underestimated and underappreciated kinds of writing. We need instructions, oral or written, for almost everything we do for the first time, whether it be assembling and operating appliances, playing games, using household products, taking medicine correctly, or maintaining a car.

Instructions can, of course, take many forms, depending in part on the complexity of the procedure, and in part on the audience and the context within which the instructions are prepared and used. The briefest instructions are the commands on signs, such as "stop," "yield," "100 km," "danger," "push," "up." A little more elaborate are the instructions on products, such as those on a can of cleaning fluid, or on hair conditioner, or on a can of frozen juice. Note that many of these are followed with warnings and instructions on what to do if they are misused. Mechanisms usually come with instructions for assembly, operation, maintenance, and sometimes repair. These vary in form from single sheets, to pamphlets, to thick volumes. Software packages come with extensive manuals that explain how to use them. Other forms you may be familiar with include instruction articles in magazines or newspapers, memos explaining new procedures at work, or "how to" books. Obviously we cannot explore all these types of instructions; instead, to familiarize you with principles that you can adapt to the situations in which you will have to write instructions, we will focus on guidelines for writing instructions for a simple procedure.

AN EXAMPLE OF INSTRUCTIONS

The following instructions for removing surface rust from a car were prepared by a student.

HOW TO REMOVE SURFACE RUST FROM A CAR

INTRODUCTION

Surface rust on a car plagues many people who live in a moist climate. To get this problem fixed professionally is generally quite expensive. However, in most cases, it is a fairly easy problem to fix. If your car does not have visible holes in the rusted area, if your rust is still in the early stages (i.e., if the rusted area is still very solid), and if you are positive that your rust has not started from the inside, then the following simple steps will help you to remove the rust, protect the area from further rusting, and eliminate most indications that there ever was any rust.

To do the job properly, you will need the following materials:

1. red or grey primer (one 142-gm can for every 40 cm² of rusted area)
2. lacquer paint to match your car colour (one 142-gm can for every 20 cm² of rusted area)
3. one 142-gm can of clear enamel
4. one 227-ml bottle of gelled rust remover
5. two sheets of emery paper (one rough and one fine)
6. an old toothbrush
7. masking tape and old newspapers
8. dry cloths or towels
9. a warm water and soap mixture in a bucket
10. a stool for sitting on (optional)

Items 1 to 5 can be readily purchased at any local automotive store.

It will take you at least eighteen hours to complete the job properly, so it is recommended that you split the work over two days. If you are in a rush, however, you can finish the job in a day if you start very early in the morning (6 a.m., for example). You will be working with paint during the job, so it is advisable to wear old clothes. Of course, it goes without saying that you will not be able to drive your car while you are removing the rust. Incidentally, in the highly unlikely case that you make a hole in the metal while removing the rust, you will either have to patch the hole yourself (if you know the correct procedure) or take your car to a body shop.

Removing surface rust from a car consists of the following steps:

1. preparing the rusted area for cleaning
2. removing the rust
3. preparing the cleaned area for painting
4. painting the area
5. matching the newly painted area with the old
6. applying the finishing touches

STEP 1: PREPARING THE RUSTED AREA FOR CLEANING

Clean the rusted area with the warm water and soap that is in the bucket; then dry the area with a soft cloth or towel. Before going any further, if there is any flaking paint surrounding the rusted area, peel it all off slowly with your fingers. Try not to peel off any more paint than necessary, as you will be painting this area later on. Cut the rough emery paper into 3-cm wide strips. Fold one of the strips of emery paper in half lengthwise, with both rough sides facing outwards. Working in a back and forth motion, sand the rusted area until it is smooth. Don't worry about scratching the surrounding paint a little; it will be covered over later. Use a fresh strip of emery paper every few minutes, even if the previous strip is not totally worn down. The purpose is not to try to remove all the rust, but merely to prepare the surface for the gelled rust remover. About 10 minutes of vigorous sanding should do the job. Wash the exposed area again with the warm water and soap mixture and dry.

STEP 2: REMOVING THE RUST

Apply the gelled rust remover generously to the toothbrush, as you would toothpaste, and spread over the exposed area. Make sure to coat the entire area with a thin film of the gel; use several applications if necessary. With the toothbrush, agitate the gel vigorously for several minutes. Try not to get the gel onto the painted surfaces, as it has no effect there. However, the gel will not harm any painted surfaces, so just wipe any off with a towel. Now let the gel sit for 10 to 15 minutes. During that time, the gel may solidify and turn into a white powdery residue. If so, don't worry; it's just the gel at work. If your gel doesn't turn white, that just means that your rust is a little deeper. Wash the gel off with the soap and water and pat dry with the towel. Repeat this step, but this time, let the gel sit for 20 minutes. If your gel has not solidified yet, repeat a third time, letting the gel sit for 30 minutes. At this time the formerly rusty area should be a dull grey or metallic colour. If not, you will have to do one of two things: (1) start again from the first step, and repeat the two procedures until the rust has been removed, or (2) take your car to a body shop, as this probably means that your rust has started from the inside, and requires treating from both sides.

STEP 3: PREPARING THE CLEANED AREA FOR PAINTING

Using the newspaper and masking tape, cover all parts of the car surrounding the newly cleaned area, leaving a 5-cm border between any painted surface and the area to be painted later (see Fig. 1). Using light, short strokes, spray the exposed area with primer. The primer is not for painting the car, but for protecting the metal from any further rusting, and to create a better surface for the paint to adhere to. With each stroke, gently feather a little primer slightly into the border area, but no further than 1 cm. Make sure never

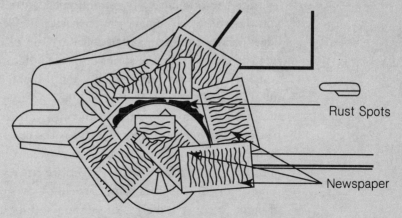

Figure 1   Preparing the Car for Painting

to hold your finger on the spray button for more than a second, or else the primer will run. With each stroke, overlap your previous stroke slightly to create a smooth surface (see Fig. 2). Apply just enough primer to cover the exposed metal. Leave the newspaper in place, and let the primer dry for at least six hours.

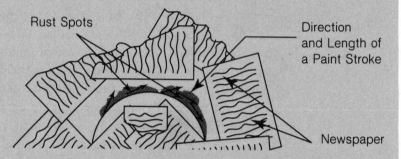

Figure 2   How to Overlap Successive Paint Strokes to Achieve a Smooth Surface

STEP 4: PAINTING THE AREA

Using the same technique outlined in step 3, apply the paint in many light strokes until the entire area is painted. Take care not to apply the paint too thickly, or you will have to sand it off later. Let the paint dry in a covered area for at least six hours, but preferably overnight.

STEP 5: MATCHING THE NEWLY PAINTED AREA WITH THE OLD

Take the fine emery paper and cut it into 3-cm wide strips like you did the rough emery paper in step 1. Gently sand down the edges where the old paint is left (i.e., the places where the paint met the exposed surface after you peeled off any flaking paint) until you get a smooth surface. This should not take more than ten minutes. If after this time you still have a very noticeable ridge, you will have to sand down the paint until you reach the primer, and paint the surface once more. If this is the case, you will not be able to finish the job until the next day. When you have achieved a fairly smooth surface, wipe the entire area with a dry towel to remove any dust or fine paint particles. Now apply a few light coats of paint to cover the signs of sanding and let it dry for two hours. Remove the newspaper and masking tape.

STEP 6: APPLYING THE FINISHING TOUCHES

Pour enough enamel into a soft cloth to coat half of it. Gently rub the enamel onto the freshly painted area. Repeat several times until the paint looks like it has been "baked on." If you can't get the whole area to shine, and it is very important to you, you might want to get the whole car painted.

Source: Timothy K. Chia, "How to Remove Surface Rust from a Car." Printed by permission.

GUIDELINES FOR WRITING INSTRUCTIONS FOR A SIMPLE PROCEDURE

PRINCIPLES. Good instructions have two general characteristics:

- *They are easy to follow.* The reader should be able to concentrate on performing the procedure correctly, not on understanding what you mean. The instructions must be readable (see Chapter 2), complete, organized, and clearly expressed. Don't let the reader guess at what you mean.
- *They lead to correct and safe actions.* Instructions must be judged by the success of their outcome. No matter how elegantly they are written, if they can be misinterpreted, or if they are actually wrong, and they lead to the reader doing something incorrectly, or to injury, or to damage to equipment, then they are bad instructions.

To achieve the above general characteristics, include the following in your instructions:

- *What not to do.* Give all cautions and warnings before you give a command. For example, if a switch must be off before the reader begins a step, then tell the reader to check that the switch is off. Although usage of the terms *caution* and *warning* is not consistent, cautions tend to be reserved for less serious consequences. Some writers use *caution* to refer to dangers to equipment and *warning* to refer to dangers of injury or death.
- *What to do.* Include each step and each substep.
- *How to do it.* An instruction such as "remove the cover" may itself need further instructions. What does the reader have to do to remove it? Are tools needed? In which directions does one push? Make sure the verbs and adverbs are precise.
- *When to do it and for how long.* Present information as the reader needs it. Present steps in sequence.
- *Where to do it.*
- *What to do if something goes wrong.*

PREPARATION. To write good instructions, you must understand the procedure and you must know your audience. The chief difficulty is to put yourself in the audience's place. Although you may know the procedure so well you can perform it almost without thinking, your reader is performing the procedure *for the first time*. Preparation, then, includes analyzing the procedure and analyzing the audience.

In analyzing the procedure, you have to break the procedure into steps and substeps and then specify exactly how to do each. Most people are unaware of how complex even the common, simple procedures are. Consider, for example, how many movements you have to make to start your car. What would you have to specify if a robot were to be programmed to do this? Let us say that you have to check that the car is in "Park." What do you do to do this? Where do you look? What do you look for? What do you do if the car is not in "Park"? How?

A good way to analyze a task is to perform the task yourself and to ask yourself the following questions:

- *What*, exactly, am I doing?
  Use the most exact verb you can for the action. Try to focus on the action (e.g., *twist*, *pull*) rather than on its outcome (e.g., *remove*, *turn on*, *close*)
- What am I doing it *to*?
  Use the most exact name and description for the object of the verb. What do you twist? What do you pull? Use illustrations and description, if necessary, to locate and identify buttons and switches that have to be pushed. In the example of starting a car, make sure the reader knows which pedal is the brake and which is the accelerator and where, exactly, the gearshift is. A common error in assembly instructions, for example, is not to label the parts clearly.
- Am I using *tools* or *equipment*?
  What is the exact name of the tool? Can I assume that a reader who doesn't know how to perform this procedure will know how to use this equipment? For example, can one assume that a person who does not know how to make a pie will know how to use a cherry pitter? Also, consider which tools and equipment are mandatory and which are optional. How else could this be done?
- *How* am I doing it?
  Quantify, as objectively as you can, such variables as
  - *duration* (How or how many times do you do this? How do you know when to stop? Remember that telling someone to stop can be just as important as telling someone to start.)
  - *force* (How hard should you hit?)
  - *direction* (Do you move to the right or left or up or down? Remember to use the perspective of the doer.)
  - *distance* (How far do you move it? How full do you fill it?)
  - *rate* (How quickly do you do this?)

The main problem in audience adaptation is deciding how full and detailed to make the instructions. On the one hand, you have to make sure that you give the readers all the detail they need, and on the other, you have to make sure that by giving too much detail you don't talk down to them or give them the impression they don't really need to pay attention to what you say. Why is your audience reading these instructions? Remember that we only read instructions if we think we don't know how to do something. But what *does* the audience know? What can you assume? Can you assume the readers have performed similar procedures? Can you assume the readers know the meaning of the verbs you are using in your instructions? Do they know how to use the tools and equipment? Put yourself in the readers' shoes and picture what they would be doing as they read each part of the instructions. Anticipate their questions and needs. Try to supply the needed information *before* they are really aware they need it. The problems of audience analysis become more complex as the audience becomes wider because there is no way to suit the needs of both the most expert and most inexperienced readers at the same time.

ORGANIZATION. For all but the most simple procedures, use the whole-parts organization in which you divide the procedure into tasks and subtasks and then the subtasks into steps. The grouping of steps helps your reader organize your instructions. In general, the particulars of format and organization should be designed to fit the procedure, the purpose of the particular instructions, and the particular audience. The arrangement described here illustrates one approach that you should adapt to the specific circumstances when you prepare instructions. The structure suggested here consists of an introduction, one major section for each major task, and then a brief conclusion if the instructions are fairly long.

In the introduction, which could be several paragraphs long, and which could contain subheadings, you should include the following:

- The *name* of the procedure and its *purpose* if that is not obvious. For example, not everyone would know why the fuel filter on a car should be checked and changed. In the example of instructions for removing rust, the last sentence of the first paragraph includes the purpose ("remove the rust, protect the area from further rusting, and eliminate most indications that there ever was any rust"). The student did not explain why rust must be removed. Do you agree that it is obvious that rust is undesirable?
- *How often* or *when* this procedure should be performed. How do you know when it is time to change the fuel filter? In the example of instructions for removing rust, the last sentence of the first paragraph specifies the conditions for which these instructions are appropriate.
- Any *special assumptions* you have made about the audience, particularly if your audience has not been well defined for you beforehand. This will help readers decide whether they should attempt the procedure and whether they can expect to understand the instructions.
- Special *warnings* and *cautions*. The example instructions caution the worker to wear old clothes.
- How *long* the procedure will take. The example instructions specify that removing the rust will take eighteen hours.

- How much the procedure will *cost*. The example instructions do not specify the cost of the procedure. The author could have included a cost estimate for every 40 cm^2 of rusted area.
- How many *people* are needed.
- What *tools* and *equipment* are needed. Which are mandatory and which are optional? Are there acceptable alternatives?
- What *materials* are needed. Be specific about special characteristics and quantities. For example, if I need nails, how many do I need? Does size matter at all? If unusual materials are needed, where can they be bought? The example instructions indicate that items 1 to 5 can be bought in an automotive supplies store.
- What kind of a *workspace* is needed. Does the area have to be well ventilated? level? sterile? The example instructions do not specify where you should work. However, since you will be using paint and rust remover, you probably should be in a well ventilated area.
- What the *major tasks* in the procedure are. These tasks will become the headings within the body of the instructions. The last sentence of the introduction in the example instructions lists the main steps. Note that the steps are grammatically parallel and that the heading for each step matches the wording used in this list of steps.

Use a separate major section for each major task. First introduce the task, using the same guidelines as for the introduction to the entire instructions, but in an abbreviated form. Then, after naming the steps in the task, give full, detailed instructions for each step. Use illustrations to clarify your instructions. In the example, the instructions for each step could be enhanced by an opening statement that indicates the purpose of the step and outlines the substeps. In step 1, the second-to-last sentence could be modified and moved to the beginning: "Preparing the rusted area for the gelled rust remover includes the following steps: washing and drying, sanding, and washing and drying again."

If the instructions are long, include a conclusion in which you give a brief summary of the main subtasks.

USE OF ILLUSTRATIONS. For some simple procedures, the instructions can be presented entirely in illustrations. Usually, though, illustrations are used together with text because words are needed to express contingencies and qualifications, and illustrations can show more clearly how something looks. There are, of course, many different ways illustrations can be used in instructions, but some of the most common ones are the following:

- *To identify and locate parts, tools, and equipment.* Photographs and drawings, together with labels that identify parts, can be a clear and economical way to "point" to things. This use of illustrations is much like that in technical descriptions. Photographs have the advantage of showing exactly what something looks like, while drawings can be used to simplify or generalize appearance.

- *To show what something should look like.* Illustrations of what something should look like at various stages of a procedure can be very reassuring to users and can also allow them to remedy errors early. Again, if exact appearance is important, use photographs. Illustrations can also be used to show what something will look like at the end of the procedure.
- *To show the position of the operator or actor.* Since words are not very economical for describing any but the most simple body positions, illustrations, and particularly photographs, are particularly useful in instructions for sports, dance, and the use of some tools and equipment.

If you use illustrations in your instructions, observe the following guidelines:

- Make each illustration *large* enough and *clear* enough for the reader to use it. What is the user likely to be doing while trying to read your illustration? Perhaps the reader will be on hands and knees in a dim garage.
- Show *actions* as clearly as possible. Simply showing a tool in an operator's hand does not illustrate what the operator is to do with the tool. If you can't show the action in an illustration, then use words to specify it.
- Label parts clearly and carefully.
- Indicate the point of view, or perspective.

LANGUAGE. Instructions are *commands* and therefore you must use what is called the *imperative* mood.

- *Imperative mood:* Open the door.
- *Indicative mood:* The door should be opened. (passive)
  The operator should open the door. (active)
  You must open the door. (active)

The indicative mood is normally used in descriptions or explanations of procedures.

DESCRIPTIONS OF PROCEDURES
INTRODUCTION

The main difference between instructions and a description of a procedure is that the reader of instructions is expected to perform the procedure, whereas the reader of a description is not. Descriptions are normally written to inform readers about a procedure or to provide a record of how a procedure was performed. Descriptions differ from instructions in the following ways:

- The mood of the verb is indicative rather than imperative.
- There is less emphasis on the *how* of actions, and so descriptions will include fewer adverbial details. For example, unless it is relevant how the top is removed, you might simply say that "the container is opened."

- Tools and equipment are not always mentioned.
- Warnings and cautions are generally less important.
- Graphics can be less detailed and less concrete.

We can also distinguish between procedure descriptions in general and what are often called procedure narratives. Table 12-1 summarizes their differences.

Table 12-1
Differences between a
Description of a
Procedure and a
Procedure Narrative

	Description	Narrative
Verb Tense Used	Present (The door *is* opened.)	Past (The door *was* opened.)
Question Answered	How do you do this action normally?	How did you do this action this time?
Nature of Procedure	Typical or Standard	Particular
Examples of Documents	– job description – textbook description of a standard laboratory procedure	– trip report – narrative in a progress report – laboratory notes – methods section in a scientific article

AN EXAMPLE OF A DESCRIPTION OF A PROCEDURE

The following description of jugular catheterization of a sheep was prepared by a student.

JUGULAR CATHETERIZATION OF A SHEEP
INTRODUCTION

Definition and Purpose

Jugular catheterization is a procedure used to prepare an experimental animal for repeated blood sampling. Blood parameters such as hormones and enzymes give valuable information about the physiological state of an animal. When many samples are required from a single animal, repeated punctures will stress the animal and cause erroneous levels of the blood parameters. The purpose of catheterization is to reduce stress by creating a temporary passage into the circulatory system so many samples can be withdrawn without multiple punctures to the skin and vein. The jugular vein is used because it lies close to the skin and is easily accessible.

Equipment

To prepare the sheep, a hammock and stand are needed to hold the animal still, and an electric razor or shears are required to shave fleece away from the neck of the sheep. For the catheterization the following equipment is needed: rubbing alcohol, cotton swabs, a 1.5-inch long 18-gauge hypodermic needle, a roll of sterile animal-tested catheter tubing, adhesive tape (1 inch wide), a suture needle and suture thread, scissors or knife, two 5-cc syringes, a syringe valve, and a solution of sodium phosphate buffer.

Sequences of Procedure

The main sequences of the procedure are preparing the sheep, inserting the catheter tubing, securing the catheter, and taking blood samples from the catheter.

PROCEDURE

Preparing the Sheep

The animal must be held still throughout the procedure. This is usually done with a hammock and stand. The hammock is a two feet by three feet piece of heavy canvas with four leg holes in it, which is mounted between two parallel poles. The sheep is walked onto the hammock while the hammock is laid flat on the floor and the animal's feet are positioned in the leg holes. Two people then lift the hammock like a stretcher and place it on the stand as in Figure 1.

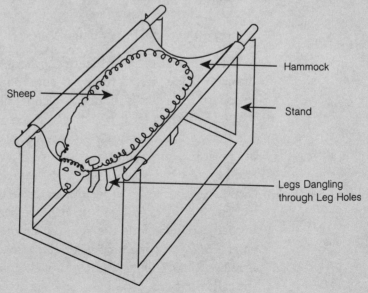

Sheep

Hammock

Stand

Legs Dangling through Leg Holes

Figure 1   Sheep in Hammock on Stand

The fleece is then shorn away from the region of the jugular vein under the neck as illustrated in Figure 2. This is done with an electric shearer which cuts the fleece off right down to the skin. The skin exposed is cleaned by rubbing alcohol over it with a piece of cloth or cotton gauze prior to catheterization.

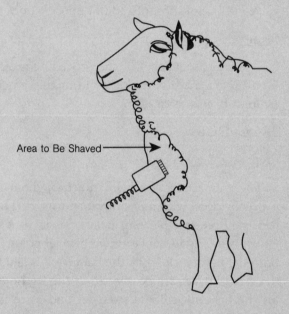

Area to Be Shaved

Figure 2   Shaving Fleece away from Area of Jugular Vein

Inserting the Catheter Tubing

Before the vein is catheterized, about 24 inches of 1/16-inch diameter animal-tested tubing is cut from the roll and the whole hypodermic needle is dipped in alcohol. Then the jugular vein is located by feeling for it with one's fingers in the shorn area. When it has been found, the needle is positioned on a downward slant, as in Figure 3, and then jabbed sharply downward through the skin and into the jugular vein, but not through it (see Figure 3).

When the needle is positioned properly within the vein, the catheter tubing is inserted into the vein through the needle and pushed carefully along the vein for about 12 to 15 inches, leaving an end of 9 to 12 inches outside the animal (Figure 4). The needle is removed by pulling it out of the skin and over the free end of the catheter. Some blood may leak out around the hole in the skin, but this is easily wiped up with a cotton swab.

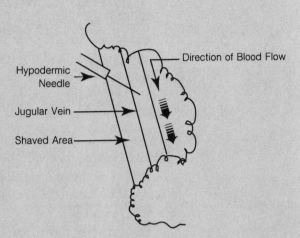

Hypodermic Needle

Jugular Vein

Shaved Area

Direction of Blood Flow

Figure 3   Position of Needle before Puncture

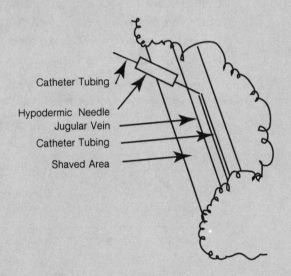

Catheter Tubing

Hypodermic Needle
Jugular Vein

Catheter Tubing

Shaved Area

Figure 4   Position of Needle after Puncture
and Insertion of Catheter

Securing the Catheter

When the catheter is in place, it must be fastened in some way
to prevent it from being pulled out or from slipping entirely into
the vein. This is done by taping the free end of the catheter to the
skin with adhesive tape. A one-inch-square piece of tape is placed
directly over the middle of the tubing. When the tape is stuck to

the skin, the four corners are stitched down to the skin so the tape cannot fall off (see Figure 5). This is done with a suture needle and thread which are pierced through only the skin and the tape. Each stitch is separate and the two ends of the suture thread are tied in a knot and cut off very short (about one-half inch).

Taking Blood Samples

Once the catheter is secured, blood samples can easily be taken without having to break the skin. This is done with a small plastic valve that is clipped to the end of the catheter. The valve forms a junction between the catheter and the syringe that is used for obtaining samples.

The catheter must first be rinsed with 5-cc of buffer solution. A 5-cc syringe is used to inject the buffer into the catheter and then the buffer is drawn back into the syringe. When the suction of the syringe is applied, blood also travels up the catheter. When the buffer is taken up, a clean syringe is attached to the valve and a 5-cc blood sample can be withdrawn (see Figure 6).

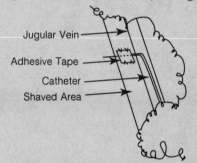

Jugular Vein

Adhesive Tape

Catheter

Shaved Area

Figure 5   Securing the Catheter

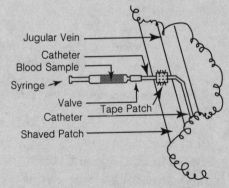

Jugular Vein

Catheter

Blood Sample

Syringe

Valve

Tape Patch

Catheter

Shaved Patch

Figure 6   Syringe, Valve, and Catheter Assembly
for Taking Samples

CONCLUSION

To catheterize the jugular vein of a sheep, the operator first suspends the animal in a hammock to keep it still and then shears the fleece away from the neck area. The catheter is then inserted in the opposite direction of the blood flow (i.e., downward) to prevent blood from flowing freely out of the catheter. This allows blood to come out only when the suction of the syringe is applied. The catheter is secured by suturing it to the skin underneath a piece of adhesive tape. When the catheter is in place and secured, many samples can easily be obtained using the valve and catheter assembly. This procedure reduces the amount of stress to which the animal is exposed, and therefore eliminates fluctuations in blood parameters.

Source: Alexandra Janssens, "Jugular Catheterization of a Sheep." Printed by permission.

GUIDELINES FOR WRITING DESCRIPTIONS OF PROCEDURES

PREPARATION. A good description is clear and accurate and as detailed as the audience needs. This means that before you analyze the procedure, you must determine who your readers will be and how they will use your document. What can you be sure your audience already knows? What do your readers know about tools and equipment and about standard or similar procedures? What questions might they have? If your readers only want a general outline of the procedure, then you don't have to be particularly careful about including detail. If the description becomes a record, you have to decide how that record will be used before you can decide how much detail to include. Include what will be relevant to your audience.

As in preparing to write instructions, first break the procedure into tasks and subtasks. Before dividing subtasks into steps, though, check how much detail is useful to your audience. Generally follow the same guidelines as for analyzing a procedure for instructions.

ORGANIZATION. Again use the whole-parts organization, but note that you will probably need fewer levels of subdivision than for instructions. Design the particulars of format to fit the procedure, purpose, and audience. Descriptions are often parts of other documents such as reports, articles, or contracts. Here we will describe a structure consisting of an introduction, then one major division for each task, and then a brief conclusion if the description is fairly long.

In the introduction, name the procedure and give its purpose, if it is not obvious, and explain when and where it is normally undertaken. In the example description above, the opening paragraph explains the purpose of jugular catheterization. Name equipment and materials at this point only if they are distinguishing features of this particular procedure;

otherwise, mention them as they become relevant in the description of the tasks or subtasks. In other words, include in the introduction the information the reader needs first. To provide an overview, end the introduction with a listing of the main tasks, as in the example description.

Use a separate section for each major task. First introduce the task, using the same guidelines as for the introduction, but in an abbreviated form. Notice how, in the example description, the first sentence of the description of a main step indicates the purpose of that step. The only step lacking such an introduction is "Inserting the Catheter Tubing." After introducing the task, describe it in as much detail as is appropriate for the audience's purposes. Use illustrations to clarify your description.

USE OF ILLUSTRATIONS. Use illustrations in procedure descriptions, but only as they are needed to clarify the description. Since the audience won't be performing the procedure, and so needs less precise information about the "how" of the actions, you will probably not need as many illustrations as for instructions, and the ones you do use can be more abstract. You are more likely to have less use for the "pointing" function of illustrations and more for the explanatory function. Flow charts may be needed to show the interrelationship of tasks and equipment in such complex procedures as paper making, for example.

EXPLANATIONS OF PROCESSES
INTRODUCTION

An explanation of a process focuses on why the process works. The desired result is the audience's understanding. Examples of explanations are found in explanatory pamphlets, in textbooks, and in encyclopedias. Elements of explanation are often included in descriptions or instructions, and they may form a large part of an expanded definition.

We can distinguish three main types of processes:

- *Natural processes.* Natural processes are those that take place in nature. They include geological processes, such as the weathering of rock or the eruption of a volcano; biological processes, such as the reproductive cycles of fish or the growth of trees; meteorological processes, such as the rain cycle; chemical processes, such as oxidation; physiological processes, such as digestion or respiration. Natural processes are characterized by the interaction of natural components and forces and often by continuity or cyclicity, so that there is no particular beginning or end. To understand these processes, one needs to understand the laws of nature.

- *Mechanical processes.* Mechanical processes are those that take place within a mechanism to make it "go," and those that the mechanism makes possible. They include the processes that make a car move, a freezer stay cold, and a computer work, as well as the processes that are performed by mechanisms such as the playing of a cassette tape by a cassette player or the taking of a picture by a camera. Usually the mechanisms are designed to take advantage of natural processes and natural forces. Mechanical processes are characterized by the presence of a mechanism and usually by the need for an operator to start, stop, and guide the mechanism. A great number of processes often take place within one mechanism.

- *Production or industrial processes.* Production processes usually use several mechanisms and require several operators. They include such processes as the production of gasoline, the building of an apartment block, the harvesting of a forest, or the operation of a slaughterhouse. These processes are characterized by a very complex interaction of materials, equipment, and operators, with many natural and mechanical processes interacting.

GUIDELINES FOR WRITING EXPLANATIONS OF PROCESSES

PREPARATION. A good explanation is clear and gives as much information as the audience needs in terms that the audience understands. To explain a process, you must analyze and understand it and you must know the background and the needs of the audience.

In analyzing the process, you will first need to identify its main stages. You may want to draw a flow chart to show how the stages interact. Determine exactly what goes on at each stage. Which mechanisms or parts of mechanisms are working? What are they doing? What is the operator doing? Which natural and which mechanical forces and processes are acting? How? What is the input and what is the output of each stage?

In analyzing the audience, first ask yourself who will read the document and why? What does this audience need to understand? How much detail does it need? What technical vocabulary, mathematics, and graphic conventions can you assume it understands? How much familiarity with basic science can you assume?

Usually, the main challenge in preparing a good explanation is to simplify the process without distorting it and to shift from an academic and technical perspective to a more general one. Many of the principles discussed in Chapter 10 (Defining) apply to the writing of explanations. Use analogies. Use the audience's experience with the processes and principles you're explaining.

ORGANIZATION. Again you can use the whole-parts organization. In the introduction provide the needed background. Give an overview of the process. Give a preview of the document by naming the stages in the order in which you will discuss them. Then discuss each stage in a manner appropriate to your audience. The main organization problem will be how to segment continuous processes and how to discuss components that interact. Note that the segmentation can be somewhat arbitrary if your audience does have an overview of the entire process.

USE OF ILLUSTRATIONS. In explanations of processes you are most likely to use flow charts and diagrams. Remember that these have a high level of abstraction and may be difficult for some audiences to understand.

EXERCISES

A. INSTRUCTIONS

1. Find at least four sets of instructions in your home.

    a. Rank them in order of their effectiveness.

    b. Identify the factors that determine the effectiveness of the instructions.

    c. Rewrite the least effective instructions.

2. Signs in public places frequently serve as visual instructions. Find one example of a sign that is unclear. How would you make it clearer?

3. An exchange student does not know how to use a standard combination lock. Prepare instructions for operating a lock whose combination is 24, 13, 49.

4. Pretend that all street signs in your town have been removed.

    a. Prepare instructions for getting from the main hospital to the main post office.

    b. Prepare instructions for getting from your college to the nearest public library.

5. Pretend that there is a computerized robot that understands instructions in English. Prepare a set of instructions that will allow this robot to prepare a cup of instant coffee in your kitchen.

6. The following instructions for replacing the battery in a Timex Marathon watch were written by a student. Review the guidelines for writing instructions and then note how the student has followed the guidelines.

    a. Does the introduction prepare you for the instructions?

    b. Is each step explained clearly?

    c. Are the warnings clear and well placed?

    d. Are the illustrations clear and well placed?

REPLACING THE BATTERY IN A TIMEX MARATHON

INTRODUCTION

A well-charged battery in your Timex Marathon is essential for the proper operation of the watch. A fully charged battery will provide trouble-free timekeeping for approximately three years. You will know it is time to change the battery when the numbers on the display begin to fade and perhaps blink out completely. Sometimes tapping the watch face will temporarily bring back the display, but this is merely a stopgap until the battery is replaced.

A steady hand and a well-lit, flat surface, such as a kitchen table, are required to ease the completion of this task. In addition, the following supplies are also needed:

1. Number 1 (0.8 mm) jeweller's slotted screwdriver.
2. Number 3 (2.0 mm) jeweller's slotted screwdriver.
3. One pair of tweezers.
4. One Eveready 3-volt number 885 watch battery.
5. One blank sheet of letter-size white paper.

The jeweller's screwdrivers can be obtained at any hardware store for under five dollars. The battery can be obtained from a jewellery store for approximately ten dollars.

The procedure will take between fifteen minutes and half an hour, and consists of the following steps:

1. Removing the back cover
2. Removing the existing battery
3. Mounting the new battery
4. Checking the operation

REMOVING THE BACK COVER

WARNING: Once the cover is removed, do NOT try to pry up on any of the metal pieces sticking up.

Place the watch face down on the table. While holding down on the strap with one hand, insert the tip of the no. 3 jeweller's screwdriver blade into the pry slot as shown in Figure 1.

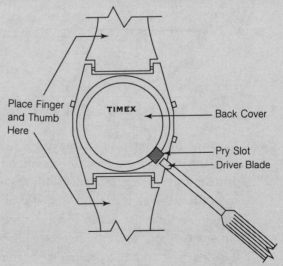

Figure 1   Back Cover of Watch

Gently push down on the screwdriver handle until you feel the back piece lift up slightly. Now insert the driver blade a bit further until it stops moving. Once again push down on the handle and the cover should pop right off. If it does not pop off, repeat the prying motion.

REMOVING THE EXISTING BATTERY

Place the piece of paper on the table a couple of centimetres away from the watch. The paper will be used as a contrasting background to put the screws on, so that they will not be lost. Locate the three screws that are holding the battery in place. Do not mistake the other two screws that hold the watch together for the battery screws (Figure 2).

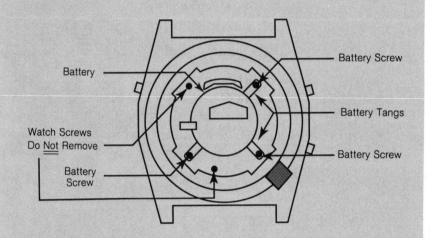

Figure 2   Back with Cover Removed

Take the no. 1 jeweller's screwdriver in your dominant hand. Now place the index finger of your other hand in the centre of the battery to steady the watch. Starting with the upper right screw, put the end of the driver blade into the slot of the screw and gently turn it counterclockwise. Keep turning until the screw does not come out any further. With the tweezers, lift the screw out of the watch. If it does not come out easily, try turning it counterclockwise one more turn. Place the screw on the piece of paper and repeat the procedure with the other two screws. Now grasp the battery between your thumb and forefinger and lift it out of the watch.

MOUNTING THE NEW BATTERY

WARNING: When reinstalling the screws do not try to tighten the screws too much or else you may strip the screw hole and have to buy a new watch.

Position the new battery in the watch until all three tangs line up with the screw holes (Figure 2). You need not worry about putting the battery in the wrong way since the three metal tangs on the new battery can only line up one way with the watch. With your index finger, press down firmly on the battery to hold it in position. Lift one of the screws from the paper with the tweezers and place it in the upper right-hand hole. If the screw does not stand upright in the screw hole, slowly take the pressure off the battery with your index finger until the battery rises enough to hold the screw upright. Once again place the blade of the no. 1 jeweller's screwdriver in the screw slot. Wiggle the screw around until it is vertical and then begin turning it clockwise. Do *not* screw it all the way in yet. When the screw is approximately one full turn from the bottom, stop turning it and repeat the procedure with the other two screws. Now go back to the first screw and turn it all the way down until it is just snug. Now tighten the other two screws in the same manner. The battery is now installed in your watch.

CHECKING THE OPERATION

Before replacing the cover, turn the watch over and see if the display has been activated. If no numbers appear on the face, try tightening down the battery screws a quarter turn more. If it still does not work, either the new battery is faulty, or the watch itself is broken. If the display is working, replace the cover by lining up the pry tab with the pry hole, and press down firmly on the cover until it snaps into place.

Source: Barrie McLaughlin, "Replacing the Battery in a Timex Marathon." Printed by permission.

7. Write complete instructions, like the examples for replacing a watch battery and removing rust from a car. Choose a procedure which you know how to perform, but which some of your classmates don't. This procedure should consist of no fewer than three and no more than six major steps. In preparing this assignment, follow the guidelines explained earlier in this chapter. The following are titles of some successful instructions written by students:

- How to Clean a Ten-Speed Bicycle Chain
- How to Assemble a Windsurfer
- How to Splice Copper Wire
- How to Give a Self-Administered Injection of Insulin
- How to Replace the Blade of an Adjustable Utility Knife
- How to Bleed the Hydraulic System of a Car
- How to Perform a Venipuncture
- How to Hot-Wax Downhill Skis
- How to Apply Prepasted Wallpaper
- How to Prepare and Assemble Scuba Equipment

8. Examine a set of instructions prepared by a classmate in response to exercise 7. Write a memo to the author giving your general impression of the instructions and suggesting how the instructions could be improved. Note what was unclear to you.

B. DESCRIPTIONS

1. Find at least two descriptions of procedures. Which one is better? Why? Suggest improvements to the weaker one.

2. Look again at the student example of instructions for removing rust from a car.

   a. What changes would you make if you were asked to write a description of how to remove rust?

   b. Rewrite the section called "Step Two: Removing the Rust" as a description.

3. Prepare a memo to your boss on how you usually perform a simple procedure that is part of your job. For example, a waiter could describe how an order is taken, placed, and delivered to the customer; a gas station attendant could describe how a car is checked for oil and how oil is added; a store clerk could describe how a refund or a delivery order is handled; a bank teller could describe how a cheque is certified; a nurse could describe how blood pressure is measured.

4. Prepare a brief pamphlet that describes a complex procedure with which you are familiar. The readers of the pamphlet will be high school students. The following topics would be suitable:

- How paper (or any other product) is made.
- How a newspaper (or the mail) is distributed to homes.
- How an ice rink is prepared for a game.
- How a safety check of an airplane (or truck) is completed.
- How a patient is assessed in an emergency ward.

5. Using the specific guidelines provided in this chapter, write a description of a procedure with which you are familiar, but some of your classmates are not. This procedure should consist of no fewer than three and no more than six major steps.

6. Write a process narrative to indicate how you performed one of the following procedures:

   • How you got into student housing.
   • How you found rental housing.
   • How you bought your car (or how you made another purchase of similar complexity).
   • How you found a summer job.
   • How you arranged your schedule of classes.
   • How you arranged a vacation.

   Prepare this narrative as a memo to your instructor.

C. EXPLANATIONS

1. In one of your textbooks find an explanation of a process.

   a. Indicate the changes you would make if you had to adapt it for a general newspaper audience and you could use only 200 words.

   b. Indicate the changes you would make if you had to adapt it for an audience of high-school students not in your discipline.

2. Write an explanation of a process studied in your discipline. Your readers are first-year students who are not in your discipline.

SUMMARIZING

INTRODUCTION

Summarizing is a process you engage in every day. When you take notes during a lecture, you are summarizing; when you tell a friend what a documentary on TV was about, you are summarizing; when you prepare for an examination, you are summarizing. In your professional life, you may be asked to write a variety of summaries, including the following:

- A summary of a meeting. Minutes are a particular kind of summary of what transpired in a meeting.
- A summary of a talk or seminar. As part of a trip report, you may have to summarize the talks or seminars you attended.
- An abstract for a report or article you have written.
- An executive summary for a report you have written.
- A summary of a report or article someone else has written.
- A review of research on a problem. This may include very brief summaries of a large number of articles or reports.

Summarizing generally consists of identifying the main points and then expressing them concisely. In addition, particularly when you are writing in the context of an organization, you will need to consider audience needs, because to some extent what constitutes a "main point" depends on the interests and needs of the audience, and the terms that can be used in the summary depend on the technical literacy of the audience. For this reason, most of the summaries you write will have to be adapted to their particular audience.

This chapter first introduces a particular kind of summary, called an *abstract*, and explains how it is used by researchers. Then it describes and illustrates two types of abstract: the descriptive, or indicative, abstract and the informative, or informational, abstract. The abstract of an article is given prominence in this chapter because it is also a prototype for the abstract and executive summary for a report or proposal and can be the basis for a review of research. After the discussion of abstracts, the chapter provides more general guidelines for summarizing written material and illustrates these with a summary of a brief article in a newsletter. Chapter 17 discusses how to write an abstract or executive summary for a formal report that you have prepared, and Chapter 22 explains how to write an executive summary of a proposal.

ABSTRACT

A special kind of summary, the abstract, has evolved to meet the needs of researchers. Abstracts are found at the beginning of articles in scholarly journals, and in special journals that publish only abstracts, such as *Chemical Abstracts*. Students and scholars can use these abstracts for the following purposes:

- *To get an overview of recent scholarship*. Reading the abstracts can provide a general sense of current research interests and methods.
- *To find the journal articles most relevant to their own research*. Reading the abstracts allows the researchers to screen out all but the most relevant articles. Because of the extremely large number of articles published on most subjects, this becomes a very important step in information retrieval.
- *To learn the results of research without having to read the article*. Since abstracts summarize the method and results, they often give all the information a researcher needs about an experiment.

As part of your professional preparation you should learn to use the most important abstracting journals in your field.

Two kinds of abstract are traditionally distinguished: the *descriptive*, or *indicative*, *abstract* and the *informative*, or *informational*, *abstract*.

DESCRIPTIVE, OR INDICATIVE, ABSTRACT

The descriptive abstract tells what the purpose and topics of the article are, but it does not give the substance of the article. Because it functions almost as a table of contents, it can be useful for screening the relevance of the article to your work, but it cannot be substituted for the article because it does not give the results of the investigation. Descriptive abstracts are relatively rare and are probably better suited to articles that are reviews of the literature than to articles that report experimental results. See Figure 13-1 for an example of a descriptive abstract.

Figure 13-1
A Descriptive
Abstract

FUTURE NEEDS AND DIRECTIONS FOR COMPUTERIZED RECORD LINKAGE IN HEALTH RESEARCH IN CANADA: FUTURE STUDY PLANS

M. Smith
Statistics Canada

This paper plots some future directions for the use of record linkage in addressing some of Canada's health problems. It is divided into three main sections. The first section reviews some of the general objectives of current health studies. A list of specific projects which have utilized the Mortality Data Base since 1979, along with references to related published papers and technical documents, is used to illustrate the kinds of studies and products possible. (The reader is referred to the Appendix, Section 4.2 for the list of studies using the Canadian Mortality Data Base.) Several new ongoing studies which are just in the planning or pilot study phase are also listed. The second section outlines the kinds and broad functions of source records used and needed in future epidemiological and genetic studies involving delayed health effects. The third section describes some main directions for our future endeavours over the next 2–5 years, with examples from some ongoing or currently planned studies. To illustrate the type of projects possible, most examples are drawn from work using the Mortality Data Base file at Statistics Canada.

Source: Reprinted, by permission, from M. Smith, "Future Needs and Directions for Computerized Record Linkage in Health Research in Canada: Future Study Plans," *Proceedings of the Workshop on Computerized Record Linkage in Health Research*, Ottawa, Ontario, May 21–23, 1986, ed. G.R. Howe and R.A. Spasoff (Toronto: University of Toronto, 1986):211.

The descriptive abstract in Figure 13-1 states the purpose of the article ("plots some future directions for the use of record linkage in addressing some of Canada's health problems"), the organization ("three main sections"), and the purpose of each section. It says that the article outlines the "broad functions of source records," but it does not say what these functions are. In other words, the abstract cannot be used instead of the article. However, this abstract does give the reader a very clear overview of a review paper that contains a great deal of specific information.

INFORMATIVE, OR INFORMATIONAL, ABSTRACT

The informative abstract summarizes the most important points in the article. If the article reports the results of an experiment, the abstract will summarize the purpose, scope, method, results, and conclusions or recommendations. It may be read instead of the article. Informative abstracts are much more common than descriptive abstracts and if only an "abstract" is called for, what is usually meant is an informative abstract. See Figure 13-2 for an example.

The informative abstract in Figure 13-2 reports on one study ("a ten year mortality follow-up of the Nutrition Canada Survey Report"). The first three sentences indicate the background, purpose, and method of the study; for a less expert audience these might have to be stated more fully. The next two sentences present the results of the study. If you were preparing a review of the literature on the effects of low serum vitamin C in females, you might be able to substitute the abstract for the article because the abstract does tell you that this variable was associated with death from all causes.

GUIDELINES FOR SUMMARIZING

To write a summary or abstract of a document, particularly of a document you did not write, you can follow these steps:

- Define the task.
- Identify the main points.
- State the main points in prose.
- Revise to meet the length requirement.

Figure 13-2
An Informative
Abstract

NUTRITION CANADA STUDY: OVERVIEW

Helen L. Johansen
Health Promotion, Health and Welfare Canada

A ten year mortality follow-up of the Nutrition Canada Survey cohort has been done by record linkage to the Canadian Mortality Data Base. The Nutrition Canada Survey took place from September 1970 to December 1972 and among the data obtained were smoking habits, body weight, a 24-hour dietary recall, a food frequency, history of present illness and drug use, and biochemical analyses. An overview analysis of those aged 40+, with no self-reported heart disease, stroke or tumors and with no accidental deaths will be presented. Age, pack-years of cigarette smoking, hypertension and either urinary glucose (male) or diabetes (female) were significantly related to death from all causes. A history of chronic conditions (male), low serum vitamin C (female), serum protein (male), and high dietary vitamin D, thiamin and alcohol (female), were associated with death from all causes. Serum cholesterol, education, income and body mass index were not strongly related to death.

More detailed analysis of coffee and alcohol are currently underway.

Source: Reprinted, by permission, from Helen L. Johansen, "Nutrition Canada Study: Overview," *Proceedings of the Workshop on Computerized Record Linkage in Health Research, Ottawa, Ontario, May 21 – 23, 1986,* ed. G.R. Howe and R.A. Spasoff (Toronto: University of Toronto, 1986):153.

DEFINE THE TASK

Identify the purpose and audience of the summary to see whether there are particular aspects you should concentrate on and whether you can retain the technical terms that may be in the original document. Determine the length required and estimate roughly the ratio of summary to text to help you determine what level of detail you'll be able to include. Length requirements are usually stated as a specific number of words. Normally a summary will be no more than ten percent of the length of the original document, but you may be asked to write a summary that is only five percent of the length of the original.

IDENTIFY THE MAIN POINTS

To orient yourself, first scan and skim the document to get a very general sense of its purpose and organization. Next, read the document, noting cues to main points, such as headings, topic sentences, and structures such as "There are ..." or "It was shown that ... ". Make marks in the margin to indicate the approximate location of main points. Then reread these areas carefully, underlining the explicit statements of main points. Sometimes main points are implied rather than stated explicitly. In this case, state the implied main points in your own words. The errors you can make at this stage are misreading the text and selecting too many main points. There are few easy cures for the first problem, but the second one you will overcome with practice as you get a better sense of how many main points your length limit will allow you to include. If the document is particularly long or complex, you may need to prepare an outline of it in order to determine its structure before you can summarize its argument.

STATE THE MAIN POINTS

Write out the main points in continuous prose. Don't just string together the exact wording of the original, but don't struggle to change every word, either. Try, instead, to assimilate the *meaning* of the original and then phrase that meaning as naturally as you can; this will give you an appropriate blend of the original wording and your own. Check that you have not distorted the meaning of the original by leaving out or changing a relationship word such as *although*, *if*, or *because* and that you have not inadvertently changed *some* to *all* or *one* to *every*. Double check all numbers to make sure you haven't misrepresented them.

REVISE TO MEET THE LENGTH REQUIREMENT

Estimate how much you are over the length limit. If you have to decrease length by more than one third, then you will definitely have to discard some of your "main" points. Make sure that you begin discarding at the level of greatest detail and work up toward what you are most certain are main points. When you think you are close enough to the length limit (within 20 percent), work on conciseness by eliminating unnecessary words and phrases. Finally, to improve coherence and increase conciseness, combine sentences.

An example of a summary

The following article, prepared by a student for *Campus Computing*, a newsletter, reports on how Dr. V. J. Modi of the University of British Columbia is using computers in his research. At roughly 1000 words, the article is itself quite a concise summary of the author's interviews with Dr. Modi. Someone else prepared the 150-word summary that follows the article. The underlining in the article identifies the passages that the summary writer first identified as potential main points. Since the underlined passages contain about 250 words, even more detail had to be removed in writing the summary.

COMMUNICATIONS SATELLITES, THE SPACE SHUTTLE, AND COMPUTERS

Timothy K. Chia

The launching of the first communications satellite in 1960, the *Echo 1*, by the United States, has propelled us into the age of instant information. Although the *Echo 1* was very crude in construction and in operation, its success in reflecting transmitted signals back to earth has led the way for the development of very sophisticated satellites. Today, most satellites average 3–4 metres in height, carry solar panels about 1 metre wide by 8 metres long to generate power, and orbit around the earth's equatorial plane at a height of roughly 35 890 km. At this altitude, the satellite's motion is synchronized with the earth's rotation, allowing the satellite to remain in one position over the earth. In other words, the period of the satellite's orbit – one day – is precisely how long it takes the earth to make one axial rotation. The continued success of these satellites, however, like most modern technological breakthroughs, depends on more research and study.

One of the research projects of Dr. V. J. Modi, of UBC's Mechanical Engineering Department, is to study the dynamics and control of communications satellites. Although extensive research has been carried out on satellites since 1962, there are many problems yet to be solved. First, a satellite is a very expensive piece of hardware (typically costing over $80 million) that operates in a very hostile environment. This environment, consisting of microgravity, extreme temperatures, non-existent atmosphere, and the earth's magnetic field, is very different than what we are exposed to here on earth. Thus, it is almost impossible to test the satellite's ability to operate in space, since it is very hard to simulate these conditions. A new satellite may operate perfectly on earth, but after launching it may malfunction or may not even operate at all and the millions of dollars spent are wasted.

Secondly, satellites are constantly being disturbed by micro-meteorite impacts, earth's gravitational and magnetic fields, solar radiation induced temperature gradients, and even light pressure. On earth, we don't feel the effect of light pressure, but at the height of synchronous orbit, the effect of light pressure equals that of the sun's gravitational force. All these disturbances cause the satellite to oscillate, disrupting the communication between the satellite and the earth. In a typical situation, a signal might be transmitted from Vancouver to London, England. The signal is sent from the ground terminal, in Lake Cowichan, to a satellite positioned over the Atlantic Ocean. The satellite then receives the signal, which is now very weak because it has covered a long distance, boosts it with a transponder, and then retransmits the signal to a ground terminal outside London. However, if the satellite starts oscillating, both the receiving and transmitting beams are affected. In fact, if the satellite rotates by 1/100 of a degree, the corresponding transmitted beam will describe an arc of 4 to 6 kilometres along the ground.

Both these problems are very hard to study physically, so Dr. Modi's research group has been using mathematical modelling to simulate dynamics of communications satellites. This modelling, however, leads to a very formidable system of differential equations. These equations are highly non-linear, non-autonomous (meaning the coefficients are time dependent), and coupled. Each system may have from 10 to 20 degrees of freedom, with each degree of freedom leading to an equation, and each equation having up to 300 terms. Thus, each model translates to a system of 15 to 20 differential equations, each with almost 300 coefficients. Without the help of computers, it would be impossible to solve such a system of equations. Dr. Modi's group derives most of their computing resources from the Computing Centre, starting with the MTS mainframe. Each model requires a researcher to write a FORTRAN program, roughly 15 000 lines long, which incorporates many of the Computing Centre's routines, such as the UBC Matrix solvers, the IMSL routines, the point specified integration routines, and many other solver packages. In addition, the researchers are anxious to use the Computing Centre's recent acquisition of the EASY5/W package from Boeing. This software is ideally suited to the type of modelling that Dr. Modi's research group is involved in, and should help in his study.

Mathematical modelling can give a fairly good estimate of how a satellite will behave after it has been launched. However, modelling still has many limitations, and at best, is highly approximate. What has been lacking for many years is a real test laboratory. In the past, there has been no way to launch a satellite, test it, and then retrieve it for analysis. But, with the space shuttle program seemingly back on track, there is an experiment scheduled to be run in the early nineties, which will use the space shuttle as the test lab for a communications satellite. The astronauts on board will suspend the satellite from the shuttle by means of a tether, which will also function as a communications link, passing data from the measuring instruments on the satellite back to the shuttle's computer. Then, if something goes wrong while the satellite is transmitting signals to a ground terminal, it can be pulled back into the shuttle, corrected, and put back into "orbit." In a co-operative effort, NASA will develop the tether and the Italian Space Agency will provide the satellite. <u>Dr. Modi's research group has been studying the control strategy for the entire system</u>. Thus, in developing the system, those lengthy equations come into play again, and much modelling must be carried out before a control strategy can be decided upon. It is anticipated that the successful completion of this experiment will lead to a much better understanding of the dynamics and control of communications satellites in space, and result in larger, more powerful, and more reliable communications satellites.*

SUMMARY

Dr. V.J. Modi uses computer assisted mathematical modelling to study the dynamics and control of communications satellites. Because the conditions of space cannot be duplicated on earth, he uses models to test a satellite's ability to operate in space and to study the effects of various disturbances in space that may disrupt communication between the satellite and earth. Each model uses a system of 15 to 20 differential equations, each with almost 300 coefficients. To solve such a system requires a FORTRAN program of about 15 000 lines that includes various Computing Centre routines. The recently acquired EASY5/W software package from Boeing is ideally suited to Dr. Modi's work. He is also using modelling and these lengthy equations to develop a control strategy for an experiment in which a communication satellite will be tethered to the space shuttle and retracted into the shuttle if it needs repairs or adjustments.

*Source: From Timothy K. Chia, "Communications Satellites, the Space Shuttle, and Computers," *Campus Computing*, 4.9 (Sept. 1989):29 – 30. Reprinted with the permission of the publisher.

EXERCISES

1. Write a descriptive abstract of 150 words for an article in a journal.
2. Write an informative abstract of 200 words for an article in a journal.

PART FOUR

REPORTS

INTRODUCTION TO REPORTS

INTRODUCTION

The preparation of reports will be an important aspect of your writing as a professional. This chapter defines reports and suggests how they can be classified on the basis of subject matter, purpose, stage of project, and form. It then provides an overview of the structure of reports and explains how reports function in organizations.

DEFINITION

It is difficult to define exactly what a report is because the term refers to such a wide variety of documents. Reports range in complexity from an accident or insurance claim report that you prepare by answering a few questions on a form, to government reports that include several thick volumes and could take teams of writers months or even years to complete. What characteristics, then, do reports share?

- All reports present an organized record of *verifiable evidence* that is assumed to be accurate. This evidence may be numerical data gathered in an investigation; or a narration of events, as in a trip report; or information gathered by consulting authorities or reference works in libraries. Chapter 15 discusses what constitutes verifiable evidence and how it can be gathered.
- Most reports also *interpret* the evidence. They discuss the *implications* of the evidence, or the relevance of the evidence to the organization.
- Many reports also *make recommendations*.

Whether a report includes interpretation and recommendations depends, usually, on the terms of reference, or the assignment, as defined by the person making the assignment.

This leads us to another characteristic of reports: almost all reports are *assigned* or *requested*. In other words, whereas a letter or memo may be writer-initiated, a report almost never is. Reports are written to fulfil a need for information – either an ongoing need, as in a routine report, or a specific need, as in a special report to help someone make or justify a particular decision.

Both the writer and the reader are communicating as members of organizations or at least as legal entities. As a result, the writer makes every effort to sound objective and impersonal. The audience is not addressed within the report as it might be in a letter or memo. In making recommendations, the writer uses objective evidence to persuade and avoids loaded language. Headings, lists, and illustrations are used to make the document more efficient.

Many criteria can be used in classifying reports, the most common being subject, purpose, stage of project, and form, and each of these has many report names derived from it. The classes of reports do overlap and many different terms can legitimately be used to name the same type of report. The kind of business an organization is engaged in will largely determine the kinds of reports that it generates. On the job, you will learn very quickly what to call the main types of reports you will write or read.

SUBJECT

On the basis of their subject, some reports can be classified as follows:

- accident
- construction
- design
- incident
- operation
- sales
- service
- trip

Another group of report names, such as the following, are derived more specifically from how the evidence was gathered:

- experimental
- inspection
- investigation
- laboratory
- research
- test

PURPOSE

The purpose of a report is sometimes used as the basis of naming the type of report. These purposes include the following:

- *Information.* An information report is the least ambitious; it presents information, but does not interpret it. Its function is to supply accurate information in a readily accessible form. Most of the reports you write early in your career will probably be of this kind. While most of them are routine, some do lead to the assignment of other kinds of reports, such as feasibility or recommendation reports.
- *Evaluative.* An evaluative report judges something and states conclusions about its value. It could assess a person, a procedure, equipment, a policy, and so on.
- *Feasibility.* A feasibility report determines whether it is possible and/ or advantageous to do something. Feasibility reports provide the basis for making such decisions as whether or not to dam a creek, build a factory, establish a new department in a university, or use natural gas as the fuel in a particular kind of vehicle. They are extremely important in many kinds of organizations and are often prepared by teams of writers.
- *Recommendation.* A recommendation report must include recommendations that are based on evidence presented and interpreted in the report. Recommendation reports are used by decision makers

both as the basis and the justification for their decisions. At the same time, decision makers are not usually bound to accept the recommendations made to them in reports. Note that feasibility reports are a subclass of recommendation reports.

Some authorities also class *proposals* as reports. However, because a proposal is often writer-initiated, and because reports and proposals are generally written in different circumstances, this book treats proposals separately in Chapter 22.

STAGE OF PROJECT

Usually a major project, such as a construction project or a research project, will require a series of reports that have the following special names:

- *Preliminary.* A preliminary report is written before activity on the project begins. It differs from a proposal in that it is written after a commitment to the project has been made.
- *Progress* (or *Interim* or *Status*). Progress reports are normally written at specified intervals to inform the client, supervisor, or granting agency about how work is progressing. They are a means of accounting for time and money and may include descriptions of problems encountered and recommendations about actions to take.
- *Final* (or *Completion*). Final reports are written when a project is finished. If the project is a research project, the final report will be a research report. If the project is a construction project, the final report will provide a final summation of the work done.

Related to the progress report, but not necessarily concerned with a project, is the *periodic* report. A periodic report is one that must be written at specified intervals and that concerns the status of an organization, department, or section. The most familiar example is the annual report prepared by a company for its shareholders. In addition, a wide variety of other periodic reports are written in most large companies.

FORM

On the basis of their form, reports are also classified as form reports, letter reports, memo reports, formal reports, and oral reports. The differences between these types of reports are discussed in the next section.

THE STRUCTURE OF REPORTS
OVERVIEW

On the basis of their structure, we can divide reports into form reports, informal reports, and formal reports.

FORM REPORT. A great deal of repetitive reporting is done on forms that are designed to record the required information in a convenient arrangement. This is the kind of report a private individual commonly makes to an organization; for example, you write a form report when you prepare your income tax return. Completing form reports poses few problems and will not be discussed further in this text.

INFORMAL REPORT. The term *informal report* is *not* to be construed as meaning "casual"; rather, the "informal" means only that the report is not presented in the special *form* of what is called a formal report. Informal reports take the form of letters or memos, with memos usually being used for reports that stay within the organization, and letters for reports that go outside the organization, such as a progress report from an engineering firm to a client. While the informal report form is normally used for shorter reports, some organizations prepare memo reports of 100 pages.

FORMAL REPORTS. A formal report is a special form that most closely resembles that of a book. Normally it will only be used for documents that are at least 2000 words long and that are particularly formal or important. This text emphasizes the formal report because it is a kind of maximal form that introduces you to all the structural features you are likely to encounter in preparing reports.

The basic structures of formal and informal reports are compared in Table 14-1. By the term *body* in Table 14-1 we mean the main developmental sections of the report – the substance of the report. In addition to the body, all reports will have an introduction and a conclusion, and may also have an appendix. While all formal reports will have either an abstract or an executive summary, an informal report usually won't have an abstract, and short informal reports going to one reader need not have an executive summary. It is really in the front matter that the two types of reports differ most. The letter of transmittal and the title page of the formal report are replaced by the headings and/or salutation of the memo or letter format of the informal report. A table of contents

Table 14-1
The Usual
Components of
Informal Reports and
Formal Reports

Informal Report	Formal Report
Memo or letter headings	Letter of Transmittal
	Title Page
(Executive summary)	Abstract (Executive Summary)
	Table of Contents
	List of Illustrations
Introduction	Introduction
Body	Body
Conclusion	Conclusion (and Recommendations)
(Appendix)	(Appendix)

and list of illustrations are unnecessary for an informal report because its brevity allows for easy scanning of headings.

Informal and formal reports also differ in layout and packaging. Probably the most striking difference is the fact that formal reports are frequently bound in covers, whereas informal reports are not. An informal report will generally also be more compact in its presentation. It will usually be single-spaced. Since the sections of an informal report are likely to be more brief, main headings may simply follow each other on the same page, while in a formal report each one will usually begin a new page. It is important to remember, then, that while the same principles apply in the formal and informal reports, it would be a mistake simply to transfer to an informal report the conventions you learn in writing the formal report. Also, remember that individual companies have their own conventions that you must observe when you work for them.

BODY

The body is the core of the report. This is where you will present information and argue your case. It is where new material is placed. All the other parts of the report, what we are calling the supplements, are derived from the body. It is the body that you will organize when you outline your report, and it is the body that you will write first, because only then can you prepare the other components.

SUPPLEMENTS

The details of the purpose, content, and form of each supplement are discussed in Chapter 17. Here we will only provide a very brief overview of what each supplement is and note that the supplements interact to make the report more usable.

- *Letter of transmittal*. The letter of transmittal, addressed to the recipient of the report, is a separate letter attached to the cover. It formally presents the report and answers the question, "What is this?"
- *Cover*. The cover helps make the report look important and also provides protection in the same way that book covers do. A label on the cover will identify the report by title, author, date, and sometimes a special number.
- *Title page*. The title page duplicates the information on the cover label when there is a cover, and replaces the cover when there isn't one. It includes the title, author, date, and other identification.
- *Abstract or executive summary*. The abstract or executive summary provides a synopsis of the essence of the report. An abstract will summarize the purpose, methods, and results, while an executive summary will highlight what is of concern to management and will phrase it in terms that management can understand. Whether you should use an abstract, an executive summary, or both, will depend on the purpose of the report and on the nature of its audience.

- *Table of contents*. The table of contents lists headings and their location in the report. It shows the basic internal structure of the report and helps the reader find particular sections.
- *List of illustrations*. The list of illustrations lists the graphics in the report and indicates their location.
- *Introduction*. The introduction, which is the first main section of the report, introduces the report by indicating its purpose, significance, scope, organization, and the background to the assignment, but it does not start the report proper.
- *Conclusion*. The conclusion summarizes the main finding(s) of the report.
- *Recommendations*. The recommendations section, sometimes combined with the conclusion, lists the main recommendations made and discussed in the report. Of course, if the report does not make recommendations, then there will not be a recommendations section.
- *Appendices*. The appendices provide supplementary material that may be needed by only some readers, or material that would disrupt the flow of the text, such as extensive data or detailed graphics.

The structure of a report, and a formal report in particular, is to some extent *repetitive*. The statement of purpose, or a version of it, is found in the letter of transmittal, the abstract, and the introduction; the recommendations are found in the abstract, the recommendations section, the body, and sometimes also in the letter of transmittal. Doesn't this mean that the formal report is an inefficient kind of document? The answer, of course, is no. The system of supplements has evolved to facilitate how reports are read and used.

In addition to accommodating the efficient use of the document, the supplements can also serve the symbolic function of adding significance to the report. Since a report may be the only visible product a client receives for his or her investment of thousands of dollars, the client may consider its size and appearance as a representation of the value of the information in the report.

FUNCTIONS OF REPORTS IN ORGANIZATIONS

We noted earlier that reports are normally written in the context of an organization. Here we will consider how reports originate, how they are used, and how they are read.

HOW REPORTS ORIGINATE

We said earlier that reports are almost never writer-initiated. When there is a need for information, the writer is assigned a report, usually by a supervisor. If the need is routine, such as the need for a monthly summary of a department's activities, or an account of what transpired on a trip, then there will be a standing assignment.

Two principles of organizational activity that lead to the need for reports are accountability and division of labour.

- *Accountability.* We cannot, of course, survey here all the kinds of accountability that operate within and between organizations. We can, however, get a sense of their complexity, particularly in large organizations, by looking at just a few examples of situations that require reports.

  A company is accountable, usually in quite different ways, to the government and to its shareholders, and must report to both. In order to do so, it must keep records, many of which are included in internal reports. In companies with several branch plants and many departments, department records are combined into larger and larger units until they finally become part of the company's annual report.

  Within the company, decisions have to be accounted for and justified, and a report is a powerful base for justifying a decision. For example, an executive may not have the authority to decide to combine two departments or to purchase new equipment, but may be able to do so if a report recommends that this be done. The report will also provide the data necessary to support the decision. Similarly, governments assign task forces to provide reports to guide their decisions.

  Reports are sent from a company to a client to justify its fees, to account for time, and to gain approval for its decisions on a project. These reports can, in turn, be used by the client, particularly if the client is another company, to account to its shareholders for the money being spent on the project.

- *Division of labour.* The report is a device that both facilitates the division of labour and derives from it. Figure 14-1 illustrates a typical use of reports to facilitate the division of labour. In this case, A has asked a subordinate, B, for a report on whether or not to open another branch store. Since this is too large a question for B to investigate alone, B asks C, D, and E to report on particular aspects of the question, and they, in turn, ask their subordinates (F, G, H, I, J) to report to them.

  In this case, nine reports are written, although A will only receive one report. The data that J reported to E became part of E's report to B, and B's report to A. Your first reports, like J's, will probably be used by your supervisor in reporting further.

  Often the investigative labour is allocated or assigned to experts who report to the manager. The report is then a document for conveying expert opinion or findings.

HOW REPORTS ARE USED

Many routine reports are simply filed for the record and consulted only if a problem arises. Others, as the previous section suggested, are incorporated into larger reports, or are interpreted in another report.

Typical questions that reports could be used to decide include the following:

Figure 14-1
Flow Chart Showing
How Nine Workers
(B–J) Participate in
B's Report to A

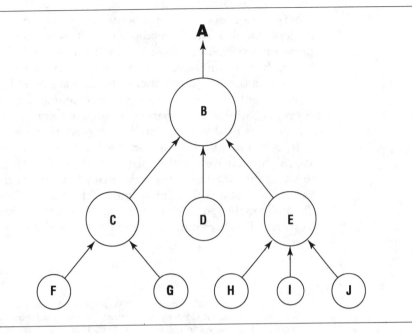

- Why did the boiler explode?
- Why have there been so many grievances from the sales department?
- Should a bridge be built?
- What will be the impact of the bridge on the community?
- Should this mine be kept open?
- How can the cafeteria be made more efficient?

HOW REPORTS ARE READ

Reports, and particularly longer reports, are not typically read from beginning to end. A study of the reading habits of Westinghouse managers reports that the most frequently read component is the summary, followed by the introduction, conclusions, body, and appendix.[1] A more recent study of how NASA reports are read by aeronautics engineers and scientists shows that the components read most often, in order, are the conclusion, results and discussion, summary, introduction, and title page.[2] It is to facilitate this kind of selective reading that the various components of a report have evolved.

What is the typical distribution and reading path for a formal report in a large organization? Regardless of who is the intended audience, the report will usually first go to your supervisor, who will have to approve it. After this, it will be submitted to a particular audience, often a single person. This person will scan, read or study anywhere from just the executive summary to the entire document. How much of the report is read and how carefully will depend in part on what the reader needs the report for, and on how the report relates to the reader's direct concerns. Usually, this first reader will also pass copies of the report to others whose jobs or departments are or may be affected by it. These readers will also usually read the executive summary and then focus on those aspects that are most related to what they do. Most readers will be much more interested in the recommendations or conclusions than in the data used to justify them; the data are most likely to be examined carefully only if the conclusions or recommendations are disagreeable. All reports also become part of an organization's permanent records and can be consulted when related decisions are made in the future.

In addition to allowing for the kind of selective reading described above, the structure of the formal report is also designed to make it easy to locate information. This is the main function of the table of contents, list of illustrations, headings, and subheadings. The list of recommendations, conclusion, and summary also make it unnecessary for the reader to worry about selecting and remembering the main points.

NOTES

1. Richard W. Dodge, "What to Report," *Westinghouse Engineer* 22 (July-Sept. 1962) Westinghouse Electric Corporation, reprinted in *Strategies for Business and Technical Writing*, 2d ed., ed. Kevin J. Harty (New York: Harcourt, 1985), 169–76.
2. Thomas E. Pinelli, Virginia M. Cordle, and Raymond F. Vondran, "The Function of Report Components in the Screening and Reading of Technical Reports," *Journal of Technical Writing and Communication* 14.2 (1984): 87–94.

GATHERING EVIDENCE FOR REPORTS

INTRODUCTION

Chapter 14 noted that reports are based on verifiable evidence. This chapter first explains what is meant by verifiable evidence and outlines the relationship between evidence and the report-writing process. Then it examines how to design an investigation. Finally it suggests some guidelines for analyzing and interpreting evidence.

VERIFIABLE EVIDENCE

A basic principle of report writing is that claims are based on *verifiable* evidence, sometimes called *hard* evidence. Verifiable evidence is independent of who obtained it; another investigator would get exactly the same results. (We will not discuss here the problems inherent in all scientific data gathering.)

Consider the following statements:

1. The room was hot.
2. The room was too hot.
3. The temperature of the room at noon was 25°C.
4. Six of the ten workers reported that the room was too hot.

Sentence 1 is a *claim*, a subjective statement. It reports the speaker's interpretation of the conditions, but says nothing about what other people might conclude. Furthermore, exactly what does it mean to say that a room is hot? Although most people will agree that a room is hot if the temperature is 30°C, will they agree if it is 22°C? In other words, sentence 1 is not verifiable. Can it be used in a report? It can be used as a claim or generalization or interpretation that should then be supported by statements like sentence 3 or 4.

Sentence 2 is also a claim, but it is even more of an interpretation than is sentence 1; sentence 2 is a judgement. To support this sentence you would have to indicate the temperature and then demonstrate why this temperature is too high for whatever is to take place in the room. If you don't do this, then you have simply stated an opinion, and unsubstantiated opinions are usually not acceptable in reports.

Sentence 3 is a statement that can be verified. Whether or not it is specific and accurate enough will depend on the circumstances. If you are concerned with the comfort of workers in the room, then you probably don't need greater accuracy. However, if you are reporting the results of an experiment that is particularly heat-sensitive, then it may be necessary to use more significant figures in the measurement, as in

25.015°C, for example. You may even need to specify where in the room the thermometer was located when that reading was taken. Note also that using sentence 3 by itself could leave the reader asking, "So what?" Your job, then, is usually both to provide the evidence and to interpret its significance.

Sentence 4 is also a statement that can be verified. Although it does not tell us what the temperature was, it provides an objective tally of subjective interpretations of that temperature. If it is legitimate to conclude that the subjective judgement of a majority of workers is a measure of the suitability of a room's temperature, then we could go on to use sentence 2 as an interpretation of sentence 4.

EVIDENCE AND THE REPORT-WRITING PROCESS

You should be concerned with evidence throughout the writing process, but it will normally require the greatest attention while you are defining the task, and organizing and outlining. For all but the most routine reports, you will have to design an investigation to gather relevant and verifiable evidence, conduct the investigation, and then interpret its results. Bear in mind that the quality of evidence and the quality of the interpretation are prerequisites of a good report; the best-written report will be worthless unless the evidence and its interpretation are sound.

DESIGNING AN INVESTIGATION

The type of report you are writing will largely determine the kinds of evidence you need and hence how you should go about getting it. Designing an investigation consists of the following steps:

- Define the information needs.
- Determine the required degree of rigour.
- Select the information sources to use.

Note that although these steps are presented linearly, you will probably follow them cyclically.

DEFINE THE INFORMATION NEEDS

To identify the information you need to gather, you must first analyze the report assignment and frame questions that will have to be answered objectively. In many cases this step consists of identifying the *variables* that must be measured. Consider, for example, how you would proceed if you were asked to report on whether bus service to your campus is adequate. The key word, of course, is *adequate*. How will you define adequate bus service? What are the variables you must consider? No doubt you would include such matters as frequency of service, location of bus stops, ease with which one can transfer to and from other buses, and how crowded the buses are. You will have to find out which buses go where and when. You might need to know where most students live.

You might also want to know what the bus users think of the service and what students and faculty in general think. What will you use as standards to determine adequacy? How long a wait for a bus is acceptable? As you can see, even an apparently simple question can become quite complex when you begin to analyze it. Although you may need to constrain your investigation later because of limited time or funds, it is very important that you don't overlook any variables at this point.

When you have identified the main questions you will answer, you are ready to examine each of them in greater detail. In considering frequency of service, for example, not only will you need to check each bus line serving the campus, but you will also want to evaluate the service at various times of the day, on weekends as well as weekdays, and in the summer as well as in the winter. What criteria will you use to determine adequacy?

In addition to the questions that you formulate before your investigation, you will become aware of new ones as you start gathering the evidence. Even as late as the draft stage you will find that you are making claims that need documentation.

Be particularly alert to the need to provide evidence for statements such as the following:

- Worker morale is *low*.
- Sales have decreased *substantially*.
- Absenteeism is *high*.
- Equipment is breaking down *frequently*.
- *A lot* of students have complained about dormitory food.
- *Several* accidents have taken place at this intersection.

In other words, remember that relative adjectives and adverbs are not specific.

When you have identified the information you need, you can decide on the rigour of your investigation and the specific sources you will use.

DETERMINE THE REQUIRED DEGREE OF RIGOUR

Rigour refers to the thoroughness and precision with which you conduct your investigation. Clearly, reports vary in the rigour required. It may help you to distinguish between the following kinds of evidence and proof:

- *Scientific proof.* A scientific proof demands the greatest rigour in experimental design and the greatest precision in measurements. Reports on research and experiments fall into this class.
- *Pragmatic business proof.* Most business proofs will be considerably less rigorous than scientific proofs. However, you are expected to have investigated the problem or question as thoroughly as possible within the prescribed constraints. You should find the *best* evidence you can and interpret it intelligently; you need not have *all* the evidence possible. Note also that most business reports deal with situations in which all the variables cannot be controlled.

- *Legal proof.* Legal proofs are designed to stand up in court. Instead of considering all variables, you may need to select those that most vividly or most convincingly support your lawyer's arguments.

You have to determine how accurate your data must be. How large a margin of error or uncertainty is tolerable? For example, if you were investigating the adequacy of bus service, how many measurements would you need of how crowded the buses are? Would it suffice to check all the buses on one day, or would you need to check them every day for a week, a month, or a year? How carefully would you have to check them? Would you need to know *exactly* how many people were on each bus?

In conducting business research you will probably have to make many compromises, either because you lack the resources to complete an absolutely thorough investigation, or because the use to which the report will be put does not warrant such thoroughness. When you do compromise, however, it is important that you realize how your study is constrained and how this may affect your results and interpretations.

SELECT THE INFORMATION SOURCES

For each question you posed when you defined the information needs, you will have to identify the best source of information. In many cases, there will only be one appropriate source. However, if you do have a choice, consider both whether a particular source provides the accuracy you need and whether you have enough time and money to use it. The following list, arranged partly in order of general accessibility, includes only the more usual sources:

- your own documents and records
- other documents and records within the organization
- specifications, price lists, manuals, regulations
- observation and measurement
- interview or letter of inquiry
- survey
- library sources
- computerized data bases

YOUR DOCUMENTS AND RECORDS. Much of your report writing on the job may be based only on your own records, such as an engineer's log book, a geologist's laboratory records, an accountant's files. A very important motivation for maintaining careful, accurate, and well-organized records is the possibility that you may need them for future reports. Many occasional reports, such as trip reports and accident reports, also require that you keep accurate records.

When you use your own records, be particularly aware of the following points:

- You must *select* the information that is relevant to your report. Only rarely will you be able to transfer your records in their entirety to a report.

- You may have to *reorganize* the information to make your report Reader-Based. Particularly if you are considering evidence acquired over time, you must be careful not just to follow the chronological order in which your notes are arranged.
- If your records are the results of observations, they must be treated with the same caution about accuracy as are direct observations.

OTHER DOCUMENTS AND RECORDS WITHIN THE ORGANIZATION. The records of other departments or individuals in an organization are often very important sources of evidence. Some examples of such documents are sales records, personnel records, union agreements, contracts, and other reports. Find out the kinds of information that are available within your organization, both in the company library and in other departments. Try to determine what kinds of research have been done and how company records are organized. Try to avoid duplicating in your own investigation what is already available elsewhere.

Using other documents and records in the organization poses the following problems:

- It may be impossible to determine how accurate the data are because you may not have enough information about how they were gathered.
- It may be difficult to gain access to them, and there may be serious political or legal constraints on your using them.

SPECIFICATIONS, PRICE LISTS, MANUALS, REGULATIONS. Specifications, price lists, manuals, and regulations can be particularly useful if you have to evaluate or recommend equipment. To get these sources, consult the company library, public libraries, government departments, or manufacturers and distributors. You can contact the latter by letter of inquiry or by telephone.

OBSERVATION AND MEASUREMENT. Observation and measurement are fundamental to gathering evidence. In fact, the very word *evidence* is derived from the Latin verb meaning "to see." Measuring, in the sense used here, includes counting, as well as the use of any measuring instrument. It could be as simple a task as counting how many broken windows there are in a building or as complex as measuring the stresses on a bridge support. The care that will have to go into using this source depends in part on the kind of data you are trying to get and the function of the data in your report.

Before making the observation or measurement, plan the details of your strategy. Are you measuring something that is relatively constant, such as the dimensions of an object, or relatively variable, such as the number of clients in a store? Generally, a constant can simply be measured once, while a variable will have to be measured several times and will require more complex planning. In either case, you will have to decide the following:

- What, exactly, will you measure?
- How, exactly, will you measure it? What instruments and/or methods will you use?

- When and how often will you take measurements?
- Where will you take measurements?

The degree of accuracy you require will determine the kind of instruments you should use and how many readings you may need.

For a more complete discussion of obtaining evidence by observation or measurement you should consult books on experimental design, scientific method, and statistics.

INTERVIEW OR LETTER OF INQUIRY. Often the best source is an authority in the subject whom you can interview in person or by telephone, or to whom you can send a letter of inquiry. To use this source you will first have to identify the required authority, then persuade that person to help you, and finally prepare specific questions to get the most useful information most efficiently.

Who is a suitable authority will depend on the kind of project you are doing. If you are interested in recent developments in theory or technology, you may need to consult researchers in a university, but if you are investigating particular applications or trends, you may need to talk to the appropriate representatives of corporations. Sometimes just finding the right person to interview can be a complex research task, but if the information you are seeking is important enough, it is well worth the care and effort. In addition to locating an authority, you should also research the interviewee's credentials and most likely biases, so that you can interpret the interview data more accurately.

Since people who are authorities are usually very busy, and since they are going to do you a favour in giving you their time, you must be careful to persuade them to agree to be interviewed. Let them know the kind of information you'll want and what you intend to do with it. Why should they bother to talk to you? How can they justify the interview to their supervisors? Can you offer them publicity? Can you exchange information? Can you offer them confidentiality? When you go to the interview, be as co-operative as you can. Arrive on time, be polite, be efficient, and thank the interviewee at the end of your meeting. Be prompt in sending any information you promise.

In preparing the actual questions for the interview, you should observe the following guidelines:
- Write the questions you want to ask, but be prepared to stray from them.
- Don't ask questions about matters that are general knowledge. Don't try to substitute the interview for library research. The interviewee rightly assumes that you have done your homework and now need special knowledge or opinion.
- Use both open-ended questions, such as "How do you foresee this company changing in the next ten years?" and questions that have specific factual answers, such as "How many employees work here?"
- Begin with more general questions and move to more specific ones. Not only are the more general ones likely to encourage a more relaxed atmosphere, but they may raise points that you can then pursue with more specific questions.

During the interview try to maintain control without offending the interviewee. This may become particularly difficult if the interviewee is forceful and insists on changing topics or on drifting away from the question.

Interviewing has the advantage of getting information that is not available elsewhere, either because it is so recent, or because it is of too narrow an interest, as is the case with information about the details of running a particular organization. However, it also has the disadvantage of being time-consuming, of not always yielding accurate and reliable information, and of presenting difficulties in recording and interpreting. At first you may find it very difficult to maintain the interview and to record answers at the same time, particularly when you are summarizing long, open-ended answers. Tape recording can help provide a record of the interview, but your interviewee may not allow you to use a tape recorder.

SURVEY. Surveys, whether face-to-face, by telephone, or by mail, are a useful means for getting comparable information from groups of people. The main disadvantages of surveys are that they take time to prepare and administer and that they are expensive.

If you want to administer a survey, you must define your sample and design a questionnaire. Although the design of surveys is beyond the scope of this text, we can note that to define your sample you must address the following questions:

- Whom do you want to survey? Do you want a sample that represents the entire population, or do you want one that represents a particular subgroup?
- How large a sample do you want? Although you have to consider the costs of gathering and processing the data, you also need to consider the usefulness of the data you collect. The larger the sample, the more useful the data will be.
- How will you select the sample from the general population? What impact does this selection procedure have on the results?

Before conducting an important survey, consult a statistician to ensure that you are not wasting time and money by collecting data that will not have statistical value.

Designing the questionnaire is a slightly less complex task. Again, the details of questionnaire design are beyond the scope of this text, but we can note the following guidelines:

- Include questions about your informants (age, sex, education) if you expect to compare answers for different sample subgroups. Err on the side of getting too much information, not too little; otherwise you may miss correlations that are important.
- Phrase questions so that answers are easy to quantify. If you don't do this, you may have to waste a lot of time interpreting answers, and your results may be less reliable.
- Try to anticipate the range of answers and test your questionnaire

to make sure that all possible answers can be accommodated. Multiple answers can be particularly troublesome.
- Check the phrasing of questions for ambiguity and lack of clarity.
- Make it easy for your informants to fill in the questionnaire.
- Spend time on layout and presentation so your questionnaire looks attractive and invites participation. A messy, amateurish questionnaire is much more likely to be dismissed.

In asking someone to participate in your survey you are asking for a favour, so be as polite as you can. Explain what you are doing. Thank the participants, and make it as easy as you can for them to comply. If you are using a mail questionnaire, include a cover letter and a stamped, self-addressed envelope in which the informant can return the questionnaire.

LIBRARY. Unless you are working in research, you will probably make much less use of a library when you are working than you do as a student. The three main kinds of libraries you are likely to use are company libraries, public libraries, and university libraries. You should be aware of how their purposes, and therefore their holdings, differ.

Company libraries must provide easy access to the printed resources that their workers need in order to keep up with developments in their field and to locate information for proposals and reports. Company libraries are very selective in their holdings; they allow for efficient information searching, provided the information relates to the narrow fields in which the library specializes, but they are not designed for extensive searches of the literature. Company libraries are also likely to stock company reports, which may not be available elsewhere. If the company you work for has a library, familiarize yourself with it as soon as you can. Most public libraries will not be useful to you as a professional because their purpose is to provide reference materials to school students and people in the community. Because university libraries must serve the needs of all their students and faculty, their collections may contain millions of items. While this tends to assure that all mainstream sources are included, it can also make the locating of information an onerous and confusing task.

As you no doubt know, libraries collect many different kinds of sources and each of them contains different kinds of information. Here we can provide only the briefest introduction to books, professional journals, standard reference works, and government publications. You should supplement this introduction by exploring those sections of your college or university library that are most relevant to your discipline.

- *Books.* You are probably familiar with how to use the library's catalogue to find books, and how to use books in searching for information. Unfortunately, books are seldom an important source for either advanced student research or for writing on the job. There are two main reasons for this. First, most books contain information that will be too general for your needs. Second, because of the two or three years it takes for a book to get from the author's desk to the library shelves, the information is usually not current.

- *Professional journals.* Professional journals are the main source for current research in your discipline. Normally, they include research articles that report the results of recent research, reviews of state-of-the-art articles that provide overviews of current developments in research on a particular topic, and professional news. As a practising professional, you will probably subscribe to a few of these journals, and your company will maintain subscriptions to others. Since in most disciplines there are hundreds, if not thousands of journals, professionals who do research have to use computer searches, indexes, and abstracting journals to conduct complete searches of the literature.
- *Standard reference works.* Every discipline has standard reference works such as dictionaries, encyclopedias, or handbooks. You should learn what the ones in your discipline are and what kinds of information they contain.
- *Government publications.* Government publications, which range all the way from simple information pamphlets, to census results, to records of legislation, to very specialized research reports, can be excellent sources of information for reports. University libraries and very large public libraries will maintain holdings of these.

To use a particular library efficiently, you need to know the following:

- What are its *holdings*? What kinds of materials does it contain? How specialized and extensive is the book collection? How many professional journals does it subscribe to? Does it have government publications? What kinds of reference resources does it have? What kinds of bibliographic resources (indexes and abstracts) does it have? What kinds of non-print materials are included? Does it have special reports?
- Which *cataloguing system* does it use? Does it use the U.S. Library of Congress system (letters and numbers) or the Dewey Decimal system (numbers only) or an ad hoc system of its own? Does it have a card catalogue, a microfiche catalogue, or a computerized catalogue?
- What is the *physical arrangement* of materials? Where and in what order are the different kinds of materials kept?

In evaluating the suitability of a particular book or article as a source of information, consider how recent the information is and how reliable the source is. Unless your interest is specifically historical, you will always want the most recent information. To get this, always look for the latest publication dates first and favour journal articles over books. To judge reliability is more difficult, but two indicators are the reputation of the author and the prestige of the journal or publisher.

Because of the phenomenal information explosion in recent years, it is very important that you know how to locate books or articles on a particular topic. As you probably know, the catalogue lists the books and journals in a library. To find a book on a topic, then, you only need to check the subject file under that topic; the card (or entry if the catalogue is no longer actually on cards) will give you all the bibliographic information and the call number, which will help you locate the book in the library. The catalogue will not, of course, allow you to locate all the books on a subject because it lists only the holdings of the particular library.

Locating articles on a topic is a more complex task that includes the following main steps:

- *Locate the main index for the discipline.* An index is a periodic publication that lists articles by topic. Each discipline has several main indexes and you should become familiar with the ones in your field. Learn what they are called, what their call numbers are, where they are located in the library you use, how broad their coverage is, and how they are to be used. The following are a few of the many important indexes:

    Applied Science and Technology Index
    Biological and Agricultural Index
    Business Periodicals Index
    Canadian Business Index
    Canadian Government Publications Index
    Canadian Periodical Index
    Cumulated Index Medicus
    Cumulative Index of Nursing and Allied Health Literature
    Engineering Index
    Social Sciences Index

Many disciplines have abstracting journals, which are periodic publications that reproduce abstracts of articles. These abstracts are arranged by topic. The following are a few of the many important abstracting journals:

    Biological Abstracts
    Chemical Abstracts
    Computer Abstracts
    Ecological Abstracts
    Forestry Abstracts
    Metals Abstracts
    Nursing Abstracts
    Personnel Management Abstracts
    Psychological Abstracts

- *Beginning with the most recent issue of the index, find the listing for your topic.* Most indexes are arranged by a *keyword,* an abbreviated subject or topic. You will want to find the keyword(s) that come closest to your topic.
- *Search the listing for promising articles and note their bibliographic information.* Indexes vary a great deal in their particular arrangements of listings. For each article you will need to know the following:

- author(s)
- title of the article
- title of the journal (journal titles are usually abbreviated)
- volume number and date of the journal
- pages on which the article is found

- *Locate each journal and article.* To find the article, you will first have to locate the appropriate volume of the journal. The card catalogue will list the title of the journal and give its call number. Some libraries have a separate listing of journals and their call numbers. Very recent issues of the journal may not yet be bound into volumes and may be located in a special area in the library.

COMPUTERIZED DATA BASES. Many indexes, abstracts, and other bibliographic resources are now available as computerized data bases, accessible either by a modem or on CD-ROM (compact disc read-only memory). The *Directory of Online Databases* (New York: Cuadra/Elsevier) lists bibliographic and non-bibliographic data bases. The rate at which the number of available data bases is increasing is reflected in the fact that the 1979 directory listed only 400 data bases, while the 1989 directory lists over 4200.

ANALYZING AND INTERPRETING EVIDENCE

After you have collected the needed evidence, you must evaluate its accuracy and its statistical significance, where applicable, and determine its implications for the problem you are discussing. Again, a definitive discussion of this topic is well beyond the scope of this text.

ACCURACY

Much of the evidence you gather will be matters of "fact" – such as addresses, dates, and scientific constants – whose accuracy need not be questioned. Beyond these examples, though, you should be aware that your data are probably not absolutely accurate.

We noted earlier that not all documents require the same degree of accuracy and that not all the data within the same document will necessarily have to be equally accurate. Be aware of the compromises you have to make in gathering the evidence. If these could have a significant impact, you should note this in the report, either in the introduction or where you discuss the data. In assessing your evidence, be sceptical and cautious, but not to the point of questioning all data. The most likely causes of inaccuracies are incomplete or inadequate sampling and research, inaccurate measurements, and the use of misleading or biased authorities.

INCOMPLETE OR INADEQUATE SAMPLING AND RESEARCH. Review the compromises you have made. We normally associate sampling with surveys whose results are analyzed statistically. However, whenever you don't examine all examples of something, you are actually sampling, and you have to be able to justify this sample as representative and adequate for your purposes. You have to be sure that your results are not over-dependent either on chance or on your own manipulation. Ask yourself the following questions:

- How extensively have you examined your own or the company's records? Have you taken into account such variables as seasonal shifts? Would someone else get very similar data from the same source? If not, why not?
- If you were researching similar products or equipment, how many did you compare? How many others did you overlook? Why? What distinguished the ones you chose?
- How many people did you interview or survey? How did you decide on this number? How did you select the particular individuals? Why?
- If you took instrument measurements, how did you decide on how many to take?
- How extensive was your library search? What proportion of books or articles on the subject did you actually consult? What were you unable to get? How many years in the index did you check? Did you consult articles as well as books?

INACCURATE MEASUREMENTS. Every physical measurement has a margin of error. For example, although something may appear to be 10 cm long, the probability is almost zero that it is precisely 10.00000 cm long; it may be, for example, 10.00023 cm or 9.9987 cm. The question is how much of an error there is and whether or not this is significant for your purposes.

MISLEADING OR BIASED AUTHORITY. If your data are derived from an authority or written material, recognize that your source could be biased or wrong. How reliable is your source? Are your data "facts" or opinions?

STATISTICAL SIGNIFICANCE

For data such as the results of a survey or experiment, statistical analysis may be needed. Even an outline of such an analysis is, of course, beyond the scope of this text. To avoid the most blatant errors in interpreting such data, observe the following guidelines:

BASE YOUR GENERALIZATIONS ON AN ADEQUATE SAMPLE. The smaller the sample, the greater the possibility of sampling error. Try to use samples of more than 30 and try to use samples that are about one-tenth of the parent population (the particular population that the sample represents).[1] If your sample is not adequate, don't try to attach too much significance to your results; instead, treat them as indications.

DISTINGUISH BETWEEN CORRELATION AND CAUSATION. If two variables correlate, they vary together. Although often the correlation may be the result of changes in variable x actually causing changes in variable y, a correlation by itself need not indicate causation. Consider the following example. Two years ago, the accounting department of an organization purchased personal computers for the five senior accountants. Since that time, four of the five have complained about vision problems, and three have had to get reading glasses for the first time. Did the personal computers cause the vision problems? While you might be tempted to conclude that they did, further investigation reveals that all five senior accountants are between the ages of 40 and 50, ages at which many people need reading glasses for the first time. In this example, then, while the time spent at a computer may correlate with the frequency of complaints about vision problems, the computers did not cause the vision problems.

AVOID FORCING INTERPRETATIONS. In interpreting data, there is a great danger of seeing what you want to see, especially if you don't have enough data to use statistical measures to determine significance. For example, if 75 percent of the workers in your department are satisfied with their work, is that good or bad?

CONSIDER ALL RELEVANT VARIABLES. If you have overlooked a variable, your data may mislead you. For example, if you questioned one group of workers on a Monday morning and another on a Friday afternoon, some differences in results might be attributable to the different interview times, and not to differences in working conditions.

IMPLICATIONS

Remember that you gathered evidence so that you could solve a problem or make a case. In other words, you had a purpose in gathering data. Now you must relate the data to this purpose. What do they tell you about the problem? The bringing together of the information and the problem is probably the key to the thinking component of report writing. You have gathered the "what?" and now you must decide on the "so what?"

NOTE

1. John T. Roscoe, *Fundamental Statistics for the Behavioral Sciences* (New York: Holt, Rinehart and Winston, 1969), 156 – 57.

EXERCISES

1. Explain how you would verify each of the following claims:
   a. Worker morale is low.
   b. Sales have decreased substantially.
   c. Absenteeism is high.
   d. Equipment is breaking down frequently.
   e. A lot of students have complained about dormitory food.
   f. Several accidents have taken place at this intersection.
   g. This intersection is dangerous.
   h. The standards in that course are too high.
   i. The waiting areas at the airport are too crowded.
   j. The afternoon shift is understaffed.

2. Pretend that you have been asked to determine whether the cost of textbooks is too high. Design a questionnaire students could complete. Explain how and when you would distribute this questionnaire. What will be some of the limitations of the data you gather in this way?

3. The following three questionnaires were prepared by students to assess the adequacy of bicycle parking facilities on campus. Discuss the strengths and weaknesses of each. The following questions may help you in your assessment:

   • Are the questions the right questions to ask?
   • Are the questions clear?
   • Are the questions easy to answer?
   • Will the answers be easy to quantify?
   • Is the questionnaire arranged attractively?

   Prepare your own questionnaire to incorporate the best features of these questionnaires.

a.   TOPIC: CAMPUS BICYCLE FACILITIES
     ATTENTION: CYCLISTS
     Please check (✓) the appropriate box for questions 1 to 4 and provide comments for 5 and 6. Drop completed questionnaires in campus mail.
     ABOUT YOU
     1. What type of bicycle do you ride to campus?
        standard _____
        racing _____
        other - please specify _____
     2. On average how many days/wk do you ride your bicycle to campus?
        1   2   3   4   5   6   7
     3. Do you use the designated bicycle parking areas?
        always   almost always   sometimes   occasionally   never
     ABOUT PARKING FACILITIES
     4. In your experience are the designated parking areas
        a) safe   yes   no
        b) convenient   yes   no
        c) available   yes   no
     5. If you answered "no" to any part of question (4), please say why.

        _____

        _____

     6. What change is needed to improve bicycle parking facilities on campus?

        _____

        _____

b. <u>QUESTIONNAIRE: BICYCLE PARKING ON CAMPUS</u>

1. Are you a cyclist?   Yes   No

2. What type of bike do you ride?
   touring   mountain   other _____

3. What day(s) of the week do you ride to campus (circle)
              M   Tu   W   Th   F

4. What area of campus do you usually park your bike? (See
   reverse for numerically designated zones on the campus map –
   circle appropriate zone.)
    1   2   3   4   5   6   7   8

5. Do you ride your bike between classes?   Yes   No

6. Do you park your bike in an area specifically designed for
   bicycle parking?   Yes   No

   If no, why? _____

7. What type of bike rack is best to put your bike in?

   concrete slabs with slits ☐
   concrete slabs with metal supports ☐

   other _____

   _____

8. Do you lock your bike?   Yes   No
   To a fixed object?   Yes   No

9. Do you think bicycle parking facilities are adequate? Yes   No

10. Would you cycle to campus more often if improvements were
    made?   Yes   No

11. Would you like to see more designated bicycle parking?
                                             Yes   No

    If so, where? (Refer to map on reverse – circle appropriate
    number(s).)
     1   2   3   4   5   6   7   8

12. Your comments on bicycle parking on campus.

    _____

    _____

    _____

c. **Student Committee To Improve Bicycle Facilities**

1. How often did you ride your bike during September?

   1–5 _____   6–10 _____   7–15 _____

   11–20 _____   more than 20? _____

2. a) Do you leave your bike parked in one spot?

   _____yes? _____no?

   b) Would you be interested in a bike check?

   _____yes _____no

   c) How often do you move your bike? _____

3. In good weather are there always spots (conveniently) available?

   _____yes _____no

4. Do you lock your bike? _____yes _____no

   If yes, have you had problems with vandalism or theft?

   _____yes _____no

5. How would you improve facilities?

   _____

   _____

   _____

6. Comments

   _____

   _____

   _____

4. If you are doing library research for a paper, prepare a very brief memo addressed to your instructor that answers parts a and b below, and attach to this memo the photocopies requested in c and d.

   a. Indicate the title of your paper and the discipline for which it is being written.

   b. List the names, call numbers, and locations of *three* important indexes or other bibliographic resources in your discipline.

   c. In *each* of these resources, find the title of at least one article related to your topic. Photocopy the page of the index on which you found the item, and circle the entry.

   d. Locate the *three* articles you noted in step c, and photocopy the first page and the last page of each.

WRITING FORMAL REPORTS: THE BODY

INTRODUCTION

This chapter explains how the writing process discussed in Part Two applies to preparing the body of a formal report and guides you through the preparation of your own formal report. It is organized around the following subassignments, some of which your instructor may omit or modify:

- report proposal
- full formal outline
- progress reports
- draft
- presentation copy

In preparing these subassignments, you will have to work back and forth between this chapter and Chapter 15 and Chapters 5 to 9. These other chapters are like subroutines in a computer program: you go to them and then return again to this chapter. An example of a report prepared by a student is presented at the end of the chapter.

PREPARING A REPORT PROPOSAL

Assignment

Prepare a report proposal in response to the following call for proposals:

CALL FOR PROPOSALS

The Technical Writing Foundation (TWF) will sponsor the preparation of student reports that could be used to improve any aspect(s) of a business or other organization. The foundation will also consider feasibility studies and investigations of procedures or facilities. The reports should be analytical. The reports should be based on the student's direct experience and primary research, although reports based on library research will be accepted if they have been approved by the instructor. The reports should represent substantial work; the minimum length for the body of the report is ten typed, double-spaced pages, excluding illustrations and supplements. Each report will be presented to the instructor, who will send a copy to the TWF and a copy to the named audience. The instructor will specify the due date for the report.

The proposal should be a memo to the instructor and should include the following headings:

- purpose
- significance
- audience
- research plan
- writing schedule

CHOOSING THE REPORT TOPIC

As was noted earlier, you will not choose a report topic when you are writing on the job; rather, the topic will be assigned to you. For the purposes of this assignment, though, you must frame a topic and it should be one that *could* be assigned to you. Choose the subject area first, then choose a broad topic, and finally focus and narrow it.

Perhaps your present job or a fairly recent one could be a source of a topic. How could your job, or a related job, or the entire division or department be improved, or made safer or more efficient? Review what you do in a shift and note all the possible improvements. Which procedures seem inefficient or unsafe? Are there problems with equipment and materials? Are there problems in how the workplace is arranged physically? Are there problems with storage? Are the schedules convenient and efficient? Are there adequate employee facilities?

If you don't have work experience, consider a social organization or sports organization you belong to. How could this organization be made more efficient or more successful? Are its facilities adequate? Could its leadership be more effective or efficient? How could its activities be improved?

If you don't belong to any other organizations, you could consider the college or university where you are taking this course; it, too, is an organization, and you are an expert on some of its aspects from a user's point of view. You could examine some of the facilities, such as the library, the cafeteria, the gymnasium, the parking areas, the residences, or even the classrooms. What are the main problems with these areas? What related procedures or rules should be changed so as to improve them?

In choosing your topic, consider the following:

- *Can the report be analytical?* Does the topic allow you to conduct an investigation?
- *Is the topic broad enough?* Is there sufficient scope for a ten-page report? Can you broaden the scope by adding related aspects?
- *Is the topic narrow enough?* Can you deal with it fully in not much more than ten pages?
- *Can you reasonably expect to complete the report by the due date?*
- *Is needed information accessible?* Will you need access to confidential records? Do you have enough time to get the needed information?
- *Are you competent to write this report?* Do you have sufficient expertise to do what you are proposing? If you don't, consider which aspects of the topic you are competent to investigate.

The following list of topics may help you:

- How to Increase Efficiency and Safety at Silver Spring Aquafarms
- How to Improve Services to Battered Women and Their Children at Red Oaks Transition House
- Evaluation of the Men's Life-Management Program at the West Side Diet Centre
- Workload Problems of the Special Care Aides at Cariboo Lodge Nursing Home
- How to Improve the Bella Coola Waste Disposal System
- How to Increase the Efficiency of the Automated Conversion Project at the King's Park Public Library
- How to Increase the Efficiency of Nursing Management on 4C at Inner City Hospital
- An Evaluation of the Information Centre in Stone Creek Park
- How to Increase Plastic Pulp Production at Big Moose Pulp and Paper Company
- How to Increase the Efficiency of the North Park Store

GUIDELINES FOR PREPARING THE REPORT PROPOSAL

The report proposal, a response to the call for proposals, is a brief memo proposal to write a formal report. See Chapter 22 for a discussion of proposals and Chapter 18 for memo format. Use a subject line and the headings specified in the call for proposals.

PURPOSE. Begin with a statement of purpose that indicates what the report you propose to write will do; for example, "This report will evaluate the safety procedures at the Richmond Packing Plant." Note that the verb (*evaluate*) should indicate your approach. Other verbs you could use include *examine, analyze, investigate*. Following the verb will be the topic of the report (safety procedures at the Richmond Packing Plant). After the statement of purpose, explain more fully exactly what you intend to do in the report. What kinds of questions will you pursue? Make sure that what you are proposing to write is a report and not a guide, or pamphlet, or instructions, or a brief, or an article for a periodical or newsletter, or an essay. A well thought out statement of purpose will help you define your topic. It will also create the impression that you know what you are doing and help to persuade the reader to approve your proposal to write the report.

SIGNIFICANCE. The significance section explains why the report is worth writing. Its purpose is persuasive. Why and how are the questions you propose to investigate important? What will be the result if your recommendations are implemented? How will your report differ from others that may have been written on similar topics? If you cannot justify writing your report, then you should, of course, consider other topics.

AUDIENCE. Review Chapter 5 (Defining the Task). To define the audience, consider who within the organization would assign this report. Instead of just saying "management," name the person and his or her position. Who else might receive the report from this first reader? Remember that "interested people" do not commission reports and do not normally receive them. You may have to check the organizational hierarchy of the company to find exactly who would have the authority to assign the report and who would implement its recommendations.

At this point you may be a little confused about the role of your instructor, who, after all, will receive and mark both the proposal and the formal report. Pretend that your instructor will read the proposal and then send it to the funding agency (TWF). Similarly, when you hand in your formal report, pretend that your instructor will send it to TWF and to the named audience. On the job, you will probably prepare reports that are first read by your supervisor and then sent on, often over your supervisor's signature, to the designated audience.

RESEARCH PLAN. Remember that reports should be based on verifiable evidence. Study Chapter 15 (Gathering Evidence for Reports) and then decide what sources of information you will use and how you will go about getting the necessary information. What will you measure or count? When? How? Whom will you interview? About what? When? To whom will you write? Make sure that you do not prepare a report summarizing what the audience already knows. In other words, do not interview the sales manager to gather evidence to present in a report to the sales manager. What will you get from library resources? Which ones?

Make a schedule showing the dates by which you expect to complete each step of the research plan.

WRITING SCHEDULE. Prepare a writing schedule you will follow. First work out a task list to include all the subassignments your instructor will set. Then decide how much time each task will require. Finally, consider your commitments to other courses and other assignments and work out a Gantt chart that you believe you can follow. The preparation of Gantt charts is discussed in Chapter 3.

When you write on the job, writing *is* your job, and the subtasks of preparing a document have to be scheduled just like the subtasks of any other project. A realistic schedule not only helps you meet deadlines, but it also shows your supervisor that you are organized and businesslike.

See Figure 16-1 for an example of a report proposal prepared by a student.

PREPARING A FULL FORMAL OUTLINE

Assignment

Prepare a full formal outline for your report. Include not only the headings and subheadings, but also the main points you will make under each heading and the titles of the illustrations you intend to use.

Figure 16-1
A Report Proposal

To: R. B. Buchan   Date: September 16, 19XX
From: Marilyn Chan
Subject: Report Topic

PURPOSE

This report will examine the summer scheduling problems in the plywood department of Great North Forest Industries Limited, Silver Lake Division. The main reason for these problems is that during July and August many of the key operators are on holiday. I will make recommendations to solve these problems economically and efficiently.

SIGNIFICANCE

The use of untrained summer employees to replace the operators who are on holiday leads to decreased production and decreased quality of product. Also, these undertrained employees pose a safety hazard. The report will suggest a plan that would ensure worker safety and also maintain efficiency. These problems have not been investigated in the past.

AUDIENCE

This report will be forwarded to Mr. Scott Brown, the Plywood supervisor in the Silver Lake Division of Great North Forest Industries Limited. He is responsible for the safe and efficient operation of the plant.

RESEARCH PLAN

I will base the report on my experience while employed in the plant during the last two summers. I will interview Mrs. B. Jones, the personnel manager, about the economic implications of hiring more support staff. In addition, I will interview my former supervisor, Mr. Brian Douglas, about the impact my suggestions would have on the efficiency of plywood production.

Research schedule:

- prepare questions to be answered – Sept. 25
- arrange visit to personnel department – Sept. 28
- arrange interview with B. Douglas – Sept. 28
- visit plant – Oct. 5

WRITING SCHEDULE

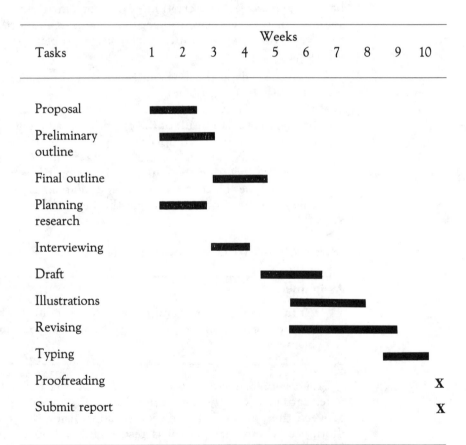

	Weeks									
Tasks	1	2	3	4	5	6	7	8	9	10
Proposal										
Preliminary outline										
Final outline										
Planning research										
Interviewing										
Draft										
Illustrations										
Revising										
Typing										
Proofreading										X
Submit report										X

Figure 1   Writing Schedule

Review Chapter 6 (Organizing and Outlining), particularly the section on the formal outline.

Your first major heading (I) will be the introduction. Include this heading in your outline, but leave the detailed planning of the introduction until you have actually written the body of the report. The second major heading (II) will begin the body. In a 10-page report you will probably need two to four major headings for the body. The following are some frequently used main headings in student reports: equipment, training, procedures, maintenance, staffing. Within each major section you will again expect to need two to four subdivisions. You may decide to organize by type of problem discussed, by physical area, or by stages in a procedure. Consider how the recommendations might be implemented and try to find an arrangement that will best suit the needs of the audience.

Do not separate problems and solutions; if you do, readers will either have to reread each description of a problem when they get to the solution, or they will have to keep turning back and forth in the report to match problems and solutions. For each problem, try to answer the following:

- *What, exactly, is the problem?* Make sure the reader understands in what way it is a problem.
- *What are the consequences of the problem?* What is happening or has happened as a result of the problem? Document accidents, losses of time and money, complaints from the public.
- *What, exactly, do you propose be done about it?* Explain your plan in detail, suggesting the what, who, when, where, how, and why.
- *What will be the consequences of the solution?* Demonstrate how it will solve the problem. Indicate the benefits and costs.

PREPARING PROGRESS REPORTS

Assignment

At the one-third point and the two-thirds point in the preparation of your report, submit a progress report to your instructor. Use memo form.

Progress reports are customary on any project that takes place over time, particularly if there is some distance (physical or organizational) between the person doing the job or supervising the job, and the authority to whom that person is responsible. Although many progress reports are written within organizations, some are written outside to a client, a sponsoring agency, or a government ministry. Progress reports arise from the need for accountability. They report how a project is proceeding, what work has been completed, what problems have arisen, how these problems were solved, what plans have changed, and what work remains. If you view your report proposal as a promise or contract to write a report, the progress reports account for how well you've kept your promise. Usually projects that begin with a proposal also have a series of progress reports and then a completion report. The intervals at which progress reports are required will vary with the length and complexity of the project.

In the progress report you need the following identifying information:

- What is the title of your project? Some projects will also have a contract number.
- Which time period does this report cover?

Very long and complex progress reports can begin with an executive summary that indicates the least that the management would need to know about the progress of the project.

The progress report can be organized either around tasks or around work that is completed. If you organize around tasks, use the list of tasks on which you based your writing schedule in the report proposal. Use these tasks as headings, and under each indicate how complete that task is and what problems, if any, you've encountered and how you've solved them. If you are organizing around work completed, your headings should be "work completed" and "work remaining." Under "work completed," indicate which tasks are complete, using subheadings if necessary, and under "work remaining," list what remains to do.

See Figure 16-2 for an example of a progress report prepared by a student.

PREPARING AN INITIAL DRAFT

Assignment

Prepare an initial draft of the body of your report.

Reread Chapter 7 (Writing the Initial Draft). When you are sure that your outline is satisfactory and your research is complete, start writing the draft. Since the outline gives you the plan of the report, you don't have to begin with the first major section (first-order heading); if you feel more comfortable with another section, begin there. To maintain a smoother flow, try to have enough time to complete a major section in one sitting.

Place *headings* as you will in the final copy. See the typing instructions on page 243.

Begin with an introductory paragraph after the main heading. Introduce the section of your report. Give the main point. Introduce the subheadings. As you write, remember to include *introductions*, *transitions*, and *summaries* to make the report more readable.

Figure 16-2
A Progress Report

TO: Prof. R. Jones   FROM: Jeff C. Brown
     Dept. of English   DATE: November 18, 1990

SUBJECT: Second Progress Report of Formal Report

INTRODUCTION

This progress report describes my progress with the formal report from October 21 to November 18. The purpose of the report was to evaluate the revised dental patient forms used at the UBC Dental Clinic and make recommendations for further improvements.

DISCUSSION

The report tasks are displayed in Figure 1 and are divided into those which are completed, in progress, and remain to be done.

Tasks	October 21 – 31	November 1 – 10	November 11 – 20	November 21 – 25
A Planning Investigation	██████			
Preparing Draft		██████		
B Conducting Investigation	████████████			
Preparing Illustrations		████████		
Revising			████	
C Typing			████	
Proofreading				████
Submit Report				█

A = completed tasks
B = tasks that are in progress
C = tasks remaining to be done

Figure 1   Schedule for the Formal Report Illustrating the Tasks and Their Time Allotment

Completed Tasks

Tasks completed since the first progress report include planning the investigation and preparing the draft. These procedures were carried out according to the schedule illustrated in Figure 1.

Tasks in Progress

Conducting the investigation, preparing the illustrations, and revising the draft comprises the work in progress. I am performing these three tasks simultaneously while compiling questionnaire results.

A slight problem arose during the investigation because the treatment plan and financial portions of the Restorative form had changed since October 1990. This created confusion in the questionnaire, as it was unclear whether the original or modified section of the Restorative form was being referred to. Thus, it was necessary to revise the questionnaire to relate some questions to the changed portion. This revision has alleviated the confusion, but has delayed the investigation by ten days. However, all three tasks in progress will be completed by November 21.

Remaining Tasks

Typing, proofreading, and submitting the report comprise the remaining tasks. I will use a word processor in preparing the final report copy. This will speed the typing process and allow corrections to be made efficiently. The formal report will be completed and submitted by the extended deadline date, November 25, 1990.

Source: Adapted from Jeff Coil, "Second Progress Report of Formal Report." Printed by permission.

Integrate the *graphics* with the text. Remember to introduce each graphic and to discuss it; graphics that are not discussed usually belong in the appendix.

Be *specific* throughout. Answer who, what, when, where, how, and why. Don't leave questions in the reader's mind.

REVISING

Since the formal report is a long, important document that will be judged on the quality of writing, you must revise it very carefully. Reread Chapter 8 (Revising) and make enough revision passes through the draft to ensure that it is as good as you can make it in the available time.

PREPARING THE PRESENTATION COPY

Assignment

Prepare the presentation copy of your report.

After revision, and after you have prepared and revised the appendices, introduction, and conclusion and recommendations (see Chapter 17), prepare the presentation copy. Reread Chapter 9 (Preparing the Presentation Copy). If you are word processing, you have fewer constraints on how you prepare the presentation copy. If, however, you are using a conventional typewriter, you should follow this order of steps:

1. Prepare the illustrations.
2. Prepare and type the introduction.
3. Type the body.
4. Prepare and type the other supplements (see Chapter 17).
5. Proofread and correct typing errors.
6. Assemble the report and make one photocopy for yourself.

PREPARING ILLUSTRATIONS

Review Chapter 3 (Graphics). Whether or not you have professional help to prepare the illustrations, you are responsible both for planning them and for checking that they are correct. If you are preparing your own illustrations, make sure that you have observed the guidelines in Chapter 3 and that each illustration is neat and clear and that any printing on it is also clear, uniform, and neat.

The illustrations should be prepared first so that you can control the layout of the report. The suggested plan is as follows:

- Prepare the illustrations on the same kind of paper as you will use to type the report.
- Measure each illustration, including photographs and tables, and leave room for it in the appropriate place when you type the presentation copy.
- Attach each illustration to the presentation copy in its designated place.
- Photocopy the presentation copy.

Avoid making illustrations smaller than one third of a page. Remember to leave the same margins on each illustration as you will on a typed page.

TYPING

Use good-quality standard paper (21.5 cm by 28 cm). Type on one side of the paper only, double spaced. If your instructor does not give you other typing and layout instructions, use the following:

- Begin each major heading, including the introduction, 4 cm (1.5 in) from the top of the page.
- Leave a 2.5-cm (1 in) margin at the right of the page and at the bottom, and a 4-cm (1.5 in) margin at the left to accommodate the cover.
- Use all capitals for a main heading (first-order) and centre it on the page.
- Use all capitals for a second-order heading, but type it at the left margin.
- Capitalize only the first letters of a third-order heading, underline it, and type it at the left margin.
- Number the pages of the body of the report in the upper right corner. The introduction is page 1, but its number is centred at the bottom. The conclusion and appendices continue the numbering of the body. The preliminary supplements are numbered (at the bottom centre) as follows:

      Letter of transmittal: no number
      Title page: count as page i, but *don't* type this on the page
      Abstract: ii
      Table of contents: iii
      List of illustrations: iv

AN EXAMPLE OF A STUDENT REPORT

The report that begins on page 244 was prepared by a student. Because of the sensitivity of the issue discussed, she had the instructor's permission to omit the specific numerical results that support her claims. If she were presenting her report to the hospital administration, she would need to include a table showing the frequency of the various types of medication errors.

1256 Bridge Road
Oakville, ON
L6L 2C1

January 26, 1990

Ms. L. Rodman
Department of English
The University of British Columbia
Vancouver, BC
V6T 1W5

Dear Ms. Rodman:

In response to your request for a formal report as the final assignment of English 301, I have prepared the attached report titled
How to Increase the Safety of the Medication System.

This report examines ways to increase the safety of the present
medication administration system at the hospital. It explains the
current system, describes the problems encountered by nurses, and
makes recommendations to reduce or eliminate the problems. I
trust this report will provide the information you require. If I can
be of any further assistance, please call me at 769-9670.

Yours truly,

Brenda Moore

Brenda Moore

Enclosure

HOW TO INCREASE THE SAFETY OF THE MEDICATION SYSTEM

submitted to
L. Rodman
The University of British Columbia
Vancouver, BC

by
Brenda Moore
January 26, 1990

ABSTRACT

This report examines ways to increase the safety of the Medication Administration Record (MAR) system, which the hospital has used for two years. The report is based on a review of the medication incident reports completed since the introduction of MAR, interviews with nurses, and the experience of the author. Although some safety modifications have already been made, more will have to be made to reduce medication errors. The report identifies problems in the processing of physicians' orders, in the dispensing of medications, and in the recording of the administration of medications. The problems in the processing of physicians' orders have led to errors in drug, dose, route, and time of administration. To reduce these errors, physicians should be instructed to write legibly and to use an official list of standard abbreviations and metric measures, the pharmacy clerk should transcribe the orders, and the messenger service between Pharmacy and the wards should be streamlined. Problems in the dispensing of medications have resulted in omissions and duplications of medications. To reduce these errors, drugs should be dispensed at the patient's bedside and every intravenous medication should have a monitor. Problems in the recording of the administration of medications delivered have led to omissions in records and to the incorrect recording of dispensing time. To reduce these errors, the record sheets should be relocated to the patient's bedside and staff should be trained in correct record keeping.

TABLE OF CONTENTS

LIST OF FIGURES

INTRODUCTION

The purpose of this report is to improve the safety of the medication administration system. The hospital adopted the Medication Administration Record (MAR) system two years ago in anticipation of the Pharmacy Department computerizing medication ordering and recording. In the interim a handwritten version of the computer system has been developed and implemented. Unfortunately, because funding for the completion of the pharmacy project has been frozen by the Provincial Government, the manual system must be maintained indefinitely. The MAR system continues to allow medication errors throughout the hospital. This report examines those problems that have been the source of documented errors.

This report is based on a review of medication error reports completed over the past two years, interviews with nurses, and the personal experience of the author working as a registered nurse on a busy ward. The author has used the system from its prototype through to its present form; consequently, she also has the advantage of knowing the evolutionary successes and failures.

This report discusses medication errors which come about due to weaknesses in the MAR. The present mode of operation is explained, each problem with the system is identified, and proposals to reduce or eliminate the problem are recommended. The following areas are discussed: processing physicians' orders, dispensing medications, and recording administration of medications.

1

2

PROCESSING PHYSICIANS' ORDERS

Processing physicians' orders is the first step in the administration of patient medications. The three main areas of concern are difficulty with reading orders accurately, errors in transcribing orders, and delays in procuring ordered medication.

READING WRITTEN ORDERS

The problems associated with reading orders start as the orders are written. Physicians use some terms and abbreviations that make accurate reading difficult. Some physicians substitute unfamiliar or obsolete imperial measures, such as "grains" or "drams," for the more widely understood metric measures. Abbreviations are a problem when physicians devise their own personal short forms. An example of this would be the use of "SubQ" for subcutaneous, instead of the standard "S.C." In this particular situation the meaning can be guessed easily, but that is not always the case. Moreover, guessing the meaning of a patient medication order is undesirable.

The solution to these problems lies in educating the physicians. The Pharmacy Department should compile an official list of metric measures and standard abbreviations to be used at the hospital and circulate it to staff and physicians. In addition, a plasticized copy of this list should be posted in every nursing station for easy reference. A hospital policy stating that only metric measures and only the official abbreviations are acceptable would legitimize complaints to offending physicians.

Another problem with reading physicians' orders is in deciphering the infamously illegible writing of some doctors. This has lead to misunderstandings between what the physician intended for a patient and what the Registered Nurse (R.N.) delivered. To guard

3

against such errors, R.N.'s have developed the time-consuming practice of verbally verifying orders with each physician. To prevent these errors and to save the R.N.'s time, the Hospital Board of Directors should send a letter reminding physicians to write more clearly, or print if necessary. To emphasize the seriousness of the problem, reports of any medication errors which are a result of illegibly written orders should be forwarded to the responsible physician for comment.

TRANSCRIBING PHYSICIANS' ORDERS

When an R.N. transcribes orders from the physicians' order sheet onto the MAR, the main problems are incomplete or incorrect transcription due to interruptions by other demands. The errors which commonly occur include forgetting to circle the time the medication is due, which leads to omissions in medications dispensed; transcribing incorrect doses; and omitting one medication when several are ordered at the same time. This crucial stage in processing orders needs to be performed by a qualified person who is in a position to concentrate on one thing at a time.

As medications cannot be dispensed until the order sheet has been to the Pharmacy Department and the order is filled, the orders could be transcribed by the pharmacy clerk. In the existing system the clerk types an adhesive label, with the patient's name and the full physician's order, for the medication package. The pharmacist triple checks this label when the order is filled. Duplicating this label with a carbon paper and returning it to the ward to be attached to the MAR would eliminate the transcription problem. All that would be required of the R.N. is to check the label against the order, attach it to the MAR, and circle the times the medication is due (Figure 1).

4

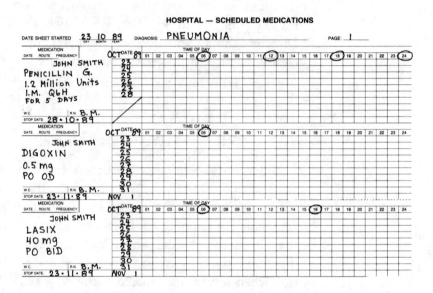

Figure 1   MAR with Adhesive Labels

PROCURING MEDICATIONS

The problem with procuring medications from the Pharmacy Department is that it can take up to three hours between sending the order and receiving the medication. The intra-hospital messenger service picks up all the ward mail and drops it off at a central mailing room where it is sorted for redistribution to the appropriate departments. On average a physician's order sheet spends 80 minutes in the mail room. This of course causes a serious delay in dispensing medications.

The transit time of physicians' order sheets could be reduced significantly if the messenger separated out these easily identifiable,

5

bright yellow-coloured order sheets as the mail is picked up. Then, instead of taking them to the mail room, the messenger could drop them off directly at Pharmacy. In Pharmacy, the filled orders could be placed in separate baskets for each ward. This procedure would eliminate the need to go through the mail room for sorting. The messenger would pick up the medications from each ward basket and place them in the appropriate section of the mail trolley.

6

DISPENSING MEDICATIONS

Dispensing medications includes delivering medications to patients according to the physicians' orders. On average, this takes up one third of an R.N's shift, and must be performed with precision to ensure patient safety. Errors occur in preparing the medication, and in administering the medication.

PREPARING MEDICATIONS

Medications are prepared on the top surface of the medication cart. The cart is usually located in the hall outside the patient's room because this location makes the nurse very visible and allows her to oversee what is happening on the ward. However, it also results in frequent interruptions in her concentration. As a contributing factor in 31 errors in the past six months, this is the main source of medication errors. The errors included pouring the same pill twice or omitting a medication.

As the medication cart is on wheels and easily portable, it could be wheeled into the patient's room and the medication prepared at the bedside. This would reduce the number of interruptions from staff and patients because it would be evident that the R.N. is attending to one patient's needs. The practice of preparing medications at the patient's bedside could be specified in the Guidelines for Using the MAR System issued by the Pharmacy Department.

DELIVERING MEDICATIONS TO THE PATIENT

Medications are generally delivered to the patient with a high degree of accuracy. However, there have been some problems with continuous intravenous medications infusing into the patient too quickly or too slowly. Often on a busy shift these problems go

7

unnoticed for up to an hour. If all continuous medication infusions were attached to an intravenous monitor, runaway infusions could be eliminated, and an alarm would alert the R.N. when the infusion stopped running. At present there are 30 such monitors in the hospital, and the demand for them varies day to day. During periods of high demand, extra monitors can be rented from Baxter, the medical supply company, for $80 a day.

8

RECORDING ADMINISTRATION OF MEDICATIONS

The R.N. records administration of medications on the MAR by placing her or his initials in the box that correlates to the medication and the time (Figure 2). Although this is a very straightforward procedure, problems arise when duplicate recording is required and when medications are given at unscheduled times.

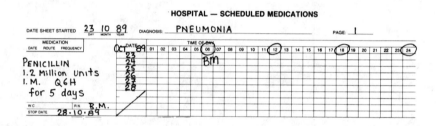

Figure 2   MAR with Penicillin Signed as Dispensed

DUPLICATE RECORDING

Insulin, heparin, and all continuous intravenous medications require an administration record in more than one place. This frequently leads to omissions in recording on the MAR or the second record sheet. The following example illustrates the kind of problems which occur. Prior to giving insulin, the R.N. will check the patient's blood glucose level. She records this measurement on the Diabetic Record Sheet in the patient's chart, along with the amount of insulin she will give. Most commonly the R.N. will forget to go back to the MAR and record it there also. Consequently, according to the MAR, it appears that the patient has not received any insulin.

9

There have been cases in which another R.N. has acted on this incorrect information.

The obvious solution is to have only one form on which to record medications. As revising the MAR would take many months, an interim solution would be to change the location of the second record sheet. Heparin, insulin, and continuous intravenous medication sheets could be kept on the clipboard at the foot of the patient's bed. If the R.N. were preparing and delivering medications at the bedside with the medication chart, the MAR and other records would be conveniently located for immediate use.

INCORRECT RECORDING

Incorrect recording of medication administration has been a big problem in the past, but, fortunately, in-service staff education has decreased the number of errors. The problem which still persists is signing on the MAR in the box indicating the time the medication was due, rather than the box indicating the time it was actually given. For example, an antibiotic due at 1200 hours, but given at 1400 hours because the drug was not available, should be signed for in the 1400 hour box (Figure 3). Judging by the success of earlier staff in-service, a short education session on recording the medication delivery time correctly is likely to resolve this problem.

10

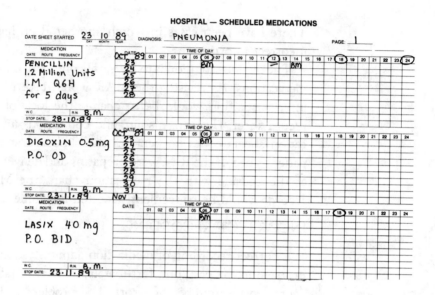

Figure 3 Correct Recording of a Medication (Penicillin) Given at an
Unscheduled Time

11

CONCLUSION AND RECOMMENDATIONS

The MAR system continues to allow medication errors in the following areas:

- the reading of written orders
- the transcribing of written orders
- the delayed delivery of medications
- the preparing of medications on the medication cart
- the delivering of continuous intravenous medications
- the recording of the administration of medications

This report makes the following recommendations:

1. The hospital should adopt a policy of using only an official list of metric measures and standard abbreviations.
2. The Pharmacy Department should prepare an official list of metric measures and standard abbreviations and send this list to staff and physicians. Each nursing station should post a plasticized copy of the list.
3. The Board of Directors should send a letter to physicians to remind them to write more clearly.
4. When illegible orders result in medication errors, the hospital should send the report of the error to the responsible physician for comment.
5. The pharmacy clerk should transcribe physicians' orders to a new adhesive label that has carbon paper. The R.N. should check the label and attach it to the MAR.
6. The messenger should separate the order sheets from other mail and deliver them directly to Pharmacy.
7. The messenger should take filled orders directly from Pharmacy to the wards.
8. The R.N. should prepare the medications at bedside.

9. The hospital should adopt a policy of attaching all continuous medication infusions to intravenous monitors.

10. The hospital should adopt a policy of keeping heparin, insulin, and continuous intravenous medication sheets on the clipboard at the foot of the patient's bed.

11. In-service staff education sessions should stress the need to record the medication delivery time correctly on the MAR.

CHAPTER 17

WRITING FORMAL REPORTS: THE SUPPLEMENTS

Overview

Appendices

Conclusion(s) and Recommendations

Introduction

References

Glossary

Abstract or Executive Summary

Letter of Transmittal

Other Supplements

Notes

Exercises

OVERVIEW

Because most of the supplements are so closely related to what is in the body of the report, you should prepare them after you have written and revised the body of the report. Note that the order in which the supplements appear in the report is different from the order in which you should prepare them.

Order of Preparation	Order in Report
Appendices	Letter of Transmittal
Conclusion(s) and Recommendations	Cover
	Title Page
Introduction	Abstract or Executive Summary
References	Table of Contents
Glossary	List of Illustrations
Abstract or Executive Summary	Introduction
Letter of Transmittal	(Body)
Title Page, Cover, Table of Contents, List of Illustrations	Conclusion(s) and Recommendations
	References
	Glossary
	Appendices

This chapter explains the purpose of each supplement, specifies its content, and describes its form. The supplements are discussed in the order in which you should prepare them. The sample report in Chapter 16 illustrates all of the obligatory supplements. Instructions for the pagination of the supplements are also provided in Chapter 16.

APPENDICES

PURPOSE

An appendix is an optional supplement that can be added to contain "extras" that would interrupt the body of the report or that only some readers would need. Whether or not you need one (or more) depends on the nature of the material in the report, on the audience(s) for which the report is designed, and on the uses to which it will be put.

CONTENT

The kinds of material that could be placed in appendices include the following:

- Complete data or complex calculations that would interrupt the report but that the reader may need in order to verify your conclusions.
- Questionnaires to support the results of a survey.
- Maps and floor plans to orient some readers.
- Supporting documents referred to in the report, such as letters, other reports, booklets, agreements, contracts, rules, and regulations. Including these in an appendix could save the reader time.

During the final revision of a report, look in particular for graphics that should be moved to appendices. If you do not discuss a graphic in the report, then it should probably be moved to an appendix. At the same time, if you can think of no important use that a reader might have for a particular appendix, then simply remove it. While appendices can be very useful, you should not use them compulsively to include all the material you have available.

FORM

Treat each appendix as if it were a main heading in the report. In other words, begin each appendix on a new page with the heading APPENDIX. If you have more than one appendix, begin each one on a separate page and use A, B, C, and so on to distinguish them. Place the appendix item below the heading; if it is a figure or table, number it as though it were the next one in the body. For example, if the last illustration in the body is Figure 7, then the first one in an appendix will be Figure 8. If the appendix item is larger than a page, or if it is itself a document, such as a pamphlet, then use one page to display the heading (APPENDIX A, for example), and attach the actual appendix material to the next page. Because appendices can include such a wide variety of materials, you may have to make some ad hoc decisions about format, or you may have to consult your instructor or supervisor.

Number the appendix pages just as you do those in the body, beginning with the page after the conclusion and recommendations. If a multi-page item, such as a booklet, is attached to a report page, then number only the report page.

Make sure that you have referred to each appendix in the text, because readers need to know that there is an appendix and when they should turn to it. If you find that you need to discuss the substance of the appendix, then consider moving the appendix material back into the text. If you cannot decide whether to have an illustration in an appendix or move it to the body, then consult your instructor.

CONCLUSION(S) AND RECOMMENDATIONS

A report must have a conclusion and may have a list of recommendations.

PURPOSE

If the findings in a report are discussed fully in the body, then the conclusion summarizes the main findings of the report, and the list of recommendations presents the recommendations that have been made and explained in the body of the report. This section does not introduce new material; it is derived completely from what is already in the body of the report. Having this section precludes the need for the readers to prepare their own summary and list of recommendations. As well, the list of recommendations, particularly if it is numbered, allows easy reference when the recommendations are discussed at a meeting, or when the report is referred to in other documents. If the body of the report is concerned primarily with presenting results, then the conclusion may introduce new material in the sense that it presents your interpretation of these results.

Some users of your report will not read the body; they may only check the introduction and conclusion. Also, when writers of subsequent, related reports are preparing their evidence, they may review the conclusions of your report without needing to review its entire text.

CONTENT

The conclusion and recommendations section will normally indicate the following:

- What was the main purpose of the report?
- What were the main methods of investigation?
- What were the most important results?
- What answers to the original question do you propose now that you have completed the investigation?
- What recommendations have you made in the body of the report?

FORM

The conclusion and recommendations section is the last main section of the report before the appendices. It begins on a separate page with the main heading CONCLUSION AND RECOMMENDATIONS. Usually the conclusion of a student report will only be a single paragraph, which is followed by a numbered list of recommendations, introduced by a statement such as, "This report makes the following recommendations."

Recommendations should be phrased as clearly and completely as possible, so that the body of the report does not have to be consulted to determine how to interpret them. The recommendations *must* be grammatically parallel.

INTRODUCTION

PURPOSE

The introduction introduces the body of the report. It is about the report itself, not about the subject of the report. It tells what the report is and what it is not. Your report proposal (see Chapter 16) may help you prepare the introduction.

CONTENT

The introduction will normally include the following:

- *Background and significance in the organizational context.* Why is it necessary to have this report? Usually reports are written because something has changed; equilibrium has been upset. Have profits decreased? Is there labour unrest? Is new equipment needed? Although your immediate audience usually knows why the report was prepared, other readers in the organization may not. As well, if your report is consulted some time in the future, no one may know what particular circumstances prompted its writing. Sometimes the statement of significance will help persuade senior managers that your report's recommendations are important and should be implemented.
- *Background of investigation.* Has this or a similar problem been investigated in the past? Why is it worth investigating again? How does this investigation differ from previous ones?
- *Purpose.* State as precisely and fully as you can the exact purpose of the report. What, exactly, are you investigating? If you prepared a report proposal, you can use a modified version of your statement of purpose here. Use a statement like the following:

  > "This report evaluates the training procedures used in the laundry rooms of the First United Hospital."

  > "This report analyzes the impact increased enrolment will have on registration procedures at Mid-Continental College and recommends changes to overcome anticipated problems."

  Make the verb in the statement of purpose as precise as you can because it indicates your main approach. Are you describing, evaluating, analyzing, or comparing? Saying "This report *is about* X" does not tell the reader what the thrust of the report is. Specify the subject fully. Indicate not only *what* you are examining, but also *when* and *where*, as appropriate.

- *Method.* Since how you gather evidence affects how accurate and reliable your results are, the decision maker who reads your report needs to know what you observed, how, when and where.
- *Scope and limitations.* As well as knowing what to expect in your report, your reader needs to know what *not* to expect. Indicate the kinds of problems, places, times, and personnel that are not

considered and the impact these omissions and constraints may have on your results. You may also want to explain why these limitations have been necessary.

- *Organization.* To forecast the structure of the report, and to define its scope further, you should list the main sections of the report in the order in which they appear.

FORM

The introduction, with the heading INTRODUCTION, is the first main section of the report. The first page of the report is usually numbered at the bottom centre. If the introduction is long, you can use subheadings, but usually they are unnecessary. Most introductions in student reports are about a page and a half long. When you have revised the introduction, you are ready to begin typing the report.

REFERENCES

The references section, which is sometimes also called *bibliography*, or *list of references*, or *works cited*, or *notes*, is part of the documentation of a report. By documentation we mean the formal acknowledgement of the work of others. You are probably familiar with using footnotes and a bibliography as a documentation system in essays. The footnote and bibliography system is generally not used in technical and scientific writing, but the various systems that are used also consist of two components (the in-text citations and a list of sources) and provide the same information (author, title, publisher or volume, year, page). In other words, while you won't be able to use footnotes and a bibliography, the documentation you will use won't be totally unfamiliar either. Of course, if you have not used the work of others in your report, your report won't have a references section.

PURPOSE

Documentation has two related purposes:

- *To provide the "address" of information so a reader who wants to examine the original material can locate it.* Any documentation system must include conventions for specifying author, title, year, and so on.
- *To fulfil the ethical and legal requirement of acknowledging the work of others.* Ideas, words, and illustrations are owned, usually by the people who produced them.

In deciding whether or not you need to document something, you have to determine whether or not you are using material that someone else owns. Many "facts," such as the following, are common knowledge and are not owned by anyone:

- The Point Lepreau generating station is in New Brunswick.
- Iron has the atomic number 26.
- A sphygmomanometer is an instrument for measuring blood pressure.

Often the distinction between common knowledge and information that must be documented is more subtle. For example, you don't need to document the fact that the population of Ontario in 1986 was around 10 million, but you would have to document the more precise figures reported by Statistics Canada.

In general the following material has to be acknowledged:

- *Direct quotations*, either from printed material or from speeches. Whenever you copy, make sure you use quotation marks and indicate your source.
- *Illustrations*. All graphics are owned in the same way as words are owned. Normally you will also need permission to reproduce an illustration.
- *Paraphrases of others' ideas*, whether or not they have been published. In technical writing it is rare to quote directly; instead, others' statements are paraphrased.
- *The results of studies*. The Statistics Canada data for the population of Ontario in 1986 fall into this category.

If you are using the results or conclusions of other reports produced within an organization you are working for, you must also acknowledge these other reports.

CONTENT

The references section must contain the full bibliographic address for each item you have used in your report.

FORM

The references section begins on a separate page with the heading REFERENCES. Beneath this heading are listed all the items you have used in your report. There are many acceptable documentation systems, the main variants being the following:

- the author-year system
- the numbered citations system
- the endnotes system

The main differences among these systems concern the following variables:

- the order in which the references are arranged
- the use of numbering in the list of references
- the format of each item in the list of references
- the content of the in-text citations
- the format of the in-text citations

If your instructor, supervisor, or editor specifies a particular system, then you must follow the conventions of that system meticulously. If you have not been told to use a particular system, then use the standard style guide for your discipline or use a respected document as your model. For academic research papers your model can be a prestigious journal in your discipline. For a report in an organization your model can be a respected report selected by your supervisor. Once you have chosen a system, follow it consistently.

AUTHOR-YEAR SYSTEM. Although there are many variants of the author-year system, the entries in the references section are always listed in alphabetical order by the author's last name, and the list of entries is not numbered. Figures 17-1 and 17-2 illustrate how three of the notes to Chapter 2 would be arranged as entries in the references section in two variants of the author-year system. These three notes illustrate the entries for an article in a journal (Flesch), for a book (Halliday and Hasan), and for an article in an anthology (Selzer). Figure 17-1 is based on the style of *The Canadian Geotechnical Journal*, while Figure 17-2 is based on the style of the *Canadian Journal of Psychology*.

Figure 17-1
Example of a References Page Using the Author-Year System in the Style of The Canadian Geotechnical Journal

REFERENCES

FLESCH, R. 1948. A new readability yardstick. *Journal of Applied Psychology*, **32**: 221–233.

HALLIDAY, M.A.K., and HASAN, R. 1976. Cohesion in English. Longman, London.

SELZER, J. 1983. What constitutes a 'readable' technical style? *In* New essays in technical and scientific communication: research, theory, practice. *Edited by* P.V. Anderson, R.J. Brockmann and C.R. Miller. Baywood, Farmingdale, NY, pp. 71–89.

Figure 17-2
Example of a References Page Using the Author-Year System in the Style of the Canadian Journal of Psychology

REFERENCES

Flesch, R. (1948). A new readability yardstick. *Journal of Applied Psychology*, 32, 221–233.

Halliday, M.A.K., & Hasan, R. (1976). *Cohesion in English*. London: Longman.

Selzer, J. (1983). What constitutes a 'readable' technical style? In P.V. Anderson, R.J. Brockmann & C.R. Miller (Eds.), New essays in technical and scientific communication: research, theory, practice. Farmingdale, N.Y.: Baywood.

In the author-year system, the in-text citations include the last name of the author and the year of publication, as in the following examples:

- Perceptual mechanisms do not automatically deliver up to us a complete rendering of an object or scene. The objects of our immediate perceptual experience inevitably require further analyses and elaboration (Rock & Gutman, 1981; Rock, Halper, & Clayton, 1972).[1]
- The causes of these slides include lateral river erosion, weak bedding surfaces in Upper Crustaceous bedrock near river level, and Saskatchewan sands and gravels in the lower half of the slopes (Thomson 1971; Thomson and Morgenstern 1977).[2]

Note that the raised "1" and "2" in the above examples, and the raised "3" and "4" in the examples below, are part of the documentation of this textbook and *not* of the author-year documentation system being illustrated. If the name of the author is part of the sentence in the text, then only the year is placed in parentheses, as in the following examples:

- Rock and Gutman (1981) and Ullman (1985) have suggested that outer bounding contours have special significance and are analyzed first, and McClelland and Miller (1979) have used outside-in processing to explain certain context effects in perception.[3]
- The geology of the Edmonton area has been documented by Kathol and McPherson (1975), Andriashek and MacMillan (1981), and Catto (1984).[4]

NUMBERED CITATIONS SYSTEM. There are also many variants of the numbered citations system, but in all of them the entries in the references section are listed in the order in which they are first cited and the list of entries is numbered. Figures 17-3 and 17-4 illustrate how three of the notes to Chapter 2 would be arranged in two variants of the numbered citations system. Figure 17-3 is based on the style of *Canadian Metallurgical Quarterly* and Figure 17-4 is based on the style of *The Canadian Journal of Surgery*.

Figure 17-3
Example of a
References Page
Using the Numbered
Citations System in
the Style of Canadian
Metallurgical
Quarterly

REFERENCES

1. R. Flesch, A new readability yardstick. *Journal of Applied Psychology,* **32,** 221–233 (1948).
2. M.A.K. Halliday and R. Hasan, *Cohesion in English,* Longman, London (1976).
3. J. Selzer, What constitutes a 'readable' technical style? in *New Essays in Technical and Scientific Communication: Research, Theory, Practice,* (edited by P.V. Anderson, R.J. Brockmann and C.R. Miller), 71–89, Baywood, Farmingdale, N.Y. (1983).

Figure 17-4
Example of a
References Page
Using the Numbered
Citations System in
the Style of The
Canadian Journal of
Surgery

REFERENCES

1. FLESCH, R: A new readability yardstick. *Journal of Applied Psychology* 1948; 32: 221–233
2. HALLIDAY, MAK, HASAN R: *Cohesion in English*, Longman, London, 1976
3. SELZER, J: What constitutes a 'readable' technical style? In ANDERSON PV, BROCKMANN RJ and MILLER CR (eds): *New Essays in Technical and Scientific Communication: Research, Theory, Practice*, Baywood, Farmingdale, 1983: 71–89

In the numbered citations system, the in-text citations need only consist of the number corresponding to the entry in the references list, as in the following examples:

- There have also been a number of studies of the antimony partition coefficient between soda and copper by groups at Helsinki [7-9], Sendai [10] and Nagoya [11, 12].[5]
- Between 1970 and 1979, CS rates in Canada more than doubled, from 6.0 to 13.9 per 100 live births.[15] Recent data for Ontario[16] show a further increase from 16.5 per 100 live births in 1979 to 19.9 in 1984, with increases reported in both teaching and community hospitals.[1,17,18] [6]

The citation numbers can be placed in parentheses or in brackets, as in the first example above, or they can be raised, as in the second example. Again, the raised "5", "6" and "7" in the examples in this section are part of the documentation of this textbook and *not* of the numbered citation system. The name of the author is only included as part of the text, as in the following example:

Kojo [8] used atmospheric pressures of carbon dioxide to fix the sodium oxide activity.[7]

ENDNOTES SYSTEM. The endnotes system is the one used in this text.

GLOSSARY

PURPOSE

If the technical expertise of the audience varies a great deal, a glossary may be included to help the less expert readers understand technical terms. If the audience is fairly uniform, a glossary should not be needed because technical terms that the audience does not already know will be defined within the document. However, if the report is so long that a reader may forget the definitions that are provided within the document, then a glossary may also be used.

CONTENT

The glossary is a list of technical terms used in the report, together with their definitions. The definitions should be designed to suit the audience. If you need to prepare a glossary, review Chapter 10 (Defining).

FORM

The glossary begins on a separate page with the heading GLOSSARY. The technical terms with their definitions are listed in alphabetical order. The details of layout are not bound by conventions. See Figure 17-5 for an example of a glossary. A glossary is an optional supplement. It can be placed either immediately before any appendices or at the beginning of the report before the introduction.

ABSTRACT OR EXECUTIVE SUMMARY

The abstract or executive summary is a bit more problematic because authorities disagree on what this supplement should be called, what it should include, and where it should be placed. What is described here is one acceptable approach. Normally you will need either an abstract or an executive summary, and for convenience we will describe both here. See also Chapter 13 for a discussion of abstracts of articles and for guidelines on summarizing.

PURPOSE

An abstract is most likely to be used with a more technical, scientific, research, or academic report. It is a self-contained document designed

Figure 17-5
Example of a
Glossary

GLOSSARY

beeper	• the auditory component of an alarm signal
cursor	• a pinpointing tool
electronic map	• a map displayed on the screen
key chart	• a visual representation of a keystroke sequence required to perform some operation
menu tree	• a diagram showing the hierarchy of a set of software commands
window	• a square on the screen in which data such as an electronic map appear

to be filed or collected separately for reference. It can be used in the following ways:

- *To decide whether to read the report at all.* Abstracts may be circulated to many potential readers, only some of whom will read the entire report.
- *To substitute for the report.* A reader who is only interested in your methods and results may not need to read the entire report.
- *To prepare for reading the report.* A reader can get a preview of the entire report from the abstract.

An executive summary, on the other hand, is more common in reports that have a greater business or administrative orientation. Normally, the executive summary is designed for management and presents a condensed version of the report; it concentrates on the implications of the report. Although management will often read the executive summary instead of the report, it is normally not separated physically from the report.

In many reports, the distinction between abstract and executive summary blurs because of the nature of the subject matter. The abstract in the student report in Chapter 16 could have been called an executive summary.

CONTENT

As the discussion of purpose implies, the content of an abstract may differ from the content of an executive summary.

The *abstract* should normally specify the purpose, scope, method, results, and main recommendations of the report. Normally it will be based on the introduction and on the conclusion and recommendations sections of the report. It will give the most central information, without elaboration or discussion.

The *executive summary* will also include purpose, scope, method, results, and main recommendations, but its focus will be on implications and costs. It may omit the kinds of technical description an abstract would include, and it will generally be more discursive than an abstract.

FORM

An *abstract* is placed on a separate page after the title page. It may begin with an identification section that gives the title, author, and identification number (if any) of the report. The abstract proper is normally a single paragraph. While there is considerable variation in length requirements – from 100 or 200 words, to 10 percent of the length of the document, to 3-5 percent of the document – an abstract is invariably short and will challenge your summarizing skills. You may find the following guidelines useful:

- Do not paragraph.
- Do not use subheadings.
- Use numerals for numbers, except at the beginning of a sentence.
- Use horizontal lists where appropriate.

An *executive summary* usually precedes the introduction of the report, and is not designed to be separated from the report. Length constraints tend to be less severe, but you should still not exceed 10 percent of the report length. You may paragraph and use subheadings if that will make the summary clearer or more readable.

LETTER OF TRANSMITTAL

The letter or memo of transmittal, usually attached to the cover of the report, "transmits" or delivers the report officially to its recipient. There should be as many letters of transmittal as there are official readers of a report.

PURPOSE

The letter of transmittal makes the delivery of the report official; it documents the submission. It also identifies the report and what the recipient is to do with it. It is not unusual for senior managers to receive several reports daily, and the letter of transmittal is their first orientation to the report.

CONTENT

The subject of the letter is the accompanying report. The letter should include the following:

- The title of the report.
- An official statement of submission. (Note that the date of the letter confirms when the report was submitted.)
- A brief explanation of why it was written. Who assigned it? When? Why? How?
- A one- to three-sentence synopsis of what the report does, a kind of summary of the abstract.
- A brief note on any particular features or sections of the report that may be of special interest to the recipient.
- An indication of what the recipient is to do with the report, particularly if the report is not directed primarily to him or her. In other words, is the recipient expected to read the report? Is the recipient expected to respond in some way to it, or to simply be aware of it and keep it on file?

FORM

The letter of transmittal, as its name implies, is a letter. Note, however, that many organizations prefer to use a memo of transmittal.

OTHER SUPPLEMENTS

The other supplements serve the same functions as those found in a book.

COVER

A cover serves to make a presentation package for a formal report and its label identifies the report by title, author, date, and perhaps number.

TITLE PAGE

The title page also helps the report look more formal and important and provides the following identifying information:

- the title of the report
- the recipient of the report
- the author of the report
- the date

TABLE OF CONTENTS

The table of contents lists the headings and subheadings in the report and the page on which each is found. The pattern of headings indicates the report's organization, and the page listings help readers locate information. As with most of the parts of the report, there are various format guidelines that can be followed. For this course, use the following:

- Begin the table of contents on a separate page following the abstract. Normally it will be numbered iii at the bottom centre.
- Centre the heading TABLE OF CONTENTS.
- Do not list the title page or the table of contents.
- List the abstract or executive summary, the list of figures, and any other front matter.
- Begin each main heading of the report at the left margin and use all capitals.
- Begin each second-order heading indented three spaces and capitalize first letters only.
- Begin each third-order heading indented another three spaces and capitalize first letters only.
- Double-space, unless you have so many headings that they won't all fit on one page.
- At the right margin opposite each heading, put the number of the page on which the heading is found in the report.

LIST OF ILLUSTRATIONS

The list of illustrations indicates what graphics there are in the report and where they are located. Follow these guidelines:

- Begin the list of illustrations on a separate page, even if you have only one illustration to list. Number the page at the bottom centre.
- List the tables and figures separately. If you have both, then use the centred heading LIST OF ILLUSTRATIONS as a main heading. If you have only tables or figures, you can use the heading LIST OF TABLES or LIST OF FIGURES.

- If you have both tables and figures, then type the heading TABLES at the left margin below the centred heading, and below this list the table numbers and captions as they appear in the report. At the right margin on the same line as TABLES, type the heading Page and below this list the page on which each of the tables appears. Next type the heading FIGURES a few spaces below the end of your list of tables, and below this list all the figures in the report.

NOTES

1. Bruce Earhard, "The Generality of Outside-In Processing Routines in the Analysis of Form," *Canadian Journal of Psychology* 44.1 (1990): 14.
2. D.M. Cruden, K.H. Tedder, and S. Thomson, "Setbacks from the Crests of Slopes along the North Saskatchewan River, Alberta," *The Canadian Geotechnical Journal* 26 (1989): 67.
3. Earhard, 15.
4. Cruden, Tedder, and Thomson, 65.
5. M.A. Kozlowski and G.A. Irons, "The Kinetics of Antimony Removal from Copper by Soda Injection," *Canadian Metallurgical Quarterly* 29.1 (1990): 52.
6. J.M. Barnsley et al., "Cesarean Section in Ontario: Practice Patterns and Responses to Hypothetical Cases," *The Canadian Journal of Surgery* 33.2 (1990): 128.
7. Kozlowski and Irons, 52.

EXERCISES

1. Consider the following pair of recommendations, which are grammatically parallel:

   a. The manager should review the duties of the accountant.

   b. The accountant should prepare a list of accounts that are more than three months overdue.

   Below are three versions of recommendation a. For each of these versions supply the grammatically parallel version of recommendation b.

   i. Review the duties of the accountant.

   ii. That the duties of the accountant should be reviewed.

   iii. The duties of the accountant should be reviewed by the manager.

2. Write an abstract of no more than 150 words for a report with the following introduction and recommendations sections:

INTRODUCTION

The exploration program carried out by the Big Rock Exploration company between May and August consisted of initial exploration, with some secondary follow-up. The purpose was to obtain as many geochemical samples as possible, but this purpose was not fulfilled, because the budget was exhausted before the program was finished. This was due to the high cost and inefficient use of equipment, poor planning, and use of time-consuming procedures. This report investigates these problems and suggests solutions that may eliminate similar problems in future programs.

This report is based on my personal experience as an assistant geologist with the company in the summer of 1988, and on commercial estimates. It is supplemented by interviews with two of the geologists Bill Chu and John Browning. Because this report is based on my personal experience, I have limited its scope to only those problems with which I was directly involved; I have excluded the problems with helicopter time management and working from hotels. I was unable to obtain an interview with Mr. George Johnson, project geologist. Furthermore, the government reports put out by the company on previous programs did not contain enough information on expenses to be of use.

The topics investigated in this report are equipment and fieldwork planning.

CONCLUSIONS AND RECOMMENDATIONS

The report makes the following recommendations to solve the cost and efficiency problems with equipment and field planning:

1. A maintenance schedule for the generator should be set up.
2. An improved fuel tank for the generator should be set up.
3. Two pickups should be rented.
4. The trucks should each be equipped with a chainsaw and winch.
5. A second U-Haul trailer should be rented.
6. Helicopter-assisted camps should be accessible by a tractor trailer.
7. Truck road trips should be implemented.

Source: Richard Haslinger, "Introduction" and "Conclusions and Recommendations." Printed by permission.

PART FIVE

BUSINESS CORRESPONDENCE

CHAPTER 18

MEMORANDA

Introduction

Memo Format

Purposes

Reader-Writer Relationship

Exercises

INTRODUCTION

The term *memorandum* is derived from the phrase "to be remembered" that was once placed on documents. In modern use, it refers both to the physical form on which a memorandum (or memo) is written and to the type of communication. Generally, a memo is used for communication *within* an organization and a letter for communication *outside* the organization. However, if two organizations are working closely on the same project, they might use memos to communicate with each other, and there are some types of messages, particularly private ones, such as congratulations or special statements of gratitude, for which a letter would be used within an organization.

This chapter is a brief introduction to the writing of memos. It begins by describing memo format and by outlining and illustrating some of the common purposes for which memos are written. Then it discusses the following three interacting aspects of the reader-writer relationship: the relative status of the reader and the writer in the organization, the you-attitude, and tone.

MEMO FORMAT

Most organizations use printed memorandum forms on which memos are to be typed or written. Like the form in Figure 18-1, they normally include the following:

- the name of the organization
- an identification block that includes
  - a *To* line
  - a *From* line
  - a *Date* line

  and will usually include a *Subject* line
- space for the message

Part of learning the corporate culture of an organization you work for will be to learn the details of how to fill in and use its memo forms.

THE TO LINE

On the *To* line give the name of the person you are addressing and the rank or position in the organization. Use the same form of name as you would in speaking to that person about that subject in a context of similar formality. Consider, for example, that you are sending a memo to your good friend Joe, with whom you play bridge. If you are sending a fairly

Figure 18-1
A Memo Form

GREAT LAKES ELECTRONICS LTD.

M E M O R A N D U M

TO _____

FROM _____

DATE _____

private or informal message, you will probably address him as Joe, but if it is a more formal message, then you might address him as Joe Black, or Mr. Black, Vice-President of Marketing. The more formal the memo, the more formal the form of address, and the more likely you are to need to indicate the recipient's rank. If a memo is going to several people, list them all on the *To* line.

THE *FROM* LINE

On the *From* line give your own name and rank or position. Use the form of your name that is appropriate to the message and your relationship with the recipient. It is a good idea to initial a typed memo beside your name to indicate you have checked it and approved it. Otherwise, there is the remote possibility that someone could send out a memo under your name without your knowledge.

THE *DATE* LINE

On the *Date* line give the date. Write out the month to avoid the confusion the use of numbers for months sometimes creates. If the time of a message is very important, you could even indicate the precise hour at which you are sending the memo.

THE *SUBJECT* LINE

The *subject* line should give a very precise and concise statement of what the memo is about, such as "New Vacation Regulations," or "Progress Report on the Black Contract," or "Company Golf Tournament." This line serves the following functions:

- It allows the body of the memo to be slightly more concise because it removes the need to introduce the subject.
- It increases readability by preparing the reader for the memo.
- It facilitates filing by clearly identifying the memo's subject.

OTHER FORMAT CONVENTIONS

- Single-space the message and double-space between paragraphs.
- Use headings, lists, and simple graphics as necessary.
- Number your points.
- If the memo is long, use plain paper for all but the first page.

A memo is usually more abrupt than a letter. Whereas a letter will normally begin gently to introduce the subject and end with a summary and some polite leave-taking, a memo will usually not, unless its purpose is largely persuasive or conciliatory. In other words, while on occasion the structure of the message part of a memo could be like that of the body of a letter, typically it is not.

PURPOSES

Since memos are the mainstay of internal communication in organizations, their specific purposes are too numerous to list. Before you write a memo, ask yourself:

- What does this memo have to accomplish?
- What will the reader do with it?

Most of the functions or purposes of memos will fall into one or more of the following categories:

- to provide a record
- to make an announcement
- to request information or assign a task
- to transact business
- to report

PROVIDE A RECORD

Memos provide a paper trail. Since oral communication is seldom recorded, the participants may forget what they said, deny what they said, or misunderstand what they heard. If the same message is in a memo, it can be filed for a permanent record, there is no denying what was said because there is a record, and any misunderstandings can be debated much more objectively. To protect yourself, always retain a copy of each memo you send. If you do *not* want a record of what you say, don't put it in writing. However, if you want to create a record of an oral agreement the other party may renege on, then prepare a memo outlining your understanding of the agreement and send it to the other person for confirmation.

When you write a memo for the record, the most important qualities to bear in mind are clarity and completeness. A memo on file could be referred to a long time after writing, when you may well have forgotten the details yourself, or when you may have left that job. Since a memo prepared for the record might be used in a legal dispute, it should be prepared carefully enough to withstand legal perusal.

Figure 18-2 is a memo confirming an individual's agreement with the payroll department. Figure 18-3 is a memo that provides a record of a meeting at which the computer needs of a municipal parking meter shop were evaluated. This memo confirms what was decided at the meeting and provides the municipal transportation engineer with the needed justification for ordering an SP/4 microcomputer and the necessary furniture, lighting, printer, and software.

Figure 18-2
A Memo that
Provides a Record of
an Agreement

DEPARTMENTAL MEMO

Date: November 10, 1989

To: Dave James, Payroll

From: C.A. Paulson, Member Relations

This is to confirm our conversation of November 3, 1989. During my maternity leave from December 15, 1989, to April 20, 1990, inclusive (18 weeks), my premium for my Group Life Insurance and my Disability Insurance will be accumulated and deducted from the first available pay cheque following my return to work on April 23, 1990.

Figure 18-3
A Memo that
Provides a Record of
a Meeting

MUNICIPALITY OF SILVER RAPIDS

INTER-OFFICE CORRESPONDENCE

May 9, 1990   File No. J653-1

MEMO FOR RECORD

TO: Municipal Transportation Engineer

FROM: A. Marshall, Systems Research

COPY TO: Parking Meter Shop Foreman

SUBJECT: <u>PARKING METER SHOP COMPUTER NEEDS</u>

On May 7, 1990, I met with M. Johnson, J. H. Wong, and W. Burgermeister to discuss the Parking Meter Shop's computer needs and system requirements. We recommend the purchase of an SP/4 microcomputer to do the following:

1. To transfer data from the traffic counters to the mainframe computer. This will replace the manual coding of forms by the staff in Transportation and the key punching by Computer Services.
2. To keep the inventory of parking meters and parking meter parts. This will eliminate the manual system that is used at present.

We chose the SP/4 because it is compatible with our other computers. The cost of the microcomputer and the necessary furniture, lighting, pointer, and software is around $12 500.

MAKE AN ANNOUNCEMENT

Most announcements in an organization will either be made directly in a memo or will be made orally and then confirmed in a memo. Any announcement has to be clear, of course, but in addition, it must reflect sensitivity to how it will be received. Consider the impact the message will have. To preserve good personal relations, use the linguistic and rhetorical resources discussed under "Reader-Writer Relationship" below.

Figure 18-4 is a routine memo announcing an increase in extended health plan premiums. The opening sentence provides some background for the announcement. The rest of the memo provides the necessary details. Figure 18-5 is a memo to an individual to announce a salary increase. A salary increase is good news, but the recipient of this memo was offended. Would you be offended? This example is included here to show you how important tone can be even in conveying good news.

REQUEST INFORMATION OR ASSIGN A TASK

Memos are often used to document requests for action. From the writer's point of view, the memo is useful because it provides a dated record of the request; from the recipient's point of view, it is important because it documents exactly what he or she is to do. Note that even though the recipients may be obliged to comply with your request or order, the tone of the memo may determine how enthusiastically and well they do so. Figure 18-6 is an example of a memo that reminds supervisors of procedures their staff must follow.

Figure 18-4
A Memo
Announcing a
Premium Increase

MEMORANDUM

TO: All employees   Date: March 14, 1990

FROM: Thérèse Rivard
            Assistant Director, Benefits

SUBJECT: Extended Health Premium Increase

After three decreases in premium rates in recent years, we have experienced an extraordinary increase in Extended Health Plan claims in 1989 and must suffer a premium increase. The rates will be increased effective May 1, 1990, by 15 percent. The employee's share of the monthly premium will increase from $3.40 to $3.91 for an employee with no dependents, and from $9.68 to $11.13 for an employee with dependents.

Figure 18-5
A Memo
Announcing a Salary
Increase

MEMORANDUM

TO: Sebastian Tello   DATE: August 15, 1989

FROM: Allan Clark

RE: SALARY INCREASE

A commitment was made to you at the time of hire that pending successful completion of your probationary period, a salary increase would be considered. Please be advised that your performance to date has been excellent and therefore your salary will be increased to Pay Grade 17 effective September 1, 1989. The Collective Agreement does not provide for a six-month increment. However, since this promise was made to you at the time of hiring, this increment will be processed as an exception.

Figure 18-6
A Memo Requesting
a Change in
Procedure

BRANCH MEMORANDUM

TO: A. Zirnajs, G. Epp, E. Rupaal DATE: October 20, 1989

FROM: K. Howlett (Local 314)

RE: PERSONNEL PROCEDURES ON FARM VISITS

Please remind your field staff that to prevent the transmission of bovine diseases from farm to farm, all field staff must adhere to the following procedures:

1. At the beginning and at the end of a farm visit wash their hands with surgical soap.
2. Wash and disinfect their boots with Bactisol Spray.
3. Carry extra coveralls so they can remove soiled ones.
4. Carry disposable gloves and boots and use them as needed.

Please call me if you require further clarification.

TRANSACT BUSINESS

Many memos are written simply to conduct the day-to-day business of the organization, including routine data exchange, requests for approval of funds or actions, explanations of actions, exchange of news within the organization, notification about problems. Figure 18-7 illustrates a response to a routine request for information.

Figure 18-7
A Memo Providing
Routine Information

M E M O

TO: W. H. Hebert   DATE: June 3, 1989

FROM: G. Rusko

Steve Nixon asked me to recommend to you some freelance writers and photographers with whose work we have been satisfied. I can recommend two writers and one photographer.

Freelance Writers
1. Pam Adachi   821-4615
2. Garth Malkin   262-9346

Freelance Photographer

Leslie Kowalchuck   337-0921
Ms. Kowalchuck is a bit overbooked, but her work is the best we've seen in years.

I wish you success with your project. Please let me know how these people work out.

REPORT

Memo reports are at the core of professional writing. For a discussion of reports, see Chapters 14 and 15. Note that in reports the tone will usually be much more neutral than in announcements and requests. Figure 18-8 is an information report on hydrogen as a fuel.

Figure 18-8
An Information
Report in Memo
Form

MEMORANDUM

TO: S. J. Levy   Date: August 4, 1986

FROM: Project Analyst (GFD)   File: 86-053-19

SUBJECT: Hydrogen as a Fuel

1. <u>Sources of Hydrogen</u>

   Hydrogen is derived almost exclusively from carbonaceous materials, primarily hydrocarbons, and water. These materials are decomposed by the application of electrical, chemical or thermal energy. Hydrogen is also produced by the partial oxidation of hydrocarbons and by such less important methods as the steam-iron process, water-gas process and separation from coke oven and refinery off-gas streams.

2. <u>Economics of Hydrogen Procedure</u>

   Hydrogen is uneconomic compared to other energy sources. The most inexpensive method of hydrogen production is steam reforming of natural gas ($4.00/MMBTU). The new direct hydrolysis of water process is the most promising of the electrolytic processes at half the cost of conventional electrolysis ($8.00 vs. $13.00). Electrolysis of water using nuclear produced electricity is one of the most expensive processes for hydrogen production ($24.00-$26.00). However, by using both the heat and electricity produced by high temperature reactors, production costs can be reduced by approximately half to $12.00-$13.00. Steam hydrocarbon reforming which produces CO_2 as a by-product may show improved economics if CO_2 demand for oil-well servicing continues strong. While hydrogen has the advantages of burning clean, being lightweight and being transportable by pipeline, it has the disadvantages of being explosive, having low energy content, and requiring heavy storage tanks.

READER-WRITER RELATIONSHIP

As was suggested in the previous section, memos differ in the degree to which they really are communications between individuals. Many memos are communications between you and the organization, and the identity and personality of the recipient are quite unimportant. For example, the official recipient of a monthly report on the progress of your research project is probably not personally concerned with its content. In most memos, though, you are communicating with an individual, and to do so effectively, you will have to pay particular attention to your relative status in the organization, to the you-attitude, and to tone. As you will see, these three concerns intersect.

RELATIVE STATUS

Every organization has an organizational hierarchy of roles; when individuals interact, they also interact in their roles. Status is marked in a variety of ways, including details of dress, type of desk and other office equipment, location of desk, and how the individual is addressed. Learning these status markers is part of learning the corporate culture. Status is also marked, usually in even more subtle ways, in how you may speak and write to others in the organization. Since most of this writing will be in the form of memos, it is in writing these that you should be most concerned about status. The main considerations are the rank of your recipient and who is accountable to whom. Are you writing up, down, or laterally? Before writing the memo, consider the following:

- Do you have to persuade the reader, or is the reader obliged to comply with your request?
- Are you obliged to inform the reader, or are you doing the reader a favour? Are you allowed to criticize the reader or not?
- Do you owe the reader an explanation or not?

Be aware that relative status relates to the kinds of verbal actions you can perform. For example, while it is appropriate to praise or thank a subordinate for a job well done, it would be presumptuous in most situations to praise a superior. Similarly, while you would ask for a supervisor's permission or approval, you would not ask this of a subordinate.

YOU-ATTITUDE

Often the same situation looks different from different perspectives. Emphasizing the writer's perspective is known as using the *me*-attitude, and emphasizing the reader's perspective is known as using the *you*-attitude. For example, let us say you must sell your furniture before the end of term so you can take a summer job. You, of course, are concerned with selling the furniture quickly. If you tell a potential buyer that he should buy it because you desperately need to get rid of it, you are using the *me*-attitude, whereas if you focus on the furniture being available to the buyer right away, you are using the *you*-attitude. The pairs of examples below should give you a better sense of the differences between the *me*-attitude and the *you*-attitude.

- *me*: I'm really desperate. I have an important meeting Thursday and my regular babysitter has the flu. Could you babysit for me?

  you: Would you like to earn a little extra money this week? I can offer you a babysitting job this Thursday afternoon, and since the time is probably a little inconvenient for you, I'm prepared to pay you 30 percent more than usual.

- *me*: Congratulations. I'm so happy one of my students won the prize.

  you: Congratulations. You certainly deserved to win the prize. You and your family must be very proud. I'm sure this will lead to many fine opportunities for you.

- *me*: I sold the store at an even greater profit than I had hoped for. This means, of course, that you will be out of work by March 1.

  you: You are no doubt concerned about your future now that I have finally found a buyer for the store. Unfortunately, the new owner will not be able to offer work to current employees and therefore your contracts will have to end on March 1.

To achieve a *you*-attitude in writing, you must first learn to view situations from the perspective of other individuals and from the perspective of your department and company. What are your reader's concerns and how does this particular situation relate to them? Try to appeal to or acknowledge these concerns when you write about the situation. Which aspects of the message are "good news" from your reader's point of view and which "bad news"? Emphasize the good news and try not to dwell on the bad news. At the same time, avoid giving the impression you are not aware of the bad news. Achieving a *you*-attitude depends as much on your "people skills" as on your language skills.

TONE

Tone refers to the "personality" that a communication conveys. The most obvious variable in tone is formality, which, of course, forms a continuum from the most informal and casual tone you use with your friends, to the most formal and stuffy tone you might use in legal statements. How formal a tone you assume in a memo will be dictated both by the relative status of you and your reader and by how "official" the document is. If you are simply sending along some useful information to your friend in the marketing department, you could be very casual and say something like "Here's the stuff I told you about." In more "official" documents, this tone would offend the recipient. Inappropriate informality can be perceived as sloppiness, insolence, immaturity, or even incompetence; inappropriate or excessive formality, on the other hand, can be perceived as pomposity, coldness, unfriendliness, stuffiness, or impersonality.

We do not understand very precisely how tone is achieved, but the formality of a document is, in part, the result of the formality of some individual words. Generally, in English if there are several near-synonyms, those of Anglo-Saxon origin are perceived as being less formal than those of Latin origin. Consider, for example, the following pairs: be sorry, regret; ask, request; find, discover; hide, conceal.

In addition to the informality-formality continuum, we can consider tone from the point of view of most of the adjectives we would apply to people's personalities or states of mind, including "friendly," "cooperative," "concerned," "abrasive," "angry," "threatening," "groveling," "humble," "mean," "insulting," and so on. In most cases, tone is created by what is mentioned and by what isn't mentioned, by the words used, and by the order of information. Remember that tone works on readers' emotions and produces emotional reactions, whether or not the writer intends to produce these reactions, and whether or not the readers can identify what they are reacting to.

EXERCISES

1. The following passages differ in the degree to which they express a *you*-attitude. Rank the passages from 1 (for the most *you*-attitude) to 5 (for the least *you*-attitude). Based on these examples, try to formulate some principles on how to achieve the *you*-attitude.

    a. We have decided to cover the parking lot this fall. To offset the cost of construction, we are increasing your monthly rental from $10 to $15.

    b. In order to offset the construction costs to cover the parking lot, we are increasing your monthly rental from $10 to $15. We regret any inconvenience this may cause, but believe you will benefit greatly from these improvements.

    c. We are covering the parking lot this fall so that your car will be protected against the seasonal elements. We regret that in order to offset the cost of construction, the monthly rental will be increased from $10 to $15.

    d. For your convenience we have decided to cover the parking lot this fall. To finance this improvement we are increasing your monthly rental by $5.

    e. Your parking area is due to be upgraded by the installation of a roof. To make this possible it will be necessary to increase your monthly rental from $10 to $15.

2. Rewrite the following passages so that they display more of a you-attitude.

    a. Our new model of calculator won't be ready for another month. Our research department took longer than expected to perfect the special 3000-hour battery and a brighter read-out panel.

     b. I have just finished another year of university and need a summer job. I would prefer work in your computer department because I would like to try out some of the programming techniques I learned this year.

     c. The library will open an hour later in the morning and close an hour earlier in the evening to reduce the amount of overtime we have to pay.

3. Your instructor in another course has agreed to an extension on an assignment. Write a memo to this instructor confirming the agreement. Supply the needed details. Use the *you*-attitude.

4. As the secretary of the campus Windsurfers' Club, write a memo to the members to announce a picnic and special race to spend a surplus in the club's budget. You may invent details. Use the *you*-attitude.

5. As the treasurer of the Young Politicians' Club, write a memo to the executive explaining that you missed the deadline for the deposit on the hall you had booked for the annual dance. Use the *you*-attitude.

6. As the president of the campus Young Politicians' Club, write a memo to the members to announce that there will be no annual dance because the treasurer missed the deadline for the deposit on the hall. You may invent details. Use the *you*-attitude.

7. Write a memo to a co-worker or a former co-worker requesting information for your formal report in this course. Ask at least three questions. Be very specific. Use the *you*-attitude.

8. Write a memo to your department head or dean to suggest a change in either your course schedule, your exam schedule, or the registration procedure.

9. Pretend that two of your classmates have been assigned to help you revise your formal report. Write memos to accomplish the following:

     a. Arrange a meeting to give them copies of your report.

     b. Define what it is you want each helper to do for you.

     c. Arrange a meeting to get your report back.

10. Pretend that you are a shift supervisor at your present place of work. Write a memo to the members of that shift asking them to keep the lunch room tidier. Be specific about what they are to do. Use the *you*-attitude. If you don't have a job, adapt this assignment to a request to the users of some specific campus area (locker room, library, cafeteria, art studio, lounge) that could be made tidier.

LETTERS

INTRODUCTION

A business letter differs from a personal letter in purpose, in form, and in the roles of writer and reader. A business letter is used to transact business between two legal entities *as* legal entities and is usually restricted to communication with a recipient outside the organization. If you write or receive a business letter at work, you are doing so in the role or position for which you are being paid, and not as an individual, even if you know the other person very well. As was explained in Chapter 18, memos are used for communication within a company. The form of the business letter is discussed in Chapter 20.

This chapter notes some of the more common purposes of letters, the legal status of letters, and the relationships between readers and writers of letters. It then examines in somewhat more detail the following four common types of business letters:

- letter of inquiry
- reply to an inquiry
- letter of complaint (claim letter)
- reply to a letter of complaint (letter of adjustment)

Business letters are an important kind of communication, both in terms of time spent writing and reading them, and in terms of their importance in maintaining good will and in transacting business. The amount of time you spend writing and reading business letters will vary with the kind of work you do, but all studies conclude that professionals at all ranks write letters, and that their ability to write good letters is likely to be a prerequisite to advancement.

You may well wonder why letters are still used to transact business when we have telephones. The main difference between a telephone call and a letter is that a letter provides a permanent record for both the writer and the recipient.

PURPOSE

Some of the specific purposes for which business letters may be written include the following:

- to get information (inquiry)
- to answer a request for information
- to refuse a request for information or action
- to make a claim for compensation

- to answer a claim for compensation (adjustment)
- to collect a debt
- to sell
- to apologize
- to place an order
- to confirm an agreement

In practice, many business letters have several purposes.

LEGAL STATUS

A business letter is a legal document that could be used as evidence in court. In writing business letters, then, you have to recognize the legal status of the document you prepare. No matter who signs a letter, if it is written on company letterhead, it becomes a letter from that company, and not from an individual. Also, the person signing the letter does so as a representative of the company, not as a private individual. For this reason you will probably not be allowed to sign letters for some time after you begin your professional career, even though you will probably have to compose many that will be signed by your supervisor. Your supervisor will be responsible for the letter, but you will be expected to write it so that it does not have to be revised before it can be signed.

You will have to learn to use language very carefully so you don't imply what you don't mean, or promise what you cannot (or do not want to) fulfil, or make an accusation you cannot support, or represent a situation inaccurately. Probably the best way to learn to conduct yourself appropriately in letters is to learn from your co-workers and supervisors. Study their letters, use them as models, and ask questions about the reasons for particular phrasing.

READER-WRITER RELATIONSHIPS

Often you will be writing to people you have not met and may never meet. The main difficulty in assessing and even in understanding the reader-writer relationship derives from the fact that your readers are acting in their role in the business transaction and yet are also reacting as people with emotions and tastes and likes. For this reason, you have to focus both on the specific *what* of what you say, and on the *how*. Often the *how* will determine your reader's reaction to your message and hence the success or failure of the transaction. As well, the *how* can affect the image you create of yourself and your employer. Since images are made slowly and destroyed quickly, it is very important to avoid blunders to which readers will react negatively. Review the discussion of *you*-attitude and tone in Chapter 18.

LETTER OF INQUIRY

The purpose of a letter of inquiry is to get information, such as statistics for a report or research project, product information to allow you to decide what kind of equipment to order, the dates of a conference, advice on how to solve a consumer problem, and so on. How carefully you have to prepare a letter of inquiry will depend on the complexity and sensitivity of the information you need and on the extent to which you are asking a favour. Your main concerns should be persuasiveness, completeness, and clarity.

PERSUASIVENESS

You must persuade your readers to co-operate and to provide you with the information you need by the time you need it. Even if your readers are obliged by the nature of their jobs to help you, you must still persuade them to do this as well and as efficiently as possible. If your readers are not obliged to send you anything, then your task is even more challenging. Remember that your readers will have to take time away from other tasks to attend to your needs. In your letters you should, therefore, convince them it is worth helping you, and you should acknowledge that you know they are doing you a favour. Consider what kinds of appeals you could use. Use the *you*-attitude to analyze the situation from the reader's point of view. What advantages could there be to the reader in helping you? Is there any potential profit? Is there publicity and good will? Is there information you could give in return? Your persuasiveness will determine, in part, whether or not, and to what extent, your reader co-operates.

COMPLETENESS AND CLARITY

How completely and clearly you state what you need determines how completely and clearly the reader can answer your request. In the letter you should answer the following questions:

- *What, exactly, do you want to know?* Never ask for "everything" or "anything" or "all the information you have." Not only are such requests difficult to answer, but they may suggest you are lazy or ignorant. Ask specific questions. If there are several questions, they will be easier to answer if you list and number them.
- *Who are you?* In what capacity are you asking for the information? How much authority do you have? Indicate your affiliation if it is not obvious from the letterhead.
- *Why do you need the information?* The reader may need to know what you plan to do with the information. Is it worth the reader's time to give you the information? Will the reader be acknowledged? Is there danger of your misusing the information? To whom will you give it? Sometimes the importance of what the information is to be used for can persuade an otherwise reluctant respondent to help you. If the information you are asking for is sensitive, then you may have to assure some confidentiality or anonymity.

- *Why did you choose this organization or person to ask?* Referring to the reputation of the organization or individual can be quite persuasive.
- *When do you need the information?* Don't rush your reader too much, but do give a particular date.

Organize your letter of inquiry into three segments, each of which is likely to be a paragraph:

1. Indicate that you are asking for information. Indicate what it is, generally, that you are asking for. Indicate who you are and why you are asking. Establish a co-operative tone.
2. Ask the specific questions. Elaborate on your background and what the information will be used for.
3. Express your appreciation.

See Figure 19-1 for an example of a letter of inquiry.

REPLY TO AN INQUIRY

Although you may write some letters of inquiry as a private individual, you would normally only answer an inquiry as a member of an organization. Your main purpose in responding to a letter of inquiry, unless the primary function of your employer or division is the dispensing of information, is to preserve or maintain good will and the spirit of co-operation, or to gain a potential customer.

If you cannot answer the inquiry, you are writing a "bad news" message that you must try to present as diplomatically as possible. If you don't have the information, try to direct the writer to someone else who might. If the information is confidential, explain why it is confidential and again try to supply a source that might give related information.

If you can supply the information, then your main concerns will be completeness, accuracy, and clarity. If your answer includes explanation or instructions, review Chapter 12. If you are at all in doubt about whether any particular information should be given out, check with a supervisor.

Again, a three-part organization will probably meet your needs:

1. Thank the writer for the request and indicate your interest in helping him or her.
2. Answer the questions in detail. Use the same order as in the request letter, if possible.
3. Offer more help if the reader has more questions. Wish the reader success.

See Figure 19-2 for an example of a reply to a letter of inquiry.

Figure 19-1
Letter of Inquiry

MUNICIPALITY OF SILVER RAPIDS

100 Front Street, Silver Rapids, Ontario, N7R 1E6

Traffic Department

November 6, 1989

Autopark Electronics Ltd.
P.O. Box 4318
Downsview, ON
M3M 3E5

Dear Sir:

The Traffic Department in the Municipality of Silver Rapids plans to convert its 57 conventional parking meters to ones with electronic displays. Since Autopark Electronics Ltd. is a recognized leader in electronic parking meter systems, I am sure you have products we should consider.

The product we select must have the following characteristics:

1. It must accept the new $1 coin.
2. It must be programmable for different rates and time limits.
3. It must operate in temperatures between 40°C and −40°C.
4. It must require very little maintenance.

To help us in our selection, could you please answer the following questions?

1. Does Autopark Electronics Ltd. have a product we should consider?
2. Can you supply this product in time for us to convert the 57 meters before February 28, 1990?

3. What is the price per unit?
4. What warranties do you offer?

Since I will have to present my recommendations on December 15, 1989, I would appreciate receiving your reply before December 1, 1989. Please call me if you would like any further information about our requirements. I hope that Autopark Electronics Ltd. has the product we are looking for. Thank you for your help.

Sincerely,

MUNICIPALITY OF SILVER RAPIDS

Janet Mahoney

Janet Mahoney
Purchasing Agent
Traffic Department

Figure 19-2
Reply to Letter of
Inquiry

AUTOPARK ELECTRONICS LTD.

P.O. Box 4318
Downsview, Ontario M3M 3E5

November 13, 1989

Janet Mahoney
Purchasing Agent
Traffic Department
Municipality of Silver Rapids
100 Front Street
Silver Rapids, ON
N7R 1E6

Dear Ms. Mahoney:

Thank you for your interest in our electronic parking meter systems. Our EM1027 is just the system for your needs. The Autopark Electronics EM1027 has all the characteristics you require:

1. It accepts the new $1 coin.
2. It can be reprogrammed for rates and time limits on site without any special equipment.
3. It can operate in temperatures between 40°C and −40°C. Our units have been tested in the Northwest Territories and in Arizona.
4. It uses a single lithium battery which operates for three years and its electronic circuits are extremely reliable.

I have enclosed a brochure that outlines the most important technical specifications.

The EM1027 has been so well received that we are in full production and can supply the units at any time with 14 days' notice. Each unit comes with a two-year warranty on parts and labour. The unit price of the EM1027 is $150. We could supply 57 EM1027's for $8550 plus tax.

Thank you for considering the EM1027. I have asked our demonstration team to contact you before December 1. If you require any further information, please call me.

Yours truly,

AUTOPARK ELECTRONICS LTD.

Mary Tomasi

Mary Tomasi
Director of Marketing
Enclosure

LETTER OF COMPLAINT (CLAIM LETTER)

A letter of complaint or claim is written when something has gone wrong. No doubt you have yourself experienced consumer problems that required such a letter. Perhaps you have bought defective merchandise, or a mistake has been made in your account, or you have had poor service. The purpose of the letter, remember, is not to calm your anger, but, rather, to solve the problem. The letter will have succeeded when you receive your refund or replacement merchandise, or your account balance is corrected, or you receive an apology or even compensation for the poor service. In writing the letter of complaint, you have to focus on persuasiveness and on completeness and accuracy.

PERSUASIVENESS

Whether or not you have a legal right to compensation, you are trying to persuade the reader to rectify what you perceive as a wrong. To do so, you will have to see the problem from the point of view of your reader and make the appeal in terms that the reader will respond to. At the same time you will have to make the reader see that you have suffered as a result of the problem.

To persuade the reader, you will have to use the *you*-attitude and manage tone very carefully. A letter of complaint is a "bad news" message. Assume that the company is concerned that its customers be satisfied and that it wants to maintain its reputation and keep you as a customer. Present yourself as rational, credible, and polite, but firm.

COMPLETENESS AND ACCURACY

Help the reader, as much as you can, to help you. To solve the problem, the reader needs to know at least the following:

- *The details of the transaction, so it can be traced.* When, where, and with whom did the transaction take place? Supply a copy of the receipt and give the order number or shipment number. If you are complaining about a product, include the model number and serial number, and note any distinctive features that might help to trace its manufacturing or handling record.
- *The details of the problem, so it can be analyzed.* Explain exactly what the problem is. Be specific. Be precise. The more clearly you describe the problem, the more likely it is that it can be solved. To say that your watch "broke" or "doesn't function properly" does not really tell the reader very much.
- *The details of the consequences to you, so you can be compensated.* Almost every problem has some consequences. Invariably you experience inconvenience and frustration, but for these you can seldom claim compensation. If you also suffer financial losses, though,

you should be able to get some compensation. Other consequences might include loss of reputation or good will because you were unable to satisfy your customers.

- *The details of the solution you propose.* Make it as easy as possible for the reader to help you. What, exactly, do you want? Do you want a refund? Do you want a replacement? Do you want repairs paid for? Do you want compensation? How much?

This time you can use the three-part organization as follows:

1. Announce that you have a problem and indicate its general nature. Use a subject line to identify the transaction and to indicate that this is a complaint. Establish a firm but friendly tone.
2. Give the details of the problem and of any consequences to you.
3. Propose a solution. Close courteously.

Attach copies of all supporting documents, such as receipts. See Figure 19-3 for an example of a letter of complaint.

REPLY TO A LETTER OF COMPLAINT (LETTER OF ADJUSTMENT)

Since letters of adjustment are always written from the context of an organization, you may never have to write one. However, you probably will have to answer some complaints of other kinds to which the basic principles of the letter of adjustment apply.

The letter of adjustment is written after a complaint has been received. Its primary purpose is to deal with the complaint by granting the request for an adjustment, by refusing it, or by granting it in part. Whether or not you grant the request will depend, of course, on the circumstances of the problem, and will normally be covered by company guidelines and policy on such matters. As well as having to deal with solving the problem, you also have to restore the customer's confidence in your company and perhaps convince the customer that the settlement is equitable. Again you will have to be concerned with persuasiveness and completeness.

PERSUASIVENESS

Remember that the reader – the person who lodged the complaint you are now dealing with – feels injured and so is not well disposed toward your company. Your job is to restore a sense of trust and good will. To do this you will have to use the *you*-attitude and control your tone so

Figure 19-3
Letter of Complaint

P.O. Box 94
Fredericton, NB
E3B 4Y6
April 28, 1990

Numbers Canada Ltd.
2921 Garden Drive
Mississauga, ON
L5S 3E2

Dear Sir or Madam:

SUBJECT: <u>Complaint about failure of ST-167 scientific calculator</u>

My Numbers Canada ST-167 scientific calculator, which has a warranty for one year, failed after four months of use and as a result I have suffered considerable inconvenience and expense. Since there are several unusual aspects to my case, I decided not to return the calculator for repair as the warranty notice instructs. I am confident that a firm with your reputation for customer service will be able to resolve this problem in a mutually satisfactory manner.

The problem arose on Saturday, April 21, as I was studying for my final exam in Physics scheduled for Monday, April 23. Suddenly, in the middle of a calculation, the display went blank and stayed that way. Without a working calculator I could not continue my studying and I would not have been able to write my final. I spent most of Sunday running around looking for a replacement calculator and finally found one for $40, a significant amount in a student's budget.

Unfortunately I do not have the bill to send you as proof of purchase because the ST-167 was a Christmas present from my grandmother in Regina. I'm sure she still has the bill, but she would be very upset if she knew that the calculator she sent me had broken already. I hope you will accept the attached photocopy of her letter as a substitute for the missing bill. I have also attached a photocopy of the bill for the replacement calculator. I realize that you cannot compensate me for the worry and frustration I have suffered and for the probable effect on my mark in Physics. I do hope, however, that you will agree that my circumstances are unusual and agree to a full refund for the broken ST-167. If you were only to repair the broken ST-167, I would be left with an extra calculator and an extra expense of $40, a situation that is not much better than the one I am in now.

Please let me know what your decision is. Please contact me if you need any additional information.

Sincerely,

Maureen Donaldson

Maureen Donaldson

Attachments

as to present yourself as co-operative, fair, and trustworthy. Consider what will soothe injured or offended customers. They will want you to acknowledge their discomfort or inconvenience and to recognize that they have suffered. They will also want to know why the problem arose. Were there any extenuating circumstances? Most people are quite understanding about others' problems and so will forgive many oversights. A customer who has suffered a loss because of your error will expect to be compensated. If you must refuse the request for compensation, however, then it may be that no amount of persuasiveness will rectify the problem.

COMPLETENESS

The complainants want to know what they will get from you, why the problem arose, and what you are doing to prevent the problem from recurring. If you do agree to compensate, indicate how much the customer will get, when, under what circumstances, and explain how you determined the sum of compensation. If you must refuse the request, explain why. Perhaps the customer has failed to follow instructions or is even misrepresenting what actually happened.

You don't *have* to give a reason for the problem, but if you do, be careful not to assign blame too readily. Don't make your organization appear incompetent, don't accuse the customer, and don't give unnecessary details. Never blame a particular employee. In deciding how much and what to say, consider legal liability and the image of your organization you may be projecting. To assure the customer that the problem won't recur, you can explain that it was caused by an unusual circumstance and suggest, in general terms, the kinds of steps you will be taking to avoid the problem in the future.

You can use the three-part organization as follows:

1. Acknowledge receipt of the complaint. Thank the writer for having brought the problem to your attention. You should, after all, be interested in what customers think and in how well your product or service meets their needs. Express understanding of the inconvenience to the customer. Say whether or not the request for compensation can be granted.

2. Explain why the problem arose and what you've done about it. Explain the details of the compensation or explain why you can't grant the request.

3. Reiterate your concern for the customer. Reaffirm the image of your organization.

See Figure 19-4 for an example of a reply to a letter of complaint.

Figure 19-4
Reply to a Letter of
Complaint

NUMBERS CANADA LTD.

2921 Garden Drive Mississauga, Ontario L5S 3E2

May 14, 1990

Ms. Maureen Donaldson
P.O. Box 94
Fredericton, NB
E3B 4Y6

Dear Ms. Donaldson:

Thank you for your letter regarding your ST-167 scientific calculator. The ST-167 is an outstanding product that has a very good record for reliability. We are concerned about the problem you experienced with your calculator and regret that the problem occurred at such an inconvenient time. We are unable to accept the solution you proposed; however, we can suggest a modification of our normal procedure that we hope you will find satisfactory.

As you know, the warranty on your ST-167 provides for repairs without charge for one year after the date of purchase and you are responsible for the shipping charges to our offices and a handling charge of $3. There is no provision for refunds and we take no responsibility for costs resulting from a calculator malfunctioning. However, in your case, Ms. Donaldson, we have decided to offer a solution that takes your special circumstances into consideration. If you return your ST-167, we will issue you a gift certificate for $32 that you can apply in the next two years to the purchase of any equipment bearing the Numbers Canada label. The ST-167 retails for $48 and you used yours for four months, or one third of the warranty period. We are offering you compensation for the two thirds of the warranty period that remained.

We hope that you will find this solution generous. We will issue the gift certificate for $32 as soon as we receive your ST-167. So that I can attend to this matter personally, please address the package with the returned calculator to me. We at Numbers Canada wish you success in your studies.

Yours truly,

NUMBERS CANADA LTD.

Ralph Brands

Ralph Brands
Customer Relations

EXERCISES

1. Find examples of business letters at home. How does each use the you-attitude and how does it achieve the appropriate tone? Do you have any examples of unsuccessful business letters? What makes them unsuccessful? Bring to class examples of a variety of business letters for discussion.

2. Your family is moving to a neighbouring province next year and you've decided to move with them. Write to a college or university in that province to find out what you'll have to do to continue your education. If you're in your final year, find out how to qualify for graduate school.

3. Write a letter to your employer (or former employer) to get information for your formal report.

4. Write a letter to your employer (or former employer) expressing thanks for the information you've received for your report.

5. Write a letter to a local gas station to arrange to hold a fundraising carwash there for your club.

6. Last summer you visited San Francisco with your sister, and while you were there, you bought a blue Jiffy Hot Pot on sale for $9.98. You've found it heats a couple of cups of water much more quickly than does a conventional electric kettle. Many of your friends have admired it, and now you've decided to buy three or four as presents. None of the water heaters on the market in Canada are quite as compact or attractive, and the cheapest sells for $15.98. You bought the pot at Disco Appliances at 155 Market Street in San Francisco. Write to Disco Appliances and find out if they will send you four Jiffy Hot Pots and how much they will cost.

7. You work for Disco Appliances. Answer the letter from exercise 6. The regular price of the Jiffy Hot Pot is now $11.98 U.S. The customers have to pay in advance and there is a $1.25 U.S. charge for shipping and handling. The Jiffy will go on sale again in February, and the price will be reduced to $9.98. Include a catalogue of appliances available at Disco.

8. You work for Disco Appliances. Answer the letter from exercise 6, this time explaining that you cannot send merchandise to Canada.

9. You decided to order four red Jiffy Pots. They arrived yesterday. When you opened the boxes, you lost your temper. Two of the pots had no lids, one of the pots did not have an electric cord, and one had a chipped handle. You wanted to give these pots as Christmas presents. Write to Disco and explain your problem.

10. You work for Disco Appliances. Answer the letter from exercise 9. You are free to choose whatever action you wish to take.

11. On December 12, just after you returned from your coffee break, you received the following telephone call:

You: Sturdy Imports. Can I help you?

Mrs. J.:   You'd better. Mrs. Jones at Northern Lights in Outpost. Those shirts you sent me are no good.

You: What do you mean? What's wrong with them?

Mrs. J.:   They shrink. They're supposed to be washable and they shrink. I've had six of them returned already and that's $90 right there, and the other four will probably come back as soon as they come out of the wash. This is a small town, you know, and I've got a reputation to worry about. You people in Vancouver may not realize how important that is. I won't sell merchandise that's no good, you know.

You: I'm very sorry, Mrs. Jones, but could you tell me which shirts these are?

Mrs. J.:   They're called Frontier something. Some frontier! It just shows me how much you people down there know. Your salesman kept saying they'd be just the thing in our weather. So I got twenty and there's another fifty coming on order. What am I supposed to do? I'm proud of my merchandise. I've been running this store for fifteen years, you know. These people here need shirts and I can't sell them these Frontier things. I just don't want them in my store.

You: I'm very sorry, Mrs. Jones. I'll look into this matter right away.

Mrs. J.:   Well, I'm sending you back these shirts and you can just send me the regular kind I always get. And tell that salesman not to push merchandise that isn't good.

After you hung up, you looked up Northern Lights General Store orders and discovered the following:

- On November 21, Neil Williams, your salesman, brought in an order from Northern Lights General Store for 70 Frontier King shirts at $9 each.
- On November 25, 20 Frontier King shirts were shipped to Northern Lights on invoice #230409.
- On December 5, 50 Frontier King shirts were shipped to Northern Lights on invoice #352673.
- For the past five years Northern Lights has been buying New Woodsman shirts. You sell these for $10 and their retail price is $18.
- Northern Lights General Store usually buys about $3500 worth of merchandise from Sturdy Imports annually.

Next, you checked your factory orders and found the following:

- On October 15, Sturdy Imports placed an order for 1500 Frontier King shirts, a new brand produced by Frontier Manufacturing Ltd. at 509 Snowshoe Road, in Winnipeg.
- On November 22, a shipment of 700 Frontier King shirts arrived on invoice #D7371. You were charged $5 for each shirt.
- On December 13, Sturdy Imports placed an order for 3000 more Frontier King shirts.

- On December 2, the rest of the first order arrived. Sturdy Imports has been doing business with Frontier for six months.

Last night, you took one Frontier King shirt home with you and washed it in the washing machine and then dried it in the dryer. The shirt shrank. This morning you checked your stock and found that you have only 30 New Woodsman shirts, 20 size small and 10 size large. Sturdy Imports has its warehouse and offices at 4901 Back Street in Vancouver.

a. Write a letter to Mrs. Jones.
   You must try to pacify Mrs. Jones and assure that she will continue to do business with Sturdy Imports. Send her the 30 New Woodsman shirts you have in stock. Agree to give her a full refund for any Frontier King shirts she returns.

b. Write a letter to Frontier Manufacturing.
   You must convince Frontier to refund your investment in the defective shirts and assure that you will not be faced with a similar problem again. Cancel the December 1 order of Frontier King shirts.

CHAPTER 20

LETTER FORMAT

Introduction

Standard Elements

Optional and Unusual Elements

Envelope

INTRODUCTION

The conventions of the business letter format have evolved to make letters more efficient and attractive. Contemporary practice uses fewer punctuation marks and tends to begin all lines at the left margin, whereas even twenty years ago neither would have been acceptable. The more modern alternative requires fewer keystrokes, and this can become a significant economy in large organizations where thousands of letters may be prepared each week. Appearance in letters is generally a matter of symmetry and balance; a letter should be framed vertically and horizontally on the page, much as a picture is in its frame.

The format used in a letter and its general appearance become part of its extra-linguistic message in much the same way as your clothing or body language does in face-to-face communication. It goes without saying that the letter should be neat. The particular format a company uses may be related to the image it projects. For example, a traditional format may suggest a company is conservative, whereas a very modern format may suggest a company is "trendy."

Since the details of format conventions will be determined by company practice and implemented by secretarial staff, the guidelines provided here are intended for your personal business correspondence and as preparation for understanding the conventions you will find on the job.

In addition to the body of the letter, there are a number of standard elements and several optional parts that may be included, particularly in some special circumstances. This chapter describes each of these parts and shows how they may be arranged in two common formats. Although these formats may have other names, this textbook will refer to them as the *full block style* (Figure 20-1) and the *modified block style* (Figure 20-2). They differ mainly in the vertical and horizontal placement of their parts, and perhaps in their punctuation; you will see many variations of these styles. To give a letter a more balanced appearance, reduce the horizontal and vertical margins for a long letter, and increase them for a very short letter.

STANDARD ELEMENTS

A business letter normally includes all of the following parts: heading, date, inside address, salutation, complimentary close, and signature. Single-space the standard elements and the body of the letter.

HEADING

If you are using letterhead paper, as you will on the job, then the letterhead is the heading. If the letter is longer than one page, use letterhead paper only for the first page.

If you are writing as an individual, then your own address is the heading:

1234 Laburnum Street
Vancouver, BC
V6J 3W3

Place the heading 2.5 cm to 5 cm (1 to 2 inches) from the top of the page. If you are using full block style, place the heading at the left margin; if you are using modified block, place it so the longest line ends at the right margin.

Observe the following guidelines:

- Do *not* include your name in the heading.
- Write out "street," "avenue," or "road."
- Place the postal code or zip code on a separate line.
- Include the name of the country if the letter is going outside Canada.
- Use the following two-letter codes for the provinces and territories:

Newfoundland	NF
Nova Scotia	NS
Prince Edward Island	PE
New Brunswick	NB
Quebec	PQ
Ontario	ON
Manitoba	MB
Saskatchewan	SK
Alberta	AB
British Columbia	BC
Yukon Territory	YT
Northwest Territories	NT

- Do not use end punctuation, but do use a comma between the city and province or state.

DATE

The purpose of the date is, of course, to indicate when the letter was written and to serve as identification if there are several letters from the same source.

Write the date in one of two ways:

- October 7, 19XX
- 7 October 19XX

Figure 20-1
Full Block Letter
Format

1560 Victoria Street
Chemainus, BC
V0R 1K0

December 15, 1988

Mrs. Anne Silins
223 Bridge Crescent
Mississauga, ON
L4Y 2V6

Dear Mrs. Silins:

Begin each paragraph at the left margin. Type the body of the letter single-spaced and use double spacing to indicate paragraph breaks.

It is customary to have somewhat shorter paragraphs in letters than in other documents. However, you should avoid single-sentence paragraphs because they don't allow sufficient development.

Sincerely,

S. Starcevic

S. Starcevic

Figure 20-2
Modified Block
Letter Format

1560 Victoria Street
Chemainus, BC
V0R 1K0
December 15, 1988

Mrs. Anne Silins
223 Bridge Crescent
Mississauga, ON
L4Y 2V6

Dear Mrs. Silins:

You may begin paragraphs at the left margin, as in full block format, or you may indent paragraphs. Type the body of the letter single-spaced and use double spacing to indicate paragraph breaks.

It is customary to have somewhat shorter paragraphs in letters than in other documents. However, you should avoid single-sentence paragraphs because they don't allow sufficient development.

Sincerely,

S. Starcevic

S. Starcevic

Note that the name of the month is not abbreviated and that in the first format a comma separates the day and year. There is no punctuation at the end of the date.

In full block, begin the date at the left margin, but in modified block, line it up with the left margin of the address. There is some disagreement about how many lines there should be between the letterhead or heading and the date.

- With letterhead, leave two to four lines, depending on the length of the letter.
- With a heading and modified block style, type the date on the line below the heading.
- With a heading and full block style, type the date two lines below.

INSIDE ADDRESS

The inside address specifies the intended recipient of the letter. It should be exactly the same as the name and address on the envelope. Place it at the left margin at least two spaces below the date.

NAME. Use a courtesy title, such as Mr. or Ms., or a title, such as Dr. or Prof. Use Mrs. or Miss if you know which is appropriate and if you are certain your reader prefers this title. Many people are very sensitive about how they are addressed. While addressing them correctly may not help you, addressing them incorrectly could make them annoyed and less receptive to your message. Obviously, you must always check that you have spelled all names correctly. For the preferred form of the actual name, check the recipient's business card or the signature of the letter you're answering. This will also help you decide among R.J., or Robert J., or R. John, or Robert, or Bob, or Rob, or Bobby. If you don't know the name of a person to address, and cannot get it readily by telephone, then address the position (Vice-President, Sales) or the department (Sales Department).

POSITION OR TITLE. If you're not sure of the recipient's position, don't include it. If you have a previous letter from this person, you may find the position listed beneath the signature.

NAME OF ORGANIZATION. If you have a letter from your correspondent, use exactly the same name for the organization as appears in the letterhead.

ADDRESS. Use the same guidelines as for the address in the heading.

SALUTATION

Type the salutation two lines below the inside address and flush with the left margin. The most common form is the following:

> *Dear* + courtesy title + last name + colon
> *Dear*   Mr.   *Smith*   :

A common error is to use a comma instead of the colon. If you always call Mr. Smith "Bob" in a professional setting, then use "Dear Bob:" as your salutation. If you are in doubt about whether or not to use a first name, check how he signed his letter to you and how he addressed you.

If you have to address the department or company because you don't know whom to address, use one of the following salutations:

- Dear Sir:
- Dear Madam:
- Gentlemen: (if you know you are addressing men only)
- Dear Ladies and Gentlemen: (usually reserved for a circular)
- Dear Sales Department:
- Dear Manager:

You can also use an attention line (see below) and eliminate the salutation. Some companies don't use a salutation at all.

Note that if you *do* know the person's name, *use* it; don't use "Dear Sir" if you know it is "Dear Mr. Smith."

COMPLIMENTARY CLOSE

The complimentary close, a social courtesy equivalent to saying good-bye, is typed two lines below the body of the letter (more lines can intervene if the letter is very short). In full block style, it is placed flush with the left margin, but in modified block, it begins either at the centre of the page or lined up below the heading. Capitalize only the first word, and put a comma at the end:

Yours truly,

Choose a close you are comfortable with and one that matches the general level of formality of the letter. On the job you may have to use a close the company favours. The following are the most common complimentary closes:

- Yours respectfully,
- Respectfully yours,
- Yours sincerely,
- Sincerely yours,
- Sincerely,

SIGNATURE BLOCK

The signature block indicates your corporate identity and the legal status of the letter. If you are writing in your professional capacity, the signature block will consist of your signature, your name, your position, and sometimes the company name. If you are writing as a private individual, then the signature block consists of only your signature and your typed name.

Place the signature block immediately beneath the complimentary close. Leave at least four lines for your signature and make sure you sign the letter before sending it out. Type your name as you want to be addressed.

Note that some authorities suggest that the typed name and the signature should be the same. Word your title or the name of your position as it is listed officially, and capitalize each main word. If you really are writing in the company's name, you may type the company name, in block capitals, above your signature, but two lines below the complimentary close. The examples in Figure 20-3 illustrate some of your options:

Figure 20-3
Three Options for the
Signature Block

Yours truly,	Yours truly,	Yours truly,
		BIG BLOCK ENGINEERING
Bob Smith	Robert Smith	
	Project Engineer	R.J. Smith
		Project Engineer
a.	b.	c.

OPTIONAL AND UNUSUAL ELEMENTS

ATTENTION LINE

The attention line indicates that you are addressing a letter to a company, not an individual, but you do want a particular individual (or position or department) to deal with it. The attention line is the last line of the inside address and should also appear on the envelope. In the example below, the writer is addressing the letter to Big Block Engineering, but wants R. J. Smith to read it:

Big Block Engineering
249-14 Avenue SW
Calgary, AB
T2R 0M2

Attention: Mr. R. J. Smith

Gentlemen:

Note that the salutation is plural because, by convention, it must agree with the inside address.

SUBJECT LINE

Opinion is divided on whether the subject line should be above, below, or on the same line as the salutation. Underlining helps to highlight the subject line. The subject line identifies what the letter is about; it increases the letter's readability and helps in filing, especially in large companies that receive a lot of mail. The subject line is particularly useful if the subject of your letter can be readily categorized, such as a job vacancy that has a competition number, a claim that concerns an order number, or a project that has a contract number.

REFERENCE LINE

The reference line, typed at the left margin two lines below the signature block, identifies the typist. Two common arrangements are as follows:

LR/jr or LR:jr

The initials in capitals to the left identify the signer, and those on the right identify the typist. Knowing who typed a letter can be especially important in a large office with word processing equipment because if any changes need to be made, it is that typist who'll know where the disk is. Remember that no matter who types a letter, the one who signs it is responsible for its accuracy.

ENCLOSURE LINE

The enclosure line, typed flush with the left margin below the reference line, indicates how many other documents (and sometimes which ones) are included with the letter. The following are some forms the enclosure line could take:

- Enclosure
- Enclosure (3)
- Enclosure: Final Report
- Enclosure (2): Questionnaire Sample
                Informant List
- Encl.
- Enc.

COPY LINE

The copy line indicates who has been sent a copy of the letter. Sometimes copies are sent simply as a courtesy to keep others informed, and sometimes because of legal reasons. Names can be arranged in alphabetical order or in order of rank or importance:

cc: R. Brown
   J. Smith

If you don't want the recipient of the original to know that a copy has been sent to anyone else, then you mark the "other" copy "bcc", for "blind copy."

ENVELOPE

The envelope should show your address on the top left corner and the recipient's address in the right middle, as shown in Figure 20-4. If you are using a letterhead envelope, type your name above the source address, just as it appears in the signature block.

Figure 20-4
Envelope

1560 Victoria Street
Chemainus, BC
V0R 1K0

Mrs. Anne Silins
223 Bridge Crescent
Mississauga, ON
L4Y 2V6

PART SIX

OTHER DOCUMENTS

JOB APPLICATIONS

INTRODUCTION

The purpose of the job application process is to persuade the potential employer that you are the *best* candidate for a job. Normally this process consists of two phases. First you prepare a résumé and job application letter, which together have the purpose of securing an interview. Then, in the interview, you must convince the employer that you are the one to hire. This chapter discusses the following topics:

- how to analyze your strengths and weaknesses
- how to analyze the requirements of the job and to match your strengths with these requirements
- how to prepare a résumé
- how to prepare an application letter
- how to fill in application forms
- how to conduct yourself in an interview
- how to prepare follow-up letters

PERSONAL INVENTORY AND ANALYSIS

The personal inventory and analysis has the following purposes:

- To gather all the relevant data about yourself in one place for reference in preparing the résumé and letter and filling in application forms.
- To understand yourself so that you can present yourself most advantageously and so that you can interpret your strengths in the résumé, letter, and interview.
- To understand yourself so that you can make wise choices in selecting jobs to apply for.

You should prepare a personal inventory now and update it as your circumstances change. Since this inventory is exclusively for your own use, choose a form and format that you are comfortable with, and that is easy to revise and expand. If you have a computer, you should probably establish a computer file for the inventory. Otherwise, you may wish to begin a card file or to use sheets of paper in a looseleaf notebook. You will need to note both the *what* (the raw data) of your personal data, education, experience, extracurricular activities, references, and also the *so what* (the significance). Ultimately you will have to analyze yourself to define your qualities, skills, and goals. When you have finished this exercise, not only will you have all the raw material for a résumé and application letter, but you will also have thought about some of the questions that could arise in an interview, and, more importantly, you will probably have a much clearer idea of how you as an individual should be approaching the job search process.

You should adapt the following guide to your own purposes.

PERSONAL DATA

- date of birth
- place of birth
- citizenship
- social insurance number
- complete address, including postal code
- telephone number, including area code
- telephone number at which messages can be left
- height in centimetres and in inches
- weight in kilograms and in pounds
- class of driver's licence
- driver's licence number
- other operator's licences
- languages spoken and degree of fluency
- languages read and degree of fluency

EDUCATION

For each postsecondary institution attended, beginning with the most recent, list the following:

- name of institution
- location (city)
- dates attended
- program completed
- courses taken (list the official numbers and titles)
- average grade
- honours or awards
- extra-curricular activities

Include high school if you have graduated within the last five years.

Now ask yourself the following questions:

- What kind of a student are/were you?
- What are your academic strengths? What do you do best?
- What kinds of academic activities do you like best?
- What are your academic weaknesses? What do you do least well?
- How, if at all, does each course you have taken relate to the work you are looking for? What special knowledge and skills did you acquire in each?
- How does your education differ from that of others with the same degree, diploma, or certificate? What is unusual about your program?

EXPERIENCE

For each job you have held, beginning with the most recent, list the following:

- exact full name of company
- address of company
- dates employed
- exact title of position
- wages
- name of supervisor
- duties

Before preparing your description of duties, use some scrap paper to list all the tasks you did and then categorize them into classes or types of activities. Think in terms of activities with people, equipment, ideas, money, company records.

- Did you supervise anyone? How many? Who? For how long?
- How closely were you supervised? Did you have sole responsibility for anything? What? For how long?
- Did you have to write anything?
- Did you do anything outstanding?

When you have prepared entries for all the jobs you have had, ask yourself the following questions:

- Which job did you like best? Why?
- Which job did you like least? Why?
- Do you like to work with people?
- Do you prefer to work inside or outside?
- Do you prefer to work with or without supervision?
- What did you learn from each job?

EXTRA-CURRICULAR ACTIVITIES

List your hobbies, volunteer work, and extra-curricular activities, including any offices held and any awards received, and then ask yourself:

- What do these activities suggest about you?
- What do you like most about each?
- How could they be related to work?

REFERENCES

List at least three people who are willing to write reference letters for you. For each, include the following:

- full name (check spelling)
- position or title in company
- business address, including postal code
- telephone

When you have gathered and organized all this material, take a global view of yourself and try to answer the following questions:

- What are your best qualities as a person? You may want to ask your friends this, too, to see how close your perceptions are to theirs.
- What are your best qualities as an employee?
- What are your worst qualities as an employee?
- What are your most important abilities related to your profession?
- What are your greatest weaknesses related to your profession?
- What skills do you have
  - related to people?
  - related to equipment?
  - related to numbers?
  - related to communication?
  - related to dexterity, fitness?

Now consider what your goals are.

- What kind of work are you looking for? Why?
- What kind of work will you accept? Why?
- What do you hope to be doing in one year? Why?
- What do you hope to be doing in five years?
- What do you hope to be doing in ten years?
- What is the highest position you hope to attain?

JOB ANALYSIS

The purpose of the job analysis is to determine what the employer is looking for so that you can decide whether you should apply and so that if you do apply, you can show how your characteristics and qualifications match the requirements. In a job ad, you normally have three sources of information you can analyze:

- the job title
- the job description
- the company

THE JOB TITLE

Part of entering your profession is learning about the general characteristics of its subdisciplines and what the various job titles mean.

Some job titles may be quite unrevealing. For example, what is a "computer-support technician," or a "communications assistant," or a "sales correspondent," or a "service writer"?

You will need to know the following about a job title:

- What does a person in this job do?
- What skills are needed?
- What personal qualities are needed?

THE DESCRIPTION

Job ads vary in the amount and kind of information they contain. Obviously, they are meant to attract the best candidates. In reading an ad, pay particular attention to the following:

- *Explicit statements of qualifications.* Many ads specify the required education or knowledge, experience or skills, and personal qualities. Consider, for example, the following: "The successful applicant will have a degree in computer science, preferably with an additional degree in business administration and a minimum of seven years' experience in a multi-user environment, augmented by demonstrated managerial skills." What are the stated minimum education, experience, and skills? What are the preferred education, experience, and skills? If you have only one year of experience, you would be foolish to apply for this particular job.
- *Explicit statement of duties.* The statement of duties not only tells you what you will do on the job, but it also suggests, indirectly, what abilities and experience would be most valuable. Do you understand what the ad means? What have you done that is like what you will have to do?
- *Tone and connotation.* Often, very important information about the job is conveyed through tone and connotation rather than through explicit statement. Interpreting some ads is as difficult as interpreting some poetry. Consider what the following might mean:

  – "Bring your raw intellect, demonstrated judgement and tireless commitment to a smaller, more flexible hands-on arena."
  – "The company requires a commonsense executive who has shown dramatic results."

Try to translate the ad into a list of qualifications that you must demonstrate in the résumé, letter, and interview.

THE COMPANY

If the company is identified in the ad, try to find out as much about it as you can.

- What is its business?
- What kinds of activities is it engaged in?
- Where does it have branches?
- Is it listed on the stock exchange?
- How well is it doing?
- What is its reputation?
- What accomplishments is it known for?

While you obviously won't do this much research for each job, this kind of information will help you decide whether or not you want to work for the company. It will also help you tailor your application more to the needs of the company, and it may help you appear better prepared at the interview. Your knowing about the company shows the potential employer that you have initiative and suggests that you are a serious candidate.

THE TRADITIONAL RESUME

INTRODUCTION

You will normally apply for a position by submitting a résumé and a job application letter, but if you apply in person, you may simply bring the résumé with you. The *résumé* (also known as a *curriculum vitae* or *data sheet*) is a summary of your qualifications presented in a conventionalized format. Its purpose from the point of view of employers is to present the relevant data about you in a convenient, efficient form to allow them to see very quickly what you can provide. Its purpose from your own point of view is to present yourself as attractively as possible and to make the most of what you have to offer. A résumé is like an application form that you have designed yourself to present your qualifications in their best light.

In preparing your résumé, observe the following conventions:

- Use headings and subheadings to locate information.
- Use various typefaces and underlining to highlight information.
- Use lists and indention to show the structure of the information.
- Use grammatical parallelism for structurally parallel components.
- Use point form and abbreviations (if they are clear) where appropriate.
- Use single spacing.
- Use no more than two pages for an entrance-level position and no more than three pages for a senior position.

While the details of how you arrange your résumé are up to you, remember that this document, perhaps more than any you prepare, functions as extra-linguistic communication about you. It is seen as a product for which you are responsible, as a sample of the kind of work you do. It must be *neat*, *clear*, and *organized*. It shows how much attention you pay to detail and how well you can organize and present information. While a very attractive résumé is no guarantee that you are a conscientious worker, a messy one does suggest that you are a messy, careless worker who will present a poor image of the company.

Most résumés are now prepared on word processors, and some are even professionally printed. It is a good idea to buy some good quality, standard size paper for the résumé and the letter of application. This paper should be of a heavier weight and could be very lightly tinted grey or buff. Note, though, that if you are using tinted paper, you should also use an envelope of the same colour. The copy you submit should be absolutely immaculate; there should be no errors, no scratch-outs, and no white-outs. Good quality photo copies are acceptable.

Ideally, you should prepare a separate résumé for each application so you can emphasize those features that are most clearly related to the particular job; when you are applying for a summer job or for an entrance-level position, you will probably use the same résumé. However, you should tailor *each* letter to the particular position you are applying for.

Two main kinds of résumés are in common use. The *traditional*, or *chronological*, résumé uses dates as an organizing principle; the *functional skills* résumé uses personal qualities as the organizing principle. Recent research in the United States shows that applicants using the functional skills résumé are less likely to be granted an interview.[1] The main reason employers prefer the traditional résumé is that its predictable form facilitates the scanning of the applicant's credentials. In the absence of evidence about the preferences of Canadian employers, we have to assume they are similar to those of Americans. For this reason, we discuss the traditional, or chronological, résumé first and in detail. The functional skills résumé is described very briefly in the next section.

A traditional résumé normally has the following sections:

- personal data
- career objective
- education
- experience
- activities
- references

Focus on your assets. Place education first if you have little related experience, and experience first if you have been out of school for a long time or if your education is not a strong point. If you have already prepared a complete personal inventory, then to prepare a résumé you will only have to select the appropriate information and present it so as to best meet the needs of the reader and your own persuasive aims.

So that you are protected in case the second page of your résumé is separated from the first, type your name at the very top right margin of each page.

PERSONAL DATA

There can be two components to the personal data section: the identifying information (name, address, telephone), which is obligatory, and further personal information (place and date of birth, citizenship, height and weight, health, marital status, sex), which is optional. Many employers prefer to have only the identifying information because additional information could leave them open to accusations of bias. Canadian legislation prohibits discrimination in employment on the grounds of race, age, sex, marital status, and physical disability.

Place the identifying information at the top centre of the first page, as in Figure 21-1. If you choose to include other personal data, you may place these on the first page, as in Figure 21-1, or near the end, before the references. Arrange the items of information clearly and attractively.

NAME. Give your name in full, but don't include more than one middle name.

ADDRESS. Give your full address as it would appear on an envelope, including postal code. If you are applying outside the country, include

Figure 21-1
Traditional Résumé

LORI ANNE ENGLISH

#105 – 2603 W. 15 Avenue
Vancouver, BC
V6K 2Z6

683-6161
or
681-6611 (Messages)

CAREER OBJECTIVE

As a social work student with a year's experience as a group home parent, I am looking for an opportunity to develop my skills in working with children. After I complete the B.Sc. and M.Sc. in Social Work, I hope to specialize in the care of adolescents in crisis.

PERSONAL

Date of Birth: July 25, 1969   Place of Birth: Winnipeg, MB
Marital Status: Married   Children: None

EDUCATION

1989-90

The University of B.C., Vancouver. Completed third year in the School of Social Work.
Important Electives: Sociology of Work, Technical Writing.
Standing: First class

1987-89

Simon Fraser University, Burnaby, BC. Completed second year in the Faculty of Arts.
Important Electives: Social Stratification, Social Issues in Psychology, Individual Psychology, Medical Sociology.
Standing: Grade point average 3.6

1987

Alpha Secondary, Burnaby, BC. High school graduation diploma.
Standing: Grade point average 4.0

L.A. English

EXPERIENCE

Feb. 1990-present

<u>Relief Group Home Parent</u>, COQUITLAM GROUP HOME,
921 Main Street, Coquitlam, BC
Supervisors: Ms. J. Brown and Mr. K. Stanley.
<u>Duties</u>: General care of home and residents; cooking; cleaning; keeping records; enforcing rules of home; counselling boys; arranging recreational activities; liaising with police, teachers, other workers, children's parents, and the community. Required ability to pace oneself through twenty-four hour shifts and emotionally stressful situations, to be firm and exercise authority of the role, to record the boys' activities and attitudes accurately.

Summer 1988 (full time) and Sept. 1988-July 1989 (part time)

<u>Sales Clerk</u>, GOURMET MEATS LTD., 6652 Hastings Street, Burnaby, BC
Supervisor: Mr. David Tomson.
Reason for Leaving: Company went out of business.
<u>Duties</u>: Serve the public, prepare trays of meat, clean up.

Summer 1985 and 1986
<u>General Worker</u>, WHITE LINEN SUPPLY COMPANY, 290
E. 8 Avenue, Vancouver, BC
Supervisor: Mr. Jack Dixon
<u>Duties</u>: Sort, count, and transport uniforms and perform various manual tasks.

SPECIAL INTERESTS

T'ai Chi, amateur photography, music.

L.A. English

REFERENCES

Mr. K. Stanley
Child Care Counsellor
921 Main Street
Coquitlam, BC
V3C 2J9
973-2707

Mrs. G. Collins
Regional Supervisor
Ministry of Human Resources
2810 Grandview Highway
Vancouver, BC
V5M 4L8
438-4489

Prof. N. Smith
School of Social Work
The University of B.C.
Vancouver, BC
V6T 1W5
228-5100

3

"Canada." If you will only be at your present address for a short time, indicate how long you will be there, and supply a "permanent address" or "contact address" at which you can be reached.

TELEPHONE. Include the area code. If you have an answering machine, check that it is working well, and use a businesslike, but friendly, recorded message. Check the machine regularly for messages and answer them promptly, apologizing for not having been able to take the call in the first place. If you are planning to move soon, give the date until when the number will be correct, and include a permanent number. If your telephone will be left unattended, supply a number at which messages can be left for you. Make sure that the person answering this number is courteous and knows how to reach you.

CAREER OBJECTIVE

The career objective section should summarize in no more than two or three sentences your education and experience, your immediate career objective, and your ultimate career ambitions. Since the purpose of the résumé is to secure only your next job, focus on the present time. Dispense with the past (education and experience) in a subordinate statement, and keep your future ambitions fairly broad. In describing your immediate objective, concentrate on those aspects that the job you are applying for would fulfil.

A well-written career objective section can be extremely powerful because it shows you can summarize, it shows you know what you want, and it suggests that the job you are applying for is well suited to your interests. However, since it is not a compulsory element of the résumé, do not include it unless you can write it well and the particular job does suit your career plans.

EDUCATION

The education section indicates in general terms the kind of education you have and highlights what is special about it. Make a separate entry for each institution you have attended, but make all entries physically and grammatically parallel. Use reverse chronological order and stop with high school. If you have had an interrupted education, you may want to organize only by institution and place dates in a very subordinate position. Remember that accounting for time should not be that important; the time only tells how recent your education is and how your education and experience are related chronologically.

For each institution, include the following information, arranged in an attractive and economical manner that uses appropriate highlighting techniques:

DATES ATTENDED. Be accurate. Try not to use up too much blank space. Include beginning and end dates if you have attended continuously except for summers (e.g., 1985–88).

NAME OF INSTITUTION. Give the full name, spelled correctly.

ADDRESS. If you are applying for a job out of town, give the name of the city in which the institution is located.

PROGRAM COMPLETED. Give the name of the degree, diploma, or certificate, along with what the major program is:

- B.A., Major in History
- B.Ap.Sc. in Electrical Engineering, Power Option
- Diploma in Chemical Technology

Check the calendar of the institution for the exact wording. If you are in your final year, use the following format:

B.A., Major in History (expected completion date, May 1994)

For earlier years, indicate year, major, and degree toward which it is to be applied:

Completed second year of a four-year B.Ap.Sc. in Electrical Engineering program.

In the first year or two you don't have to be very specific about majors and options.

SPECIAL COURSES (OR RELEVANT COURSES). Use this section either to highlight how the courses you have taken relate particularly to the requirements of the job, or to show how your education is unusual. In the first case, note especially those courses that are related to requirements stated in the job ad. If the ad specifies familiarity with computers and with drafting techniques, for example, then you should highlight the courses you have in these areas. Do not expect the reader to know what the normal curriculum at your institution is. It is *your* job to emphasize relevant information. As well, though, you should also show how your education differs from that of your classmates. In this case you might want to use the heading "Electives" to indicate that you studied psychology as part of your program in agriculture, for example.

STANDING. If your standing is particularly good, include it. If you have won awards or prizes, you may want to list these separately.

EXPERIENCE

The purpose of the experience section is to indicate your employment record and to highlight what is most relevant, important, or positive in that record. Make a separate entry for each employer you have worked for and make all entries physically and grammatically parallel. Use reverse chronological order. Do not give the same attention to trivial jobs or jobs held a long time ago unless they are directly related to the work you are applying for; rather, use the saved space to expand the entries for the more important and more recent jobs.

For each employer, include the following, arranged in an attractive and economical layout that uses appropriate highlighting techniques:

DATES EMPLOYED. Be accurate. Avoid using up too much space for the dates.

NAME AND ADDRESS OF EMPLOYER. Give the full name and the address of the employer.

POSITION OR JOB TITLE. Give the job title accurately.

SUPERVISOR. Give the supervisor's full name.

DUTIES AND RESPONSIBILITIES. The description of duties and responsibilities is the most important part of the experience section of the résumé. Try to present your experience in the best possible light without exaggerating and without ignoring what is important. Remember that your résumé may be read first by a personnel officer who may not know what duties are implied by a particular job title. List your main duties, trying to make your verbs as accurate as possible, being precise about their objects, and specifying equipment when relevant, as in "used XYZ software to select routes for the dump trucks." Include skills as they relate to people as well as to equipment and machinery. State responsibilities for people (how many), equipment (which kind), money (how much), security, budget, safety, communication (reports, presentations). State whether you trained anyone. State whether you made any innovations or won any awards.

ACTIVITIES

The activities section allows you to show that you are an interesting, well-rounded person. It can suggest that you are sociable, fit, adventuresome, and that you are a leader or a good team person. If you do not participate in sports or other organized activities, and don't have serious hobbies, leave this section out. List the activities you are genuinely involved in. If you play softball once a year, don't list it, but if you are a member of the university ski team, make sure that you do. Include offices you hold in organizations. Don't list more than three activities unless you really are seriously involved in more, and consider whether too many activities may not interfere with your doing a job well. Be aware that some activities and sports enjoy greater prestige than others.

REFERENCES

Give the full name, position, address, and telephone number for three references. Before listing someone as a reference, though, get that person's permission, because giving a reference is a time-consuming favour. Also, you should ask first to determine whether the referee is willing to give you a reference. Try to keep each referee informed of the jobs you're applying for and what the requirements of each are.

FUNCTIONAL SKILLS RESUME

The functional skills résumé has a personal data section and a career objective section. The education, experience, activities, and references sections, however, are replaced by listings organized by personal qualities (leadership, mechanical ability), skills (management skills, organization skills), or accomplishments. Figure 21-2 is a functional skills résumé that corresponds to the traditional résumé shown in Figure 21-1.

JOB APPLICATION LETTER

PURPOSE

The job application letter is a sales or persuasion letter whose purpose is to present your qualifications so that you will appear to be a sufficiently attractive candidate to get an interview. At the interview you have to rely on face-to-face persuasive skills to get the job.

PRINCIPLES

In preparing the job application letter, observe the following principles:

- *Interpret your résumé.* Relate your qualifications to the requirements of the job. Focus on linking your qualities to what the employer needs. Select the *what* from the résumé and then focus on the *so what*, on how this fact is related to the job. Since applications may be screened by very busy personnel clerks, if you don't *show* that you are special, they may not *see* that you are. Even when the application is read by the employer, don't expect him or her to have either the time or the interest to search out reasons for choosing you. Remember that it is not unusual for an employer to interview fewer than one candidate in ten.
- *Use the you-attitude.* Focus on how the employer will gain from hiring you, rather than on how you will gain from getting the job. What do you have to offer? See Chapter 18.
- *Control tone to present your voice and personality.* The tone of your letter will convey an impression of you. How do you want to be perceived? Is this the impression of you the letter creates? Test your tone on friends or classmates and adjust it until you achieve the one you want. Although the tone you adopt is up to you, it is generally appropriate to aim for one of confidence and competence. If you try to be too humble, you may be perceived as groveling and not worthy of the job, whereas if you push too hard, you may be seen as aggressive and perhaps even abrasive.
- *Display your business communication skills.* Your letter is a sample of your professional communication skills; it should show the highest quality the employer can expect from you. Obviously it cannot contain any errors in typing, spelling, or grammar.

FORM AND APPEARANCE

The application letter must follow the format conventions outlined in Chapter 20. It should be typed or prepared on a letter-quality printer.

Figure 21-2
Functional Skills
Résumé

LORI ANNE ENGLISH

#105 – 2603 W. 15 Avenue
Vancouver, BC
V6K 2Z6

683-6161
or
681-6611 (Messages)

CAREER OBJECTIVE

As a social work student with a year's experience as a group home parent, I am looking for an opportunity to develop my skills in working with children. After I complete the B.Sc. and M.Sc. in Social Work, I hope to specialize in the care of adolescents in crisis.

SKILLS IN DEALING WITH PEOPLE:

- completed three years of university courses in the social sciences (psychology, sociology) with a grade point average of 3.6
- supervised and counselled boys as a relief group home parent
- liaised with police, teachers, other workers, and children's parents as a relief group home parent
- served the public as a sales clerk in a food store

ORGANIZATION SKILLS

- kept accurate records of boys' activities and attitudes in group home
- arranged recreational activities in group home
- arranged meat trays in a food store
- sorted and counted uniforms in a linen supply company

COMMUNICATION SKILLS

- studied technical writing at university
- wrote assessments of boys in group home

Write the letter by hand *only* if the advertisement specifies "reply in handwriting." ("Reply in writing" means "submit a letter of application.") Use the same good quality, standard size paper as for the résumé. Normally the letter should fit on one page, single spaced. Note, in particular, the following:

- Do not put your name above your address. The signature block includes your full name.
- If you know the name of the recipient, use it in the salutation.
- Use a subject line to indicate which competition or position you are applying for.
- Sign the letter.
- Place the letter symmetrically on the page; retype it until you get it right. It's a good idea to keep a photocopy of every letter you send out.

STRUCTURE AND CONTENT

The application letter normally consists of three or four paragraphs.

The *opening paragraph* is an introduction. Announce your candidacy by identifying the job you are applying for, indicating how you found out about it, and saying that you are an applicant. Then summarize your education, experience, and any outstanding personal qualities. Don't be too aggressive.

The *middle paragraphs* develop the summary given in the opening paragraph and provide the main evidence for your implicit claim that you are the ideal candidate for the job. The résumé lists facts; the letter selects the most important facts and interprets their relevance to the job. When you show the relevance of your qualifications, don't exaggerate or grasp at straws. If you are clearly not qualified for a job, you are wasting your time applying for it. Normally you will devote one paragraph to education and one to work experience; the stronger one should appear first. You may also want to refer to extra-curricular activities, but usually you would not discuss them in a separate paragraph.

The *closing paragraph* is a conclusion. Reiterate your interest in the position and ask for an interview. Be positive, but don't put doubt in the reader's mind by saying "If you should find my qualifications attractive..." Indicate when and where you can be contacted.

Figure 21-3 is a sample job application letter that could have been submitted with the résumé shown in Figure 21-1 to answer the following ad:

JOB POSTING

Family Support Program, M.H.R. – Child Care Counsellor 1.

<u>Duties</u>: Under direction of District Office Supervisor and in cooperation with social workers as well as Regional Family and Children's Service Co-ordinators, to assist parents in developing their

child care family skills; to assist families/children in using appropriate community services; to provide supportive services to children-in-care; to prepare reports and maintain chronological records; and other related duties as required.

<u>Qualifications</u>: A high degree of maturity; preference will be given to those with demonstrated ability to work with families and the community. A Child Care Counsellor 1 must have a minimum of secondary school graduation, preferably with some undergraduate training in behavioural sciences plus some directly related experience.
Quote job posting 90:1586.

APPLICATION FORMS

When you have submitted a résumé and a letter, you may still be asked to fill in an application form. Don't argue about the need for this, and don't appear resentful. Follow these guidelines:

- *Be prepared.* To save yourself time and to show you are businesslike, prepare a fact sheet which you bring, together with two pens and a small notepad, to every interview and every visit to an employment or personnel office. This fact sheet should be complete because the application form may ask for information that is not included in your résumé. Try to anticipate what you could be asked.
- *Read the form carefully.* Demonstrate that you are a careful worker and that you follow instructions and plan your tasks. Does the form specify whether you are to print, handwrite, or type? If you are filling in the form at home, always practise on a photocopy first. Are there word limits placed on any answer? Are questions repeated?
- *Be neat.* There are very few jobs in which neatness is not important, and a neat application form suggests that you are careful in your work. Make sure your answers fit into the spaces provided.
- *Be complete.* Answer every question completely. Make full use of opportunities to express yourself, but do so concisely and carefully. Use your notepad to plan your answer. Your earlier analysis of your personal inventory should have prepared you for answering questions about your career goals or your outstanding personal qualities.

You may also be asked to write 10 or 20 lines to explain how your experience and education are relevant to the position for which you are applying.

INTERVIEW

PURPOSE

While the purpose of the résumé and job application letter is to sell yourself so that you are invited to an interview, the purpose of the

Figure 21-3
Job Application
Letter

#105-2603 W. 15 Avenue
Vancouver, BC
V6K 2Z6
April 3, 1990

Director of Personnel
Public Service Commission
544 Michigan Street
Victoria, BC
V8V 4R5

Dear Sir:

RE: <u>Job Application for Competition No. 90:1586</u>

I am very interested in filling the Child Care Counsellor 1 position you have recently posted. I believe my education in the School of Social Work and first and second year concentrations on psychology and sociology have helped prepare me for the tasks of the position. Moreover, my experience with children and families during my student practicum and relief work at a group home have exposed me to some of the needs of the clients and to various helping approaches.

The concentration on social science courses in my first two years of university broadened my perspective and gave me an understanding of people and how their lives are affected by personal characteristics and trends in their socio-economic environment. My year in the School of Social Work gave me experience in applying these theories and taught me to analyze critically the work I was doing with the client. Also it provided me with techniques for working with people. These skills are particularly valuable to a worker in the Family Support Program since the clients are often in, or on the verge of, a crisis. Also, working with other professionals on the case is enhanced with the attainment of these skills since understanding and critical analysis of all methods used to help the clients enables workers to co-ordinate their services.

Furthermore, I have one year of closely related experience. During my student practicum I was exposed to children and families with severe emotional problems and learned the importance of overcoming frustration and exhaustion when working with such demanding clients. I learned how to help families work toward their goals. In addition, experience at the group home prepared me for work with children. Being a house parent requires patience, understanding, and firmness. The attached resume outlines the details of my experience and education.

I find the goals and tasks of the Family Support Program very interesting and attractive. I look forward to the opportunity to discuss my qualifications with you at an interview. I may be reached at 683-6161, or messages may be left at 681-6611.

Sincerely,

Lori Anne English

Lori Anne English

Enclosure

interview is for you to persuade the interviewer(s) that you are the *best* candidate. At the same time, it also allows you to meet the potential employer and to decide whether you really do want this job.

The purpose of a job interview from the point of view of employers is to find the best candidate for the job. The interview allows the interviewer to meet you and to see what you are like. The company wants to know whether you can do the job and how well you will fit in to the company. People tend to hire in their own image; companies usually want to hire more people like the ones they already have. The interview also allows the company to sell itself, to convince you that you should work for them.

If there are many candidates for a job, you may have to attend a series of interviews. The first, which will be designed to screen out unsuitable candidates, will be brief and will usually be conducted by personnel officers. In this case, your aim is to avoid doing or saying anything that will make you seem unattractive. Subsequent interviews will be directed at finding the best candidate. These will be more extensive, may include more than one interviewer, and will be more concerned with finding out what you are like and what you can do.

PREPARATION

In preparing for interviews you will need to do at least the following:

- Select appropriate dress.
- Research the company and the job.
- Review your qualifications.

APPROPRIATE DRESS. A candidate may be judged in the first few minutes of the interview. This suggests that appropriate grooming, dress, and manner are extremely important. Don't offend the interviewer. Avoid unusual haircuts, too much jewellery, or too much perfume. Whether or not you are being interviewed for an office job, wear the kinds of clothes you would wear in an office. Be absolutely certain everything you wear is clean and pressed. It is a very good idea to have a photograph or video of yourself in your interview clothes so you can see exactly how you look.

COMPANY. Find out as much as you can about the company so you can ask intelligent questions at the interview and so you can make a sounder decision about whether or not to take the job if it is offered to you. Use the following resources:

- The campus placement office. Large companies have specially prepared promotional literature. Your placement officer will direct you to this and to other sources, such as Scotts Industrial Index and Financial Post Surveys.
- The public library.
- The company. Call the company and ask for annual reports or other materials that will tell you more about them.

Formulate questions you might ask at the interview.

QUALIFICATIONS. Review your résumé and letter of application so you remember exactly what you said in them. Review how your education, experience, and personal qualities relate to the job you are applying for.

STRUCTURE

Most job interviews have the following components:

- creation of rapport
- information exchange based on interviewer's questions
- information exchange based on interviewee's questions
- termination

CREATION OF RAPPORT. The first few minutes of the interview are critical to your success because of the force of first impressions. Make sure that your grooming and dress are immaculate and that you carry yourself confidently. Shake hands firmly, and smile. Sit comfortably, but don't slouch, and try to avoid nervous mannerisms. Again you may find it helpful to watch a video of yourself to see how you can make yourself appear more confident and relaxed.

Usually the interviewer's first few comments and questions will be meant to relax you and to create rapport for the rest of the interview. This is an opportunity to show your social skills and to gain the interviewer's support.

INTERVIEWER'S QUESTIONS. After giving you a little background about the job and the company, the interviewer will begin to question you. Some of these questions, such as "Tell me about yourself," are non-directive and are designed to allow you to speak for several minutes. In addition to eliciting information, such questions are meant to show how well you organize and how well you express yourself. Take a moment to think about the question and then give a fairly full answer. Watch the interviewer's response. Judge when you have said enough. Don't be afraid of some silence. Recognize that the interviewer may use what you say to formulate further questions. Other questions, such as "How many people did you train?" are directive questions and are designed to elicit quite specific answers, though these should generally be more than a single word or sentence.

You may find it useful to practise answering the following frequently asked questions:

- Why did you apply for this job?
- Why do you want to work for this company?
- What are your career goals?
- What do you hope to be doing in five years and in ten years?
- What do you think determines an employee's progress in a good company?
- What kind of people do you like to work with?
- What kind of people do you find it most difficult to work with?
- What qualities would your ideal supervisor have?
- What would your ideal job be like?
- How do you define success?

- What is your greatest achievement?
- What is the most difficult challenge you've met?
- Why did you continue your education beyond high school?
- How did you choose your major?
- How do you spend your spare time?
- Why should we hire you?

Other questions will normally relate more directly to your education and experience and will be designed to determine whether your background has prepared you to do the job. As well, you may be asked some problem-solving questions. These ask you what you would do if faced with a particular problem, such as a conflict between a co-worker and your supervisor.

INTERVIEWEE'S QUESTIONS. The interviewer will ask you whether you have any questions. This is your opportunity to demonstrate your sincere interest in the job and your preparation for the interview, but also to find out whether you have judged the job and the company correctly. The following are particularly good subjects for your questions:

- the specific duties and responsibilities of the job
- the training program
- the opportunities for advancement
- the future of the company
- the expected impact of current legislation or current market trends on the company

You should have prepared several specific questions when you were researching the company.

TERMINATION. At the end of the interview you should be told when you can expect a decision. Thank the interviewer.

FOLLOW-UP LETTERS

You should write follow-up letters after the interview and after you have been offered or refused a job. The main purpose of these letters is to create a good impression. Use the you-attitude and a friendly tone.

AFTER THE INTERVIEW

The follow-up letter after an interview reminds the interviewer of you and clarifies any misunderstandings that may have arisen in the interview. Express your gratitude for the interview and your continued interest in the position and the organization. Add any relevant information you think you should have mentioned in the interview. Clarify any misconceptions. For example, if you think the interviewer thought you weren't willing to accept supervisory responsibilities, you could emphasize your interest in the opportunity to supervise. Don't, however, make this letter too long or too effusive. Make sure you are enhancing the interviewer's impression of you, not destroying it. See Figure 21-4 for an example of a follow-up letter after an interview.

Figure 21-4
Follow-up Letter

#105-2603 W. 15 Avenue
Vancouver, BC
V6K 2Z6
April 30, 1990

Ms. E. Dzugalo
Public Service Commission
544 Michigan Street
Victoria, BC
V8V 4R5

Dear Ms. Dzugalo:

Thank you very much for meeting with me yesterday to discuss my application for the Child Care Counsellor 1 position. Now that I know more about this position, I am even more eager to qualify for it. I am confident that my report writing ability will meet your standards. Unfortunately, I may not release the reports I have prepared for the Coquitlam Group Home. However, I have attached a photocopy of a formal report I prepared for the technical writing course I took at university.

If there is any further information I can provide, please call me at 683-6161.

Sincerely,

Lori Anne English

Lori Anne English

AFTER AN OFFER

If you are accepting an offer, the letter is a very routine document. Accept the offer, express your enthusiasm about the position, and clarify any details such as the date when you will start. If, however, you are refusing the offer, express your gratitude for the offer, explain briefly why you are refusing it, and allow for the possibility you might work for that organization in the future.

AFTER A REFUSAL

Although a follow-up letter won't give you a job you have been refused, it could lead to a different or later offer. Express your disappointment at not getting the job, but indicate your continued interest in the company, and your optimism about future opportunities.

NOTE

1. Steven M. Ralston, "A Response to 'Teaching Résumé Writing the Functional Way,'" *The Bulletin of the Association for Business Communication*, 46.1 (1986): 18–20. Ralston cites results reported in Howard M. Sherer, "Effective Entry Level Organizational Communication as Assessed through a Survey of Personnel Recruiters," (diss., Indiana University, 1984) and Barron Wells, "Fortune 500 Chief Personnel Officers' Views on Hiring" (Organizational Policy and Development Conference, Louisville, 24 May 1985).

EXERCISES

1. Analyze the following job ads. Which qualities will the successful applicant need to have?
   a. TUTOR/COMPANION
      College student required for the summer (May – Aug.) to travel with family (children ages 10, 12, 14, 16) through South America, Australia, South Pacific, and Africa. Should have strong background in mathematics and science and be prepared to supervise children's activities. Remuneration for the summer: $3500. All travel expenses and food and lodging paid.
   b. RESEARCH ASSISTANT
      College student to conduct survey of tourist facilities throughout the province. Must be free to travel. The successful candidate will prepare the survey, conduct it, and then report the results in writing. Should be able to work with minimal supervision. Salary: $2400/mo. and contribution to living and travel expenses.

2. Select three job ads from the financial pages of a major newspaper and analyze the qualities each is asking for. Select at least one ad you find difficult to interpret and bring it to class for discussion.

3. Write a description of duties and responsibilities for your most recent job.

4. Prepare three layout versions for an entry from the experience section of your résumé. Vary the spatial layout, the use of boldface, and the use of underlining. Rank the effectiveness of these three versions. Ask a classmate to rank them. Compare the two rankings.

5. Write a career objective statement.

6. Prepare an application letter for one of the positions advertised in exercise 1 above.

7. Prepare four questions you would ask the interviewers if you were called to an interview for the job you applied for in exercise 6.

8. Pretend that you are a personnel officer asked to screen the following four responses to the first ad in exercise 1 above. Which candidate do you think should be invited to an interview? Why? Indicate why you would reject the other three. Prepare four questions to ask the candidate you've chosen.

a. I would like to offer myself as a suitable candidate in filling the position of a tutor and a companion to the children touring Australia, South Pacific, South America, and Africa during the oncoming summer months. I feel that my experience in handling my four younger brothers and sisters (ages 9, 10, 13, 16) will prove invaluable in assessing the intellectual and practical needs, as well as facilitating communication with your children.

My exceptional advantage for this position is that not only do I have experience with children, but in addition, I have resided in Africa for the last seventeen years and am presently specializing in cell biology at university. This puts me in a position whereby I can perform the role of a tour guide around the various African countries, especially because I speak Swahili, the native language, fluently. Moreover, my acquired academic knowledge of science, in general, will make this tour both an intellectual and entertaining experience for the children.

I find the idea of a travelling and working summer vacation very appealing. If you decide that my knowledge and experience qualify me for the position of a tutor, companion, and a tour guide, please call me to arrange an interview at your earliest convenience.

b. I am very interested in filling the tutor/companion position you have recently advertised for. I believe my education in science and my second, third, and fourth year concentrations in biological science, mathematical statistics and child development have helped prepare me for the tasks of the position. Furthermore, my experience with counselling children at camp, teaching my nieces, as well as tutoring people in mathematics have helped prepare me to deal with the needs of the children.

My concentrations at university have given me insight into the ways children and adolescents think through situations. By combining this knowledge, my mathematical skills and my experience working with teenagers, I feel I have a more complete insight into problem situations as compared to a knowledge where I lacked one of these qualifications. In Child Development courses we were taught to explain why children act a specific way, consider life from the perspective of the child, and design techniques to teach children (teenagers) specific things. These techniques would be important because they would help me to teach the adolescents the skills they need. If a crisis situation arose I feel I have the ability to deal with it adequately because of my education.

I also have experience which could be important to the adolescents in their travels. I have a bronze medallion in swimming, a first-aid certificate, I speak fluent French, I'm an amateur photographer of wildlife, and I enjoy all types of physical activities. This knowledge will help me enhance the children's knowledge of the world in a broader aspect rather than just in scholastic terms.

I find the objectives of this job very interesting and attractive. I would welcome the opportunity to discuss my qualifications further with you. If you decide my experience and education qualify me, please call me to arrange an interview at your convenience.

c. I am very interested in filling the position of tutor/companion that you advertised for in Saturday's paper. I feel that my education and extensive work with children qualify me for the job.

I have done a great deal of work with children, primarily with the mildly to severely disabled. I started five years ago as a volunteer and have worked my way up to director of two programs for learning disabled children and teens. In these programs I have had the responsibility of supervising up to 15 children as well as two staff and some volunteers. I have learned to plan activities, games, and learning activities for these children. I also have some camping experience with children from regular schools in outdoor education settings. In this I worked with normal children, ages 8-15, for two months. This gave me the opportunity to expose children to nature through hikes, swimming, horseback riding, and nature studies.

I am presently in my third year of study in the Special Education program. I attended a private all-girls high school with an academic focus and took many grade 11 and 12 science courses including biology, chemistry, physics, and math. In my first year at university I studied chemistry and math. I feel that, because of these studies, I have a fairly firm rooting in the sciences area. This grounding, when added to my studies in Education would enable me to help your children while away from their regular schools.

I find this opportunity challenging as well as interesting. As I have travelled to New Zealand and Australia a few years ago, I am not a stranger to the area and feel I can be an asset to you and your children. I look forward to discussing this job with you further in the near future.

    d. I am most interested in filling the Tutor/Companion position that you have recently advertised. I believe that both my experience and education make me an attractive candidate for this post.

    While studying at the University of Guelph in Ontario, I worked as a senior tutor for the biological and chemical sciences. This provided me with the opportunity to effectively deal with others on a one-to-one basis and also to improve my instructional skills. In addition, I have been employed as a tennis instructor and swimming instructor/lifeguard. This experience undoubtedly will be most valuable for your children during this four month period. Having only limited travel experience, I would look upon this position as a chance to further both my education and the education of your children.

    To date, I have completed an honours Bachelor of Science degree in the biological sciences from the University of Guelph. Courses that I have taken, such as calculus, chemistry, biology, botany and zoology, will be a definite asset for this position. In addition, I have given oral reports on research projects that I have conducted.

    I find this position that you have advertised to be both interesting and attractive. I would welcome the opportunity to further discuss with you this post and my qualifications, at an interview. I have enclosed a copy of my résumé for your perusal. Please do not hesitate to contact me at the above address and telephone number. I look forward to hearing from you.

9. Revise the letter you thought was the weakest one.

10. List the assumptions each of the writers in exercise 8 has made about the children and about the family.

11. Select an advertisement from the newspaper for a job for which you think you are qualified now. Cut out the advertisement and submit it with this assignment. Prepare a résumé and the job application letter.

12. Obtain a UCPA (University and College Placement Association) application and fill it in.

CHAPTER 22

PROPOSALS

Introduction

Guidelines for Preparing a Proposal

An Example of a Proposal

Exercises

INTRODUCTION

The importance of proposals varies from discipline to discipline and depends on the kinds of business transactions a company or organization engages in. Since you are unlikely to be asked to prepare a major proposal alone, particularly in the early years of your professional life, this chapter is designed more to inform you about what proposals are than to prepare you to write any but the briefest ones on your own. This chapter defines what a proposal is, outlines some common purposes of proposals, and explains the difference between solicited and unsolicited proposals. It also provides an overview of the preparation of a proposal, suggests some guidelines on format and organization, and then presents an example of a short proposal for supplying a product.

DEFINITION

Like reports, proposals include a wide variety of documents. The simplest proposals can be brief memos, such as the one you may have prepared in Chapter 16 to gain approval of your report topic. Complex proposals, such as ones that are prepared to win contracts to design and build large projects, extend to several volumes, each of which may be hundreds of pages long. Some proposals are prepared for an audience within an organization; these are called *internal* proposals. For example, college instructors who want to offer new courses prepare proposals for an audience of departments and deans within the college. More frequently, though, proposals are prepared for an audience outside an organization; these are called *external* proposals. For example, a civil engineering firm that wants to win a contract to build a bridge might prepare a proposal addressed to the appropriate government department.

What characteristics, then, do proposals share?

- *Proposals are offers of products or services.* Because they are offers, they commit the source (whoever issues the proposal) to the delivery of the products or services specified. In the examples mentioned above, the college instructors are offering to teach a new course and the engineering firm is offering to build a bridge.
- *Proposals are sales documents.* From the point of view of the source of the proposal, the objective is to secure a contract (as in the case of the external proposal) or the approval of a plan (as in the case of an internal proposal). The writer's job is to persuade the audience to accept the proposal.

- *Proposals include detailed descriptions of the product or service that is offered and also detailed descriptions of how and by whom the product or service will be delivered.* In other words, proposals specify the "how" as well as the "what."
- *Most proposals are source-initiated.* While some clients may specifically invite proposals from particular companies, those companies must nevertheless decide whether or not they wish to prepare a proposal.
- *Large proposals are major undertakings that may occupy teams of specialists for months.*
- *The structure of proposals is often similar to the structure of reports.*

To summarize, we will use the term *proposal* in the following two related senses:

- a document that offers specific products or services to a specific client in a contractual agreement.
- a document that makes a single, integrated suggestion, and describes a plan for executing or implementing that suggestion.

PURPOSE

Many proposals are similar to job applications in function. When you write a proposal, you are trying to persuade the audience that your company can do a particular job better than someone else or that the audience needs a job done and your company is the best candidate to do it. In most technical fields, proposals are extremely important as a means of getting contracts and as a means of finding companies that will do work or provide products.

The most common purposes of proposals from the point of view of writers are the following:

- *To get a design contract.* Consulting firms write proposals to get contracts to solve various technical problems, whether or not these firms also become responsible for constructing what they have designed. For example, a consulting firm might write a proposal to design a new waste disposal system for a chemical plant. They may or may not actually construct the system they design.
- *To get a construction or manufacturing contract.* Construction firms and firms that produce various kinds of machinery or instruments or software write proposals to get contracts. For example, an engineering firm might write a proposal to build a waste disposal system that another firm has designed.
- *To sell a product.* For example, a company that manufactures electronic sensing equipment might write a proposal to sell this equipment to an aircraft manufacturer.
- *To sell a service.* Many companies write proposals to get contracts

to supply a service. For example, a tree planting company may write a proposal to win a tree planting contract.

- *To get a research contract.* Researchers write proposals to get funding for their research. For example, a cellular biologist might write a proposal to a pharmaceutical firm to get funding for a research project.

SOLICITED AND UNSOLICITED PROPOSALS

Solicited proposals are written in response to a call for proposals. Sometimes this call is as informal as the one you may have responded to in Chapter 16. More often, though, particularly if the proposal is for a complex project, a client will issue a request for proposals (RFP). If an organization – let us call it Timberline Logging – decides to hire a contractor to build a new facility, it may issue an RFP so it can find the best contractor. Contractors that want to do this job will each submit a proposal. Timberline will award the contract to the company whose proposal indicates that it can do the best job or that it can do an equally good job at less cost.

The RFP will specify what the client's needs are, and what the proposal must include, and it may specify how the proposal itself is to be organized and presented. Usually, a solicited proposal has to compete with other proposals for a contract, and the challenge for the proposal team is to prepare the winning proposal. In this case the proposal writers don't have to convince the clients that the clients require a product or service; instead they have to convince the clients that their particular product or service is in some way superior to all others, or that their company is superior.

An unsolicited proposal is not submitted in response to a request for proposals, and there is usually no competition among companies. Rather, the proposal writer must convince the potential clients they need something the proposing company has to offer. Let us say Innovative Electronics is trying to sell a new product or procedure it has developed. It finds out that Horizon Communications has some projects that could be made more efficient using this new product or procedure. It contacts someone at Horizon who expresses interest in principle and suggests Innovative submit a proposal. If Horizon is persuaded by the proposal, it may award a contract to Innovative.

GUIDELINES FOR PREPARING A PROPOSAL
PREPARATION

As in preparing a job application, you have to analyze the audience's needs, both for the proposed product or service and for information in the proposal; determine exactly what you have to offer; and then match the two. However, the form in which your proposal is presented will be completely different from that of a job application.

If there is a published request for proposal, analyze it to see what the client wants. Sometimes a client simply indicates the problem that has to be solved, and proposals are judged on the quality of the design or of the technical solution. Try to assess the audience's needs as accurately as possible. Try to meet with your client to confirm the accuracy of your assessment.

If the proposal is not solicited, you have to research the client's needs more fully to derive your own equivalent of a "request." Again, you may be able to get a lot of help from your client.

Since proposals are very detailed documents, and since your company will be legally bound to deliver what the proposal promises, major proposals are prepared by teams of specialists. Most proposals will have to include, in detail, the following kinds of information:

- The *full technical specifications* of the product. The more complex the product, the more complex these specifications will have to be. The completeness and accuracy of the specifications will help the client determine your technical credibility.
- An explanation of how the product meets the client's *technical needs*. The client needs to know that you do understand what the client's specific technical problems are.
- A detailed *development schedule* for the product so that the client can tell which development steps you propose to include and when they will be completed. A realistic schedule tells the client that you really do know what steps are required and how long each will take.
- A project *cost schedule*. The project will have to be broken down into steps, and the following costs will have to be assessed for each step: materials, equipment, labour, management. A realistic cost schedule will again assure the client that your company knows what it is doing.
- A *management plan*. Key technical and management personnel have to be identified and their expertise described.
- A *description of your company*. The client will have to be convinced that your company can be relied on to do the job. You will have to demonstrate the stability of the company and its ability to summon the financial, technical, and management resources needed to complete the project.

When you have worked out the details of what you have to offer, you must develop a persuasive strategy. Determine what the main strengths of your offer are. Remember that if there is a competition for a contract, you have to show the clients why they should choose your proposal. What are your selling points? If you have articulated these explicitly, then you can plan your proposal so as to focus on them.

FORMAT AND ORGANIZATION

In general, proposals can have the same forms as reports – letters, memos, and formal report format. Usually, a letter would be used for a very simple and relatively short external proposal and a memo for all but the most complex internal proposals. The RFP of a complex solicited proposal will usually specify the required format for the proposal. It will include the headings that are to be used and the kind of information that should be supplied under each heading. For example, it might specify that the proposal be organized as follows:

1. Introduction
2. Personnel Qualifications
3. Technical Approach
4. Company Background
5. Management
6. Budget

As well, it might specify such details as the maximum length of the proposal, the size of margins, the number of copies of the proposal that must be submitted. These specifications must be followed very carefully.

If there is no RFP, or if the RFP is not very specific about format, you can use the guidelines outlined here. The proposal should begin with the following components:

- *Letter of transmittal.* The letter of transmittal should identify the document as a proposal, indicate which RFP it is responding to, and include a brief persuasive overview of the proposal. If possible, the letter should introduce the sales strategy that informs the proposal; it should include the main selling points.
- *Cover.* The cover should include your legal name for contractual purposes, the title of the proposal, the date of submission, and any other necessary identification. A well-designed cover can help to create a good company image. Some companies include an illustration on the cover; a photograph of a product you are promoting might be quite persuasive.
- *Table of contents.*
- *List of illustrations.*
- *Summary.* The summary should provide a persuasive overview of the most important features of the proposal. It should outline the problem the proposal is addressing and the solution it is offering. It should indicate the main strengths of your company, of the technical proposal, and of the management plan, as well as the total cost of the project.

The proposal proper will provide the full details of the proposal. It should include the following sections:

- *The company background.* Provide a concise description of your company, but emphasize the qualities that make it a strong competitor for this contract. How long has it been in operation? What is its main line of business? What products does it produce? Who are the directors? Is the company public or private? Who are the major shareholders? Who are the company's financial and legal advisors?
- *The project overview.* Describe the problem as you understand it and indicate how your company proposes to solve it.
- *The technical proposal.* Give the full technical specifications of the product or service you are offering. In the case of proposals to develop or supply complex equipment, the technical proposal may be an entire volume. Explain what is special about your offer; don't expect the audience to recognize the significance of unusual features. Persuade the audience that yours is the superior product.
- *The development schedule.* Provide an overview of the tasks and subtasks that will constitute the project and provide a detailed schedule of when the subtasks will be engaged in and when they will be completed. You will probably want to use a Gantt chart to illustrate your schedule (see Chapter 3). The schedule helps the audience assess whether you really know what you are doing. Also, if you win the contract, it serves as a target, or gauge, against which progress can be measured when you write progress reports.
- *The management proposal.* Convince the audience that you have the best management resources for the project. Provide the résumés of the key personnel and their responsibilities in the project. Demonstrate that you have the equipment, facilities, and expertise to complete the project. Indicate the safeguards that your company is providing to assure the successful completion of the project.
- *The price proposal.* Provide a detailed projection of all costs. Include full details of the cost of equipment, materials, facilities, subcontracting, and all labour costs. In labour costs, show how many workers in each category (engineers, mechanics, secretaries) will be used, as well as how many hours or days they will work and at what rate. For very large projects, the price proposal may be broken down into the costs for each major substep.

AN EXAMPLE OF A PROPOSAL

Figure 22-1 is a short unsolicited proposal for supplying a product. This product was also described in the reply to a letter of inquiry in Chapter 19. Such a proposal might be written when Autopark learned that Silver Rapids was planning to convert some of its conventional parking meters to ones with electronic displays.

Figure 22-1
An Unsolicited
Proposal

AUTOPARK ELECTRONICS LTD.

P.O. Box 4318
Downsview, Ontario M3M 3E5

November 13, 1989

Traffic Department
Municipality of Silver Rapids
100 Front Street
Silver Rapids, Ontario
N7R 1E6

Dear Sir:

Autopark Electronics has learned that Silver Rapids is planning to convert 57 conventional parking meters to ones with electronic displays. As a recognized leader in the manufacturing of electronic parking meters, Autopark invites you to consider the attached proposal to supply and install 57 of our EM1027 electronic parking systems for a total cost of $8550 plus tax.

Yours truly,

AUTOPARK ELECTRONICS LTD.

Mary Tomasi

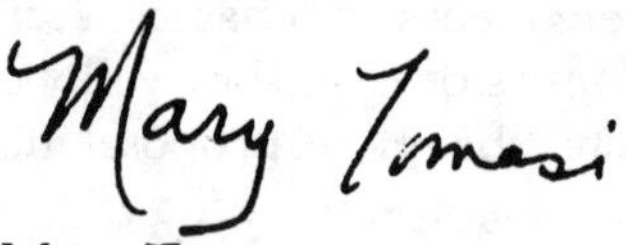

Mary Tomasi
Director of Marketing

PROPOSAL TO SUPPLY
ELECTRONIC PARKING METER SYSTEMS

Summary
Autopark Electronics Ltd., a recognized leader in the manufacturing of electronic parking meter systems, proposes to supply and install 57 EM1027 electronic parking meters at a cost of $8550 plus tax.

Company Description
Autopark Electronics is a publicly held Canadian company whose head office is located in Downsview, Ontario. Autopark began operations in 1979 and has been manufacturing electronic parking meter systems since 1981. Its list of clients includes most larger municipalities in Canada.

Project Overview
The Municipality of Silver Rapids plans to convert its 57 conventional parking meters to ones with electronic displays. They require a product with the following characteristics:

- It must accept the $1 coin.
- It must be programmable for different rates and time limits.
- It must operate in temperatures between 40°C and −40°C.
- It must require very little maintenance.

Autopark Electronics' Solution
Autopark Electronics proposes to supply and install 57 EM1027 electronic parking meters in the Municipality of Silver Rapids. The EM1027 has the characteristics Silver Rapids requires:

- It accepts the $1 coin.
- It can be reprogrammed for rates and time limits on site without any special equipment.
- It can operate in temperatures between 40°C and −40°C.
- It requires very little maintenance.

Technical Proposal

The EM1027, developed in 1986, grew out of the very successful and reliable EK1001, which was first introduced in 1984. The EM1027 is an electronic parking meter system with the following special features:

- It has an especially clear digital display of parking time remaining.
- When the parking time expires, the display shows the time at which the violation began.
- It accepts Canadian $0.25 and $1 coins.
- It can be programmed for time limits at ten-minute intervals from 10 minutes to 1 hour.
- It operates on a single lithium battery with a life of three years.
- It has a low-battery indicator.
- It comes with a two-year warranty on parts and labour.

Schedule

Autopark Electronics can supply the units at any time with 14 days' notice. Our crews will need four days to install the meters and one day to train Silver Rapids' maintenance staff.

Cost Proposal

> 57 EM1027's @ $150 = $8550 plus tax

Terms: 30 days

2

EXERCISES

Pretend that three students, one of whom uses a wheelchair, want to spend next summer conducting a wheelchair accessibility study of the campus and prepare a report for the college administration. They want to earn as much from this project as they would doing other summer work.

Working with a proposal writing team of at least five or six classmates, prepare the full, formal, unsolicited proposal to get funding for this project. You will have to conduct several meetings to complete the proposal. The following suggestions may help your team.

1. Choose the leader of your team; this student will co-ordinate the work of the other members. Determine which three students in your group would want the summer job. In the proposal you will have to convince the administration that these three students have the credentials to complete the study and prepare the report.

2. The product that you are proposing to produce is a report. Determine what will be included in the final report that the three students propose to present at the end of the summer. The least that the report should include is a detailed map of the campus showing any paths or sidewalks that are not accessible to wheelchairs and a detailed inventory of classrooms, laboratories, and offices that are not accessible. What, exactly, will be the product that you are asking the administration to finance? The details of this product will form the basis for the Technical Proposal section of the complete proposal.

3. Subdivide the proposal writing task into subtasks and determine who is responsible for each one. Who will prepare the Cost Proposal? Who will prepare the overview of the problem? Who will prepare the Gantt charts? Who will prepare the Executive Summary? Who will co-ordinate the writing of the proposal?

4. Determine your persuasive strategy. What are your project's greatest strengths?

5. Prepare the section of the proposal that you have been assigned.

TECHNICAL SPEAKING

PART SEVEN

TECHNICAL SPEAKING

CHAPTER 23

TECHNICAL SPEAKING

Introduction

Differences between Technical Writing and Technical Speaking

Speaking Tasks

Preparation of Technical Talks

Presentation of Technical Talks

Notes

Exercises

INTRODUCTION

In addition to writing, and often in conjunction with writing, you can expect to spend much of your professional time speaking. A recent study reports that, on average, professionals spend half of their working time speaking, with the time spent by each of four subgroups varying as follows:[1]

agriculture	59%
business	59%
engineering	43%
physical sciences	33%

This chapter first reviews the differences between technical writing and technical speaking and outlines the types of technical speaking tasks you are likely to encounter. Then it discusses in some detail how to prepare and present technical talks.

DIFFERENCES BETWEEN TECHNICAL WRITING AND TECHNICAL SPEAKING

Consider the ways in which writing differs from speaking. The three key differences from which other differences derive are the immediacy and the transience of the speaking situation, and the lack of visual cues.

IMMEDIACY

Speaking is immediate in the sense that both the audience and the speaker are physically present at the time of communication. This, in turn, has the following consequences:

- *The listener reacts to the speaker as a person.* Your appearance, personality, and body language – including stance, gestures and facial expressions – will affect how your listener perceives and reacts to your message. A positive personal impression can compensate for an otherwise weak communication, but a negative impression may also detract from your message.
- *The speaker can gauge the audience's reaction.* The listeners' body language will often indicate whether they are bored, lost, resistant, interested, or supportive. Try to be sensitive to your audience's reactions and adjust what you are saying so as to get the most positive reaction. Be aware of the difficulty of getting people to listen and keeping them listening.

- *The speaker and listener can question each other.*
- *The speaker can use tone of voice and stress to alter a message.* Often a very slight change in the tone of voice can alter a message. That is why people say "Don't use that tone of voice around here." Consider how the meaning of the following sentence shifts as you move the stress from word to word: "I like that." In how many ways can you say this sentence? What does this do to the meaning? Remember that your tone of voice can create a negative impression without your being aware of it.

TRANSIENCE

Normally a speaker makes only one pass through a speech and the listeners cannot go back to an earlier part they did not understand or cannot remember. Also, the larger the group of listeners, and the less the immediate motivation to listen, the more likely it is that the listener's mind will wander. Almost anything, including a neighbour's shoes, can distract a listener. Consider what distracts you in class, for example. For how many minutes do you pay attention if you are not immediately engaged in what is going on? The reader whose mind wanders can always go back to the top of the page and start again, but the listener whose mind wanders has no way to recover what has been said.

To overcome the problems of transience when you are speaking, you should try to make the text more *listenable*. Make the organization explicit. Preview, indicate transitions, and summarize. Use visual aids to emphasize organization. Keep lists short, and keep sentences relatively short and free of complicated structures.

As a listener you should take notes to help remember what is said. That is why minutes are kept at formal meetings. You should also keep your private notes of what transpires at meetings and of what is agreed to on the telephone or in informal meetings. If you are uncertain about whether you remember what was said, or if you want to make an agreement more binding, you can send a letter or memo asking the other individual to confirm or contradict your interpretation of what happened.

LACK OF VISUAL CUES

Speech lacks visual cues such as paragraph indentions and headings. As we will see later, one of the functions of visuals in speeches is to overcome this lack.

SPEAKING TASKS

Precisely which speaking tasks you will encounter on the job and how much of your working time they will occupy will depend on the kind of job you have. A special kind of "speaking" you may have to do, particularly if you have to produce a lot of correspondence, is dictating.

Dictating is special in the sense that instead of speaking to someone, you are composing a spoken version of a text for a typist to type. In preparing to dictate, you must, of course, define the task and organize the discourse, just as you do in preparing a written text. As you dictate, you must speak clearly and indicate paragraph breaks and any punctuation that is not obvious from your intonation.

The other common speaking tasks can be distinguished on the basis of formality of the context, with the informal ones including face-to-face conversations, telephone conversations, and informal meetings, and the formal ones including formal interviews and formal meetings. The informal speaking tasks constitute the regular day-to-day communication on the job among participants who know each other. In all speaking situations you must be courteous and you must be a good listener. In addition to using the ordinary conversation skills, you should try to use the you-attitude and observe corporate manners. Corporate manners, the details of which vary from corporation to corporation, concern such conventions as whether or not you shake hands, how formally you address each other, how you seat yourselves in a group, and so on.

Formal speaking situations are more rare in most jobs, but they may be extremely important. They are specially scheduled and arranged, have some official status, and have a clear agenda. The participants need not know each other, but do come prepared for the agenda. There are clear expectations of behaviour, and there may be rituals that participants must observe. Usually forms of address will be more formal, permitted topics will be restricted, and turn-taking will be fairly formal.

For each of these speaking situations there are some guidelines you should observe.

FACE-TO-FACE CONVERSATIONS

Learn to shake hands firmly, to make eye contact, and to remember names. Cultivate a friendly manner. Use the you-attitude. Listen.

TELEPHONE CONVERSATIONS

If you are making the call, plan what you want to accomplish. What is your agenda? Define your task. Begin the call by identifying yourself and make sure you know to whom you're speaking. If you know the listener, you may want to make some small talk to establish a friendly, co-operative mood, but don't waste time with gossip. Then set the context for your main business. Establish common ground by referring to the last time you talked, or to a memo, or to the project you are working on. If you are receiving the call, make sure you know to whom you are talking and what the common ground is before you get to the "business" portion of the call.

During the "business" portion of the call, be very clear and specific in what you say and make sure you understand everything that is said to you. Take brief but careful notes of what you agree to and what your listener agrees to. Make sure you have all the information you may need, such as complete addresses, complete and correct order numbers, and so on. Avoid the embarrassment of having to make another call to get more information. Make sure, also, that you don't promise what you don't have the authority to do.

At the end of the conversation, summarize any agreements. What have you said you will do? What has the listener agreed to? Close cordially. Thank the listener.

INFORMAL MEETINGS

You may have to participate in an informal meeting almost every day. Observe the following guidelines:

- Learn the corporate manners that apply to the various kinds of meetings that your job requires. Where are you to sit relative to others? When are you to speak? How are you to address others?
- Pay attention to the group dynamics, to how the individuals interact. How do they assert power? Where do you fit in?
- Listen carefully and look interested, no matter what. Make eye contact with the speaker and with others in the group. Don't doodle, slouch, or look at your watch or out the window.
- Don't speak just for the sake of speaking, but when you do speak, be clear, precise, and careful. Make eye contact with the people you're addressing.

INTERVIEWS

An interview is a formal, planned information-seeking meeting. Usually the interviewer and interviewee are strangers. Before the interview, both parties should prepare – the interviewer by phrasing key questions, and the interviewee by reviewing relevant information. Two special kinds of interviews are discussed elsewhere in this text: job interviews in Chapter 21, and information-gathering interviews in Chapter 15. Whether you are the interviewer or the interviewee, be courteous, clear, and efficient. If you are the interviewer, keep careful, but quick notes, and before you leave, check the accuracy of your understanding of key points.

FORMAL MEETINGS

Formal meetings are called by administrators to keep others informed, to announce and justify changes, and sometimes to make formal decisions. They are more common in large organizations that have a democratic decision-making mandate. Observe the following guidelines:

- Learn the corporate manners that apply. Where should you sit? How do you indicate you want to speak? How do you address and refer to others? To learn corporate decorum, observe and copy others and ask your supervisor about the points that are unclear to you.
- Learn how business is conducted. Are Robert's Rules of Order followed? Must you direct your remarks to the chair?

- Prepare for meetings. Study the agenda; determine what the issues are; gather any additional evidence you may need. How do the issues affect you? What is at stake? What is your role at the meeting? What interests are you representing? What does your supervisor expect of you? What is your personal stance? How will your stance affect others? How will others perceive your stance?
- Be alert and look alert. Keep notes of the main points made. Observe any unusual or unpredictable shifts in the line of arguments. Keep track of the issues.
- Speak only if you have something relevant to say and if it is appropriate for you to speak. If you speak, observe the six Cs:

    be confident
    be courteous
    be constructive
    be cautious
    be clear
    be concise

    Remember that what you say will be recorded in minutes.
- Overcome stage fright by knowing beforehand what you will say, by speaking more slowly at first than seems natural, by breathing naturally, and by not being afraid of silence.

PREPARATION OF TECHNICAL TALKS

Prepare a formal presentation in much the same way as you prepare a document. It has been suggested that you should spend one hour preparing for every minute you will be speaking.[2]

DEFINING THE TASK

Review Chapter 5. Define your purpose as precisely as you can. Find out as much as you can about your audience. Determine whether you are expected to speak from notes or read a manuscript, how much delivery time you will have, and whether or not there will be a question period.

ORGANIZING

A presentation must be organized very carefully, and the organization must be made explicit to help the listener. Review Chapter 6. Before making your outline or plan, check your time limit to decide how many main points you will be able to make. Convert the time into equivalent pages of double-spaced text. You can probably deliver four to five pages in ten minutes, or eight to ten pages in twenty minutes. How many key points can you make and develop in ten pages? If you are reading a manuscript, you can probably include more points than if you are speaking from notes.

CHOOSING AND PREPARING VISUALS

As you plan your presentation, you should also be designing and preparing your visuals. For the general principles governing graphics, review Chapter 3. Designing visuals for oral presentations is, however, somewhat different from designing visuals for documents. In particular, you must consider the following matters:

- the media to use
- the demands of the speaking context

MEDIA. In written documents, graphics have to be presented on paper. In talks, however, many media may be used, including the following:

- handouts
- overhead transparencies
- slides
- flip charts
- blackboards
- posters
- models
- films or video tapes

In choosing the medium, consider the following questions:

- *What equipment will be available in the room?*
- *How large will the room be and how large will the audience be?* Make sure that everyone in the audience will be able to see your visuals clearly.
- *What resources do you have for producing visuals?* Don't forget you can probably use colour. Avoid amateurish visuals, even in fairly informal talks.
- *What will the visuals be like?* If your graphics are complicated and your listeners will need time to study them, then use handouts rather than slides or overhead transparencies.

SPEAKING CONTEXT. As we noted earlier, there are some important differences between speaking and writing. Resulting from these differences are several additional purposes that visuals can serve in oral presentations. In fact, special kinds of visuals can be used to overcome some of the limitations of the oral context, particularly transience and the lack of visual cues. These special visuals, usually transparencies, consist mainly of words, as in Figure 23-1.

These visuals are used, first of all, to focus the listeners' attention. As we said before, listeners are distracted very easily, and this is perhaps the main obstacle for a speaker. However, a visual is almost like a magnet in that it is almost impossible not to look at one. In using visuals, then, the speaker regains the listeners' attention. At the same time, however, the visual can distract the listener from what the speaker is saying; if the visual simply repeats what the speaker is saying, then the listener may feel insulted, and will neither look nor listen.

Figure 23-1
A Visual for an
Oral Presentation

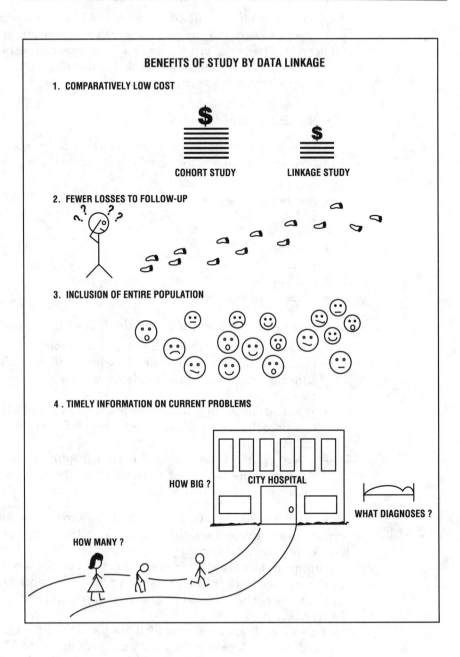

Source: Reprinted, by permission, from L. Wynn, F. White, Nova Scotia Saskatchewan Cardio-vascular Epidemiology Study Group, "The Nova Scotia Saskatchewan Heart Study," *Proceedings of the Workshop on Computerized Record Linkage in Health Research Ottawa, Ontario, May 21-23, 1986,* eds. G.R. Howe and R.A. Spasoff (Toronto: University of Toronto, 1986) 182.

A more important function of visuals in talks is to compensate for the lack of visual cues to organization. As we said before, there are no headings, paragraph breaks, or other visual cues to organization in a speech. We have stressed from the beginning how important these are in technical writing. Visuals can be used to show organization and thereby to overcome this lack. A visual presented early on can show the main points or headings and serve as a forecasting statement. As you move from main point to main point, you can use the same visual to show where you are. You can also use visuals to highlight the main points within major sections. However, if you overdo this, you may lose your audience to boredom. Give them a reason to listen, but don't make them listen too long without help.

In designing visuals for your talk, bear in mind the following special features of using visuals in oral contexts:

- *Speaker control.* A great advantage of the speaking situation is that you can control when your audience sees the graphic and for how long. In planning the talk, plan exactly when you will show a particular visual and how long you will let the audience look at it. You can also choose visuals that are dynamic rather than static. For example, you can draw on the blackboard or transparency, and add to the drawing as your talk progresses. Similarly, you can uncover a transparency to reveal more, or use overlays to show developments.
- *Limited time for reading a visual.* Since it would be very awkward and disruptive to stop a talk while the audience examines a complex visual, most visuals have to be designed so they can be read quickly. This eliminates not only most tables and complicated graphs, but also diagrams with many parts or numerous labels. More complex graphics can only be presented on handouts or posters, and then the audience has to be allowed time to study and discuss them.

PREPARING NOTES OR A MANUSCRIPT

Whether you speak from notes or read a prepared manuscript will normally depend on the formality of the occasion and on whether or not you have been asked to read. Speaking from notes has the important advantage of a more spontaneous delivery because you are composing sentences as you go. The audience will feel that you are talking to them, and this in itself will help to engage their attention. The disadvantage of speaking from notes is that unless the notes are very good and you are quite an experienced speaker, you may stumble or lose your train of thought. For this reason, and to make sure you are within the time limit, you should practise your speech at least once before you give it. Also, to ensure a smooth beginning and conclusion, you may want to have full written versions of the first four and last four sentences to read. Notes require very careful organization. In fact, the notes should be rather like a note version distilled from a text that you will have to reconstruct as you speak. Include all the major and minor points in their appropriate sequence. It is a good idea to use overhead transparencies to display your main points, but normally these transparencies won't be as full as will your notes. Make your notes large enough to see comfortably and yet as unobtrusive to the audience as possible. As you speak, convert the points to sentences and insert the necessary transitions. Use a lectern for your notes if possible.

Prepare a full manuscript only if you will be reading it. Before preparing your manuscript, review Chapter 7. Also review the differences between speaking and writing and try to make it easier for your listeners to follow what you are saying. To make your presentation more listenable, observe the following guidelines:

- Explicitly preview the structure of the paper and use overheads to show your headings, if appropriate.
- Use explicit introductions, transitions, and summaries throughout the presentation.
- Avoid sentences that are difficult to process. Complex subordinations, multiple negatives, and very long clauses are particularly difficult. Break up long sentences. Replace negatives with positives. Read your manuscript to a friend to help you identify passages that need to be simplified.
- Keep lists short.
- Use pronouns only if their antecedents are obvious.
- Use terms your listeners know. If you must use unfamiliar terms, define them and try to include them in overheads to show how they are spelled.
- When you document references, try to make the name of the author part of the sentence. For example, instead of "This phenomenon has received considerable scholarly attention (Brown, 1950; Jones, 1973; Smith, 1986)," write "This phenomenon was first examined by Brown in 1950. Later studies include those by Jones in 1973 and Smith in 1986."

To make the manuscript easier to read, you can triple-space or you can enlarge the type on a photocopier. Always practise reading the manuscript to make sure you don't stumble on a word or lose your way in a sentence. Indicate exactly when each visual should be shown and for how long. Mark the manuscript to indicate emphasis and to highlight main points.

PRESENTATION OF TECHNICAL TALKS

Making the presentation includes not just delivering your talk, but also overcoming nervousness, establishing and maintaining rapport, and using visual aids.

OVERCOMING NERVOUSNESS

It is normal to be a little nervous about giving a presentation. Review what it is you are most nervous about. Are you afraid that your audience won't like you? To overcome this reason for nervousness, think about speakers you have not liked, and why, and try not to be like that. Check that you are appropriately dressed and carefully groomed so that you won't feel self-conscious about your appearance. Are you afraid that you will lose your place in your talk or that your audience won't like your presentation? To reassure yourself about how the actual talk will go, be as prepared as you can. Know your material, but don't try to memorize it. Rehearse your presentation. Have good notes or a good manuscript and good visuals.

The most difficult time is always the beginning. You may find the following hints helpful:

- Try to get to the room before the talk and familiarize yourself with the general layout, the lectern, the audio-visual equipment, and how the room looks when you are at the front. Try to feel at home in the environment.
- Know whether you will be introduced. Prepare a very brief introduction in case you'll need to introduce yourself.
- Look at your audience. Don't let your audience become a sea of faces. Instead, focus on particular individuals and make eye contact.
- Keep your body relaxed. Raising one foot can help you relax, but make sure the audience cannot see you are doing this.
- Breathe normally. Try to establish normal breathing before you begin to speak.
- Smile.
- Speak slowly. Most inexperienced speakers try to speak too quickly. Don't be afraid of silence. Realize that your sense of time while you are speaking is very different from that of your audience.
- Write out your first four sentences so you can be absolutely sure you'll get a good start.

ESTABLISHING AND MAINTAINING RAPPORT

An audience that likes you will be more attentive and more receptive of your ideas. For this reason, try to give the impression that you are making the presentation for them and not for yourself. The following suggestions may help you establish and maintain rapport:

- Be aware of your audience. Observe the audience's response and adjust your presentation as needed. If they look puzzled, slow down a little and explain your points more fully. If they look bored, speed up and shorten your explanations.
- Let your audience know you are aware of them. Make an opening remark that relates to common ground, such as what a previous speaker has said. Make eye contact. Smile.
- Look like you really want to give your talk.

DELIVERY

A good way to improve your delivery is to listen to tapes of yourself and to watch yourself on video. Make sure that you can be heard and that you don't do things that will distract your audience from what you are saying. Let your personality determine your individual speaking style. You should, however, observe the following guidelines:

- Stand so as to look poised and calmly confident.
- Avoid any distracting physical mannerisms such as touching your hair.
- Except in the most formal contexts, move from the lectern for emphasis. Don't, however, distract your audience with too much movement.
- Speak in a well-modulated voice, enunciate clearly, and maintain a natural speed.
- Avoid fillers such as "OK, then," or "and, uh," or "well, uh." Learn to be comfortable with silent breaks between sentences.
- Show enthusiasm. If you don't think your subject is interesting, why should your audience?

USING VISUAL AIDS

The main challenge in using visual aids in a presentation is to integrate them into the talk. Practise using them so that the transitions to and from the visuals are smooth. Mark your notes or manuscript with the point at which each visual is to be shown and turned off. You may find the following hints helpful:

- Make sure your audience has enough time to read the visual. When you prepared the visual, you should have made it as simple as possible, but now you have to consider how long it will take the audience to read it. Again, don't be afraid of silence.
- Help the audience read more complicated visuals by directing their attention to what they are to notice. Focus their attention by using a pointer and by covering what is not necessary at that time.
- When the audience is not supposed to be looking at the visual, remove it and turn the projector off.

NOTES

1. Larry R. Smeltzer and Kaylene A. Gibert, "How Business Communication Needs Differ among Professions," *The Bulletin of the ABC* 49.3 (Sept. 1986): 5.
2. Terry C. Smith, "Conquering Unspeakable Fear," *The Bulletin of the ABC* 49.3 (Sept. 1986): 29.

EXERCISES

1. Introduce a classmate to the class as though that classmate were a guest speaker. You will have two minutes for the introduction. To complete this assignment you have to interview the classmate to find out the kind of information your audience will find interesting and relevant.

2. Prepare an oral summary of your major report. You will have five minutes for your presentation.

3. Present one recommendation from your major report. Provide the necessary background, explain the problem you are addressing, and explain your recommendation. Use appropriate visuals.

4. a. Interview two people whose work includes public speaking. The purpose of the interview is to elicit advice on public speaking. You could pursue any of the following questions, or you could add others that particularly interest you.

   • What are some strategies for overcoming nervousness?
   • What qualities must a good speaker have?
   • How should one prepare for a presentation?
   • What are the most difficult aspects of making a presentation?

   b. Prepare a five-minute summary of the advice you elicited in part a.

MECHANICS

SPELLING

Although spelling errors almost never lead to misunderstanding, they can have a very strong stigmatizing effect. How many times have you heard a statement such as "He can't even spell" used to dismiss someone's competence? While very few people never make errors in spelling, careful writers know when they are uncertain about how to spell a word and will look it up in a dictionary. If you want to improve your spelling, you might try keeping a personal list of the words you have trouble spelling. You may be surprised at how few words you really do have trouble spelling, or you may discover that you are not applying one or two of the rules that apply to English spelling. You should also try marking the place in your dictionary every time you look up a particular word, because this will both save you time when you look it up again, and provide you with another record of words you have trouble spelling. If you are using a word processing program that allows you to check spelling automatically, by all means take advantage of it. Be aware, though, that such spelling programs will only tell you whether the letter sequences you have used are in their listing of legitimate words. They will not help you with two common kinds of errors: the misuse of the apostrophe and the confusion of homonyms. Two additional aspects of spelling to consider are hyphenation and the differences between Canadian and American preferred spellings.

APOSTROPHE

The apostrophe has three main uses:

- *To indicate the possessive form of nouns*

	Singular	*Plural*
Subject form:	friend	friends
Possessive form:	friend's	friends'

Examples:

My friend has a car.
My friend's car is in the garage.
My friends have a car.
My friends' car is in the garage.

If the subject form of the singular noun ends in *-s*, you must still add *'s* to make the singular possessive:

	Singular	*Plural*
Subject form:	class	classes
Possessive form:	class's	classes'

If the subject form of the plural noun does not end in *-s*, add *'s* to make the plural possessive:

	Singular	*Plural*
Subject form:	woman	women
Possessive form:	woma<u>n's</u>	wome<u>n's</u>

Treat pronouns ending in *-one*, *-body*, and *-other* as nouns.

Subject form:	somebody
Possessive form:	somebod<u>y's</u>

Do NOT use an apostrophe in the possessive form of *he, she, it, you, who, they*:

Subject form:	he	she	it	you	who	they
Possessive form:	his	her	its	your	whose	their

Examples:

I left my car at home because <u>its</u> clutch is broken.
She knows <u>whose</u> book that is.
The students have already written <u>their</u> essays.

- *To indicate the omission in contractions.* Contractions with negatives (*isn't, can't, don't*) are acceptable in most contexts. However, contractions such as *it's* (*it is*), *they're* (*they are*), *man's* (as in *The man's here*, for *The man is here*) may be considered too informal for some professional writing.
- *To indicate the plural of a number or letter*, as in: *His 7's look like 1's.*

HOMONYMS

Homonyms are words that sound the same but differ in spelling and meaning. Check, in particular, that you do not confuse the following homonyms or near-homonyms:

affect	effect	
already	all ready	
altogether	all together	
anybody	any body	
anymore	any more	
anyone	any one	
beside	besides	
everyday	every day	
everyone	every one	
its	it's	
maybe	may be	
principal	principle	
than	then	
their	they're	there
to	too	two

HYPHENATION

The use of hyphens in compound words is particularly important in technical writing because the professional vocabularies tend to include many compound words. Consult the specialized dictionaries and style guides for your discipline and keep a record of those terms you use frequently. A further difficulty is the general lack of uniformity in current practice; in recent years, the trend has been away from hyphenation in compounds. Perhaps the most important rule is to be consistent; never treat the same compound in different ways within the same document.

The following general guidelines should help you hyphenate correctly:

- Use a hyphen in a compound adjective if that adjective precedes a noun:

      solenoid-operated switch
      zero-energy reactor
      lock-and-key theory
      15-inch ruler
      5-kilogram bale
      two-thirds empty.

- Use a hyphen in most compounds in which the first element is a letter:

      U-bolt
      f-stop
      C-layer
      t-distribution
      A-frame

- Use a hyphen in units of measurement:

      kilowatt-hour
      foot-pound
      foot-candle

- Use a hyphen in compound numbers:

      twenty-five
      seventy-five

CANADIAN SPELLING

For a few words the preferred spelling in Canada is different from the preferred spelling in the United States. The authority on Canadian spelling is *The Gage Canadian Dictionary*. Usually the Canadian preferred spellings are also listed in American dictionaries, either as the less preferred form or as a British spelling. Some of the differences in preference are listed below:

Preferred Canadian	Preferred American
axe	ax
cheque	check
jeweller	jeweler
manoeuvre	maneuver
plough	plow
traveller	traveler
centre	center
fibre	fiber
metre	meter
theatre	theater
mould	mold
moult	molt
smoulder	smolder
defence	defense
pretence	pretense
analyse	analyze
paralyse	paralyze

The software you use to check spelling is probably checking for American spelling. You may want to add the words for which the preferred spelling in Canada differs from the preferred spelling in the United States.

There are also some words whose preferred spelling is the same in Canada and the United States, but whose second spelling is marked in American dictionaries as being British. These include the following:

Preferred Canadian and American	Other Canadian (not American)
color	colour
flavor	flavour
honor	honour
neighbor	neighbour
program	programme

CAPITALIZATION

Use your dictionary to check capitalization. The following guidelines should help you with some of the special problems that frequently arise in technical writing:

- In titles, headings, and the titles of figures and tables, capitalize all words that are not articles, prepositions, or conjunctions:

    Writing from a Legal Perspective
    The Composing Processes of an Engineer

Some conventions require that only the first word of the title of a figure be capitalized.

- Capitalize *Figure* and *Table*, both in the caption and in references in the text. For example: "See Figures 7 and 8."
- Technical terms derived from proper names are usually capitalized; when in doubt, check in your dictionary:

  Bunsen burner
  Gantt chart
  Celsius, Fahrenheit, (but *centigrade*)
  Einstein-de Haas effect
  Ohm's law (but *ohm*)
  Volta effect (but *volt*).

- Do not capitalize *north*, *south*, *east* and *west* when they simply refer to compass directions:

  The road is 10 miles east of the river.
  House prices are rising more rapidly in Ontario than in the West.

- Whether or not you should capitalize the items in a list depends on the structure of the items and on how they are presented. Horizontal lists are not capitalized unless the items are numbered sentences. Vertical lists are capitalized if they are numbered or if each item is a sentence. If vertical lists are not numbered, and the items consist of more than one word, capitalization is optional. Again, make sure that you are consistent throughout a document.
- The technical terms in some disciplines such as zoology and geology are governed by special conventions.

PUNCTUATION

Learn the most common uses of the punctuation marks and use a handbook to check on the less common ones. Pay very careful attention to errors your instructor marks in your assignments.

COMMA

Most uses of the comma in English can be covered by the terms *series*, *movables*, and *removables*.

- *Series.* Commas are used to separate the elements in a series or list:

  (1) The mechanic inspected the engine, drove the vehicle around the block, and wrote a report.

  Note that a comma is used before *and*.

  In a compound sentence (two main clauses joined by a co-ordinating conjunction), there is a series of two, and a comma is necessary:

(2)   The mechanics inspected the engine, but they did not find the source of the problem.

- *Movables.* When a sentence element is moved to the front of the sentence, a comma is used to mark the end of that element:

(3)   At the beginning of the spring term, the instructor announced the due dates for all assignments. (The phrase *at ... term* could have followed *assignments.*)

(4)   Because most of the students had already finished their drafts, the instructor decided to modify the schedule. (The clause *because ... draft* could have followed *schedule.*)

- *Removables.* Elements that are in apposition (also known as non-restrictive modifiers) can be removed from a sentence without altering the meaning of the main clause. They are enclosed in commas:

(5)   The truck, which has already broken down twice, should be sold. (Note that the sentence refers only to one truck.)

(6)   The truck that has already broken down twice should be sold. (In this case there is more than one truck, and the sentence refers to the one "that has already broken down twice." In this case commas are not used because the clause is a restrictive modifier.)

Conjunctive adverbs (*however, therefore, nevertheless, moreover, thus*) and various other adverbs must be enclosed in commas, or in a comma and a period or semicolon. For example:

(7)   The salesman wanted to rent a car; he did not, however, ask his supervisor for the necessary voucher.

(7a) The salesman wanted to rent a car; however, he did not ask his supervisor for the necessary voucher.

(8)   He should, of course, have realized his mistake; nevertheless, he didn't.

SEMICOLON

The semicolon has two main uses:

- *To separate the items in a series* if these items have internal punctuation:

(9)   The mechanic inspected the engine, but didn't check the suspension; drove the car around the block, but didn't take it up any hills; and wrote a report.

- *To separate main clauses that are not joined by a co-ordinating conjunction.* See sentence (7). Note that if you join two main clauses with a comma, you make an error called a *comma splice:*

(7b) The salesman wanted to rent a car, he did not, however, ask his supervisor for the necessary voucher. (There is a comma splice before *he.*)

(7c) The salesman wanted to rent a car, but he did not ask his supervisor for the necessary voucher. (Because *but* is a co-ordinating conjunction, sentence 7c does not contain a comma splice.)

COLON

The colon has three main uses:

- *To introduce a list* When you use a colon to introduce a list, check that you have a complete sentence before the colon:

  We have bought the following:

  2 zoom lenses
  3 flash units
  10 rolls of film

- *To end the salutation in a business letter*:

  Dear Mrs. Robinson:

- *To separate two main clauses if the second one illustrates or clarifies the first*:

  John has become a liability to the company: his sales are down, and his customers have lodged at least a dozen complaints.

Colons are seldom used in this way in business and technical writing.

NUMBERS AND UNITS

Check that you have used numbers and units correctly and consistently. In reports and scientific articles you should favour figures, whereas in letters you will probably use words, unless figures are compulsory. Use words rather than figures in the following situations:

- If the number is the first word of a sentence. However, if the number is a specific measurement followed by units, and therefore must be written as a figure, then you may have to change the sentence so that some other element will come first:

  Twenty-nine vehicles have had to be scrapped already.
  Already, 31.4 tonnes have disappeared.

- If the number is either an integer smaller than 10 or a proper fraction, and if the number is not followed by a unit of measurement:

  We need seven part-time tellers.
  They will work 24 hours a week. (Use figure for number greater than 10.)
  They bought 7 kg of strawberries. (Use figure because unit is indicated.)

Her income has increased 2.4 times. (Use figure because the number is not an integer.)
The class is three-fourths full.
They used 3/4-inch pipe.

ABBREVIATIONS

Check that you have used standard abbreviations correctly. Are the capitals, periods, and spacing correct? Check that you have defined any abbreviation your audience might not know. Usually this is done by introducing the abbreviation in parentheses, as in the following example:

The International Phonetic Alphabet (IPA) is used.

SUPPLEMENTARY EXERCISES

SUPPLEMENTARY EXERCISES

1. Identify the subject and verb in the following sentences. Correct the error in subject-verb agreement.
    a. Notice that the list of words at the top of the screen have been replaced with the words "File Name."
    b. The treatment for allergies vary greatly with the specific condition.
    c. The cost of fixed assets are usually quite high.
    d. The pattern of thick and thin rings are matched to the master chronology.
    e. Symptoms of the allergic reaction depends on the location of the invasion.
    f. The movement of the exhaust gases around the fan cause it to rotate.
    g. The dynamic forces induced during the start and completion of the swing causes fluctuating stresses in the boom chords, which may induce fatigue cracks.
    h. In general, three to four models per object is adequate.

2. Correct the lack of parallelism in the following sentences:
    a. The position also provided me with experience in motivating and communicating with staff, maintaining controls, and security procedures.
    b. The ticket issued as a result of the test should be checked for clarity, completeness and is it printed on the blank side of the ticket stock.
    c. She would be able to use it to show to potential silkscreen candidates, to increase her sales of graphic supplies to customers who are considering extending their hobbies into a profession, as well as being a good reference source for instructing her Saturday morning silkscreening workshops.

3. Correct the following comma splices. Then rewrite the sentence or passage to make it concise, clear, and direct.
    a. Antibiotics are complex, large molecular weight molecules, therefore, they have similar chemical structure, however, they differ in their mode of action upon different pathogenic microbes.
    b. Footnotes are at the bottom of the page, there may be many and there is no list of references at the end of the article.
    c. Bacteria differ in oxygen requirements, some require oxygen, some can use it or not use it, and some will even die in its presence.
    d. Heat lightning is essentially the same as sheet lightning, however its effects are much fainter.
    e. Heritabilities vary from 0 to 100 percent for different traits, therefore the response to selection also varies.
    f. Usually the slide is left in the solution for 20 to 40 seconds, otherwise the cellular constituents will become overstained when the slide is removed, the excess stain is rinsed off with distilled water and

the slide is left to be air dried. Once dry, the cover slip is glued over top of the tissue sections with Canada Balsam glue.

g. Antibiotics are classified into many groups, two of the common ones are the penicillins and the tetracyclines.

h. When the pathogens mutate, some are still affected by the antibiotics, those which aren't rapidly reproduce and make the infection harder to control.

i. Some antibiotics are most effective against G+ infections and others work best for G− infections, these antibiotics are called limited spectrum antibiotics.

j. Because there is one less wheel assembly, the vehicle is inherently more fuel efficient than a conventional car, also, the comparatively low overall weight enhances acceleration and cornering.

k. Not all of the sentences were clear, some were very confusing, and some could be more concise.

"AVOIDING SEXIST PRONOUNS"

MICHAEL P. JORDAN
JENNIFER J. CONNOR

BACKGROUND

During a recent tour a gracious host proudly pointed out to his female guest one of his city's many liftbridges, noting that it was designed by a woman engineer and worked very well. After a pause he quickly added, "Of course, they *all* work well." Evidently he realized that in his enthusiasm he had inadvertently uttered a patronizing sexist statement.

This kind of subconscious sexism – a "gee whiz" attitude to a woman's professional ability – is still legion; nevertheless, as this anecdote also shows, there is an increased awareness of the problem. Awareness of sexism – especially in language – has grown out of the discussions and publications of the last two decades. In this paper we will briefly review some of the major themes in the literature, referring to Canadian works whenever possible, and offer practical ways to overcome one of the most common problems of sexism in writing: the inappropriate use of gender-specific pronouns.

Although inappropriate sexist language is that which discriminates against either sex, historically it tends to exclude (or to imply exclusion of) women, or to stereotype women in certain roles. A wealth of material has been published on sexist language, ranging from early anecdotal or impressionistic works to more recent research studies. While the following overview is not by any means exhaustive, it refers to works which are representative of the types available. Publications on sexist language in general include linguistic, communication and philosophical studies [1–11], practical "how-to" works for professionals [12–16], publishers' recommendations [17–20], and the recommendations of special interest groups and federal government departments, particularly in Canada [21–30]. Increasingly writers' manuals are devoting brief sections to sexist language [31–34], and whole manuals on the art of nonsexist and other nondiscriminatory language have appeared [35–37]. One study suggests that editors of company newsletters, at least, may have heeded the advice provided in such works [38]. American business and technical communication literature, including textbooks, also demonstrates the concern for nonsexist language (although much of the discussion in this field is still derivative and prescriptive) [39–45]. Unfortunately, more needs to be done in Canada.[1]

FOUR AREAS OF SEXISM

Generally speaking, the focus in all these publications has been on four main areas of sexism in English: different courtesy titles for men and women; separate occupational titles for men and women performing the

---

1. Few Canadian works on business and technical communication exist, and those that are available do not include discussions of sexist or nonsexist language. One notable change has occurred, however: Ron Blicq's popular *Technically-Write!* reflects nonsexist usage in its subtitle. Originally published as "Communication for the Technical Man" in 1972, it became "Communicating in a Technological Era" in its second edition in 1983 [46].

same job; the use of "man" to refer to people in general; and the use of "he," "his," and "himself" to include women. Handling the first three problems has been relatively straightforward.

First, many women adopted the courtesy title "Ms" to denote a status equivalent to men ("Mr."); by removing the indication of marital status of the traditional titles "Mrs." and "Miss," use of this neutral title sought to change a perception that an indication of women's marital status somehow subordinated women to men. (This trend is reversing: many women now do not use "Ms" [41, p. 25; 11, p. 164], probably because of its association with early strident feminism or because they choose to indicate marital status.) Perhaps another approach is to change men's courtesy titles using the rather archaic "Master" as well as "Mister." In business correspondence, however, it is becoming customary to eschew courtesy titles altogether: both women and men use full names in the signature line and sometimes in the salutation (as in "Dear John Smith").

Second, organizations have changed position titles so that they are no longer gender-specific; and in some countries, including Canada, governments have published dictionaries of new occupational titles [47]. Noticeable changes in Canada, for example, include "flight attendant" in place of the former "steward/stewardess"; "police officer" for "policeman/policewoman"; "letter carrier" for "mailman" and "server" for "waiter/waitress." Most of these titles happily avoid the clumsiness of changing the "man" suffix to "person." Whole government agencies and other organizations have also changed their names to reflect their actual constituency: Canada Manpower has become Canada Employment Centre; the Workmen's Compensation Board has become the Workers' Compensation Board; and the National Museum of Man has become the Canadian Museum of Civilization.

Third, writers have consciously avoided using "man" to refer to everyone. A notable, and now classic example, is anthropologist Peter Farb's 1978 work *Humankind*, in which he explained his deliberate choice of the nonsexist noun in his title [48]; only ten years earlier Farb had used the conventional generic noun in his *Man's Rise to Civilization as Shown by the Indians of North America*. In addition to "humankind," other collective nouns avoid the implication that women are excluded: people, society, human race, humanity, etc. However, we still need to resolve such problems as *manhole, man overboard, one-upmanship, horsemanship, manslaughter, man-eater, man-hunt*; the "man-girl" inequality as in *man Friday/girl Friday*; and the unnecessary qualifier in "woman engineer," "woman lawyer," etc.

Other problems with sexism have been identified in the literature, including the demeaning reference to women according to their physical attributes (e.g., "the blonde"), their lower occupational status (e.g., "the girls in the office"), and their implied possessive relationship to men as in "man and (his) wife". These problematic descriptions are harder to correct, except the last one, which we now accept as "husband and wife." More subtle problems sometimes occur: a recent example in an Ontario university newsletter informed readers that at the Learned Societies Conference "the expected attendance of the Royal Society of Canada is 350 people, including wives and children." In a letter to the editor, a scientist expressed her dismay at the implication that either there were no female fellows of the Royal Society or husbands do not attend conferences.

THE PRONOUN PROBLEM – COMMON SOLUTIONS

Despite such occasional slips, the above solutions for courtesy and occupational titles and the generic use of "man" clearly show that much has been achieved toward the goal of nonsexist language, particularly in the workplace. A continuing concern which has no easy solution, however, is the use of the generic pronoun "he" and its variants to refer to a collective noun or to one which is not gender-specific. For example, in the sentence "The applicant must bring his resume" the pronoun "his" is grammatically correct but tends to imply that women are not included in the statement. Attempts to overcome this problem can sometimes lead inadvertently to stereotyping; for example, the use of the female pronoun in an advertisement for a community nurse – "The successful applicant must have her own car" – can leave the erroneous impression that only a woman can fill the position. Unfortunately, the use of "he" consistently with an explanatory note indicating that the pronoun refers to both sexes, though common in legal documents, shows a lack of concern for the reader; moreover, this attempted solution does not remove the perceived inequity in the language. Studies have indicated, in fact, that the word "he" does *not* conjure up images of both sexes in the minds of readers, but only the single image of "male" [9, pp. 73 – 74; 35, pp. 35 – 38; 43, p. 87]. To avoid these potential pitfalls, writers have advanced a variety of solutions. The most common suggestions, perhaps, are the following:

1. invent a new pronoun;
2. alternate male and female pronouns;
3. use "he or she";
4. use "they" as a singular pronoun;
5. pluralize the noun;
6. use the second-person pronoun or the neutral "one";
7. eliminate the pronoun reference.

While these suggestions can be useful, they can also be problematic, especially for use in functional communications.

1. Since the eighteenth century writers have proposed upwards of eighty new English pronouns to convey the meaning of both sexes in the same singular word [10, p. 190]. Here are just a few of the suggestions [4, p. 131; 10, pp. 205 – 209; 11; 35, p. 47; 49]:

thon/thons   tey/tem/ter(s)
co/cos/coself   hesh/hizzer/himmer

E/E's/Em	hir
na/nan/naself	heshe/himer/hiser
e/es/em	on
she/heris/herim	s/he
she/shis/shim	ho/hom/hos/homself
ve/vis/ver	hue/hues/hume

While the intent behind their invention is laudable, these neologisms have failed to gain support or interest, have been treated with contempt or derision, and have been used only rarely, if at all. Without general acceptance they become barriers to communication themselves and so are not suitable solutions for any genre of writing.

2. Some writers have alternated pronoun gender from sentence to sentence or within larger units (paragraph to paragraph or chapter to chapter) to refer to both sexes equally. However, this technique can lead to confusion and tedium for the reader, and so is not recommended for functional communications.

3. Using "he or she" and similar expressions can also give equal attention to both sexes, but can clutter up writing and generally is clumsy. Too many can mar any communication, and so "he or she" (or "s/he") must be used sparingly.

4. "They" and "their" are used frequently as singular pronouns in everyday speech – it is simpler and more natural to say "Everyone must bring their own beer" than to use "Everyone must bring his own beer." Although the use of the plural pronoun has been sanctioned by well-known writers for centuries, and has been proscribed by grammarians only in the last two hundred years [2], it is still often censured for formal writing. Therefore, using the plural form is not recommended in formal technical or business communications.

5. A more efficient and less clumsy method is to pluralize both the noun and the possessive pronoun. Thus "Everyone must bring his own beer" becomes "Partygoers must bring their own beer." Yet this approach may not always be ideal – especially if you want to personalize the communication.

6. To personalize, the second-person pronoun can be used. Thus "Everyone must bring his own beer" becomes "You must bring your own beer," which is suitable for singular or plural *you*.

7. Often writers eliminate the pronoun altogether. Thus "Everyone must bring his own beer" becomes "Everyone must bring beer." However, the sense may change in the process. For example, if this revision does not convey exactly the same message (since it is conceivable that someone does not drink beer, why bring it?), then minor changes are required to improve the sentence, depending on the context: "Anyone who wants to drink beer at the party must bring it."

These suggestions applied singly do not always achieve the goal of non-sexist communication. Nevertheless, conscious attempts to combine them and other approaches will increase the nonsexist tone throughout a piece of writing. The aim should be to minimize sexist expressions in an efficient, invisible way, to write in as neutral a manner as possible. The reader should neither be conscious of awkward attempts at unbiased writing nor feel the attempts overpower the message through overuse [38].

THE PRONOUN PROBLEM – OTHER SOLUTIONS

In addition to these seven commonly identified ways of reducing the number of sexist pronouns, writers often offer examples of "writing around the problem" or "recasting" the sentence. In general, however, they do not identify the specific grammatical techniques used; moreover, seldom do they offer more than one or two examples of "recasting." Perhaps the most detailed exception so far is that of Christian [43], who shows eight ways to substitute other pronouns and four ways to eliminate troublesome pronouns.

The following list represents an attempt to identify more fully the specific ways to avoid the use of generic pronouns. The list offers a preliminary classification of techniques with examples. In each pair of examples, the first phrase uses a male pronoun and the second gives an alternative which avoids it. The main goal of the list is to outline specific methods for writers and teachers of writing to achieve nonsexist communication. Perhaps it might also form a basis for detailed research into gender-specific pronouns, their use and their effects on tone, style and propriety in technical and business writing. Finally, teachers may find that an in-class analysis of the large variety of methods used to avoid sexist pronouns can form an interesting and informative introduction to sentence and clause structures in expository prose. To encourage teachers to try these analyses, a brief exercise with suggested answers follows the list of solutions.

THE PRONOUN PROBLEM – OTHER SOLUTIONS

DEFINITENESS AND PLURALITY

1. DEFINITE ARTICLE

If the teacher is aware that his lesson will be assessed ...

If the teacher is aware that the lesson will be assessed ...

2. INDEFINITENESS

... for the teacher to walk into his class ...

... for the teacher to walk into ___ class ...

3. INDEFINITE ARTICLE

Perhaps <u>the student's</u> problem is more basic still: <u>his</u> inability to ...

Perhaps <u>the student's</u> problem is more basic still: <u>an</u> inability to ...

4. UNARTICLED PLURAL

<u>The teacher</u> should use visual aids in presenting <u>his</u> lessons.

<u>The teacher</u> should use visual aids in presenting __ lessons.

5. UNARTICLED SINGULAR

<u>The successful applicant</u> must send <u>his</u> acceptance within a month.

<u>The successful applicant</u> must send __ acceptance within a month.

6. CONSISTENT PLURAL

<u>The</u> successful language student can be encouraged to explain how <u>he has</u> analyzed <u>his</u> exercise.

Successful language student<u>s</u> can be encouraged to explain how <u>they have</u> analyzed <u>their</u> exercise<u>s</u>.

7. INCONSISTENT PLURAL

<u>No one</u> failing this course can complete <u>his</u> program.

<u>No one</u> failing this course can complete <u>their</u> programs.

CONTINUITY

8. FULL REPETITION

How can <u>the teacher</u> help language learners? <u>He</u> can ...

How can <u>the teacher</u> help language learners? <u>The teacher</u> can ...

9. PARTIAL REPETITION

<u>The child who has been well nurtured</u> becomes a well-balanced adult. <u>He</u> is better able to ...

The child who has been well nurtured becomes a well-balanced adult. <u>The well-nurtured child</u> is better able to ...

10. GENERIC NOUN

When <u>a student</u> makes an utterance that needs expansion or rephrasing, <u>he</u> can be encouraged to do this.

When <u>a student</u> makes an utterance that needs expansion or rephrasing, <u>the speaker</u> can be encouraged to do this.

11. SYNONYM

The <u>student</u> needs to acquire the ability to infer meanings in words. <u>He</u> must also discover ...

The student needs to acquire the ability to infer meanings in words. <u>The pupil</u> must also discover ...

12. ACRONYM

The <u>psychologically deprived child</u> can become a serious problem in society. <u>He</u> often later resorts to violent and criminal acts.

The <u>psychologically deprived child</u> can become a serious problem in society. <u>The PDC</u> often later resorts to violent and criminal acts.

13. UNTRIGGERED ASSOCIATE/PERSPECTIVE

The diligent student can expect to receive good grades for <u>his</u> work.

The diligent student can expect to receive good grades.

DESCRIPTIVE CLAUSES

Note: The following examples of descriptive clauses are all non-defining; however, it is probably possible to use defining clauses for these categories to avoid sexist pronouns. e.g. "Teachers <u>who</u> always consider the use of visual aids may nevertheless find them unsuitable for some purposes."

14. RELATIVE CLAUSE

The <u>teacher</u> should always consider the use of visual aids. <u>He</u> may find them unsuitable for some purposes, however.

The <u>teacher</u>, <u>who</u> should always consider the use of visual aids, may find them unsuitable for some purposes.

15. -ED CLAUSE

The <u>language learner</u> may be faced with living in the target country. <u>He</u> will then undergo "culture shock."

The <u>language learner</u>, when fac<u>ed</u> with living in the target country, will undergo "culture shock."

Notes:

1. -ed clauses can often be reduced to a single adjective (e.g., "questions which he has attempted" becomes "questions attempted" or "attempted questions").

2. -ed clauses are, of course, agentless passives.

16. -ING CLAUSE

The <u>teacher</u> writes the vocabulary on the board. <u>He</u> then separates the different parts of speech.

The <u>teacher</u> writes the vocabulary on the board, separat<u>ing</u> the different parts of speech.

17. VERBLESS CLAUSE

The <u>student</u> is usually eager to learn real-life language. But <u>he</u> may be less keen to learn grammar.

The <u>student</u>, usually eager to learn real-life language, may be less keen to learn grammar.

18. TO-INFINITIVE CLAUSE (PASSIVE)

The <u>winner</u> will be announced next class. <u>He</u> will be presented with the award on Founders' Day.

The <u>winner</u>, <u>to be announced</u> next class, will be presented with the award on Founders' Day.

19. TO-INFINITIVE CLAUSE (ACTIVE)

The <u>writer's</u> aim is to create a plausible sales message. <u>He</u> can only achieve this by providing convincing information.

The <u>writer's</u> aim, <u>to create</u> a plausible sales message, can only be achieved by providing convincing information.

20. APPOSITION

The <u>whale</u> is the largest mammal on earth. <u>He</u> constantly migrates along continental shorelines.

The <u>whale</u>, the largest mammal on earth, constantly migrates along continental shorelines.

21. WITH

We were dealing with the highly motivated <u>student</u>. <u>He</u> generally had a broad linguistic background.

We were dealing with the highly motivated <u>student</u>, generally <u>with</u> a broad linguistic background.

ELLIPSIS

22. SUBJECT ELLIPSIS (ACTIVE)

The <u>teacher</u> can collect sentences of various structures and <u>he</u> can group them ...

The teacher can collect sentences of various structures and __ can group them ...

23. SUBJECT ELLIPSIS (ACTIVE – PASSIVE)

<u>The student</u> pays fees to the Home University; <u>he</u> is classed as a "visiting graduate student" at the Host University where no fees are paid.

<u>The student</u> pays fees to the Home University and __ is classed as a "visiting graduate student" at the Host University where no fees are paid.

24. SUBJECT-MODAL ELLIPSIS

<u>The student</u> must attend regularly and <u>he must</u> submit all assignments on time.

<u>The student</u> must attend regularly and _____ submit all assignments on time.

25. SUBJECT-VERB ELLIPSIS

<u>The student may feel</u> that certain things are inadequately expressed in English. <u>He may also feel</u> that some things are not adequately expressed in Ciluba.

The student may feel that certain things are inadequately expressed in English and _____ that some things are not adequately expressed in Ciluba.

26. ADJUNCT REPLACEMENT

<u>The teacher</u> can help students use actives and passives together by analyzing formal description. <u>He</u> can also help them do this by having them write such texts.

<u>The teacher</u> can help students use actives and passives together by analyzing formal description and _____ by having them write such texts.

27. LIST

<u>The teacher</u> can bring humour into the classroom. <u>He</u> can change the pace. <u>He</u> can make learning a joy ...

<u>The teacher</u> can bring humour into the classroom, __ can change the pace, and __ can make learning a joy ...

INFORMAL USES

28. YOU/YOUR

<u>The student's</u> assignment is to learn a new tense. <u>He</u> is given a list of regular verbs to select from.

<u>Your</u> assignment is to learn a new tense. <u>You</u> are given a list of regular verbs to select from.

29. WE/OUR

<u>The teacher</u> seldom gets ready-to-use directions from grammarians. <u>He</u> can, however, produce <u>his</u> own.

<u>We</u> seldom get ready-to-use directions from grammarians. <u>We</u> can, however, make <u>our</u> own.

30. I

If <u>the teacher</u> had to express the same ideas, could <u>he</u> use the same structures and words?

If <u>I</u> had to express the same ideas, could <u>I</u> use the same structures and words?

31. IMPERATIVE

<u>The student</u> should answer the easy questions first. <u>He</u> should then re-read and answer the rest.

<u>Answer</u> the easy questions first. Then <u>re-read</u> and <u>answer</u> the rest.

FORMAL USES

32. ONE/ONE'S

<u>The student</u> should always re-read <u>his</u> examination responses.

<u>One</u> should always re-read <u>one's</u> examination responses.

Note: The U.K. system <u>one</u> ... <u>one</u>, though frequently considered rather pompous, must now be preferred over the U.S. <u>one</u> ... <u>he</u>.

33. AGENTLESS PASSIVE

<u>The teacher</u> asks a question, and throws a ball to a student, who answers and returns the ball. <u>He</u> can vary this procedure in a number of ways.

<u>The teacher</u> asks a question and throws a ball to a student who answers and returns the ball. This procedure <u>can be varied</u> in a number of ways.

(Also see -ed clauses earlier.)

34. AGENTIVE PASSIVE

The student sometimes submits essays written by others. To receive credit, all work <u>he</u> submits must be <u>his</u> own.

The student sometimes submits essays written by others. To receive credit, all work <u>submitted by a student</u> must be <u>written by that student</u>.

Note: The agent in an agentive passive can be any form of continuity except, of course, a personal pronoun (e.g., by him); here repetition is used.

SUBSTITUTE CLAUSES

35. INVERTED

The writer may wish to delay stating the agent as long as possible. He can do this by using a by-phrase at the end of the sentence.

The writer may wish to delay stating the agent as long as possible. A by-phrase at the end of the sentence can serve this purpose.

36. COMBINED

The teacher can guide learners into habits of intelligent guessing from context. He does this by a kind of catechism of leading questions.

The teacher can guide learners into habits of intelligent guessing from context, ___ by a kind of catechism of leading questions.

(Also see Adjunct Replacement earlier.)

IMPLICIT CONNECTION

37. INDIRECT OBJECT

It is easier for a student to remember the correct use of expressions if they are presented to him in meaningful sentences.

It is easier for a student to remember the correct use of expressions if they are presented _____ in meaningful sentences.

38. OBJECT

If the student is asked for the passive counterpart, it does not help him much to know the transformational "rules."

If the student is asked for the passive counterpart, it does not help ___ much to know the transformational "rules."

39. REFLEXIVE

If a student misbehaves himself on the trip, appropriate action will be taken.

If a student misbehaves _____ on the trip, appropriate action will be taken.

40. SUBJECT WITH ANTICIPATORY "IT"

At some time the teacher can simply state that something is wrong. At other times it may be worthwhile for him to ask the student to explain the answer.

At some time <u>the teacher</u> can simply state that something is wrong. At other times <u>it</u> may be worthwhile _____ to ask the student to explain the answer.

41. TEMPORAL -ING CLAUSE

It is inadvisable for <u>a trainee</u> to use a new aid if <u>he</u> is giving a practical test.

It is inadvisable for <u>a trainee</u> to use a new aid <u>while giving</u> a practical test.

42. TIME ADJUNCT

<u>The gifted student</u> may lose interest in academic work <u>in his</u> youth.

<u>The gifted student</u> may lose interest in academic work during youth.

OTHER

43. MODAL INFINITIVE

<u>The student</u> needs to be seated so <u>he</u> can see all information presented. (or "to enable <u>him</u> to see")

<u>The student</u> needs to be seated so as <u>to be able</u> to see all information presented.

44. EXISTENTIAL "THERE"

<u>The teacher</u> often has difficulty teaching articles and prepositions to ESL students from China. <u>He</u> can, however, simplify the task.

<u>The teacher</u> often has difficulty teaching articles and prepositions to ESL students from China. <u>There</u> are ways, however, of simplifying the task.

45. NOUN COMPLEMENTATION

The student may, within two days, rewrite the essay rejected by <u>the teacher</u> and require <u>him</u> to accept it.

The student may, within two days, rewrite the essay rejected by the teacher, and require <u>its acceptance</u>.

46. DEFINING COMPLEX SUBJECT

If <u>a student</u> is aware of damage being done in residences, <u>he</u> has a duty to report it.

<u>Any student aware of damage being done in residences</u> has a duty to report it.

Notes:

1. Relative, -ed, -ing, and verbless clauses can form part of the complex defining subject; a verbless clause is used here.

2. Triggered reflexive associates ("a student <u>whose grade</u> is ....") are also used.

47. NOMINATIVE NOUN

Should <u>a student</u> prove disruptive during a practice session, <u>he</u> will be required to withdraw from the program.

Should <u>a student</u> prove disruptive during a practice session, <u>withdrawal</u> will be required.

48. PURPOSE CLAUSE

<u>The local successful applicant</u> will be sent an application form and <u>he</u> will be asked to complete and return it for the regional competition.

<u>The local successful applicant</u> will be sent an application form <u>to</u> complete and return for the regional competition.

49. DIRECT VERB

<u>The student</u> may make <u>his</u> selection of electives from those listed for the department.

<u>The student</u> may <u>select</u> electives from those listed for the department.

50. INTRANSITIVE VERB

<u>The graduate student</u> needs a supervisor who can <u>assist and stimulate him</u> effectively throughout the program.

The graduate student needs a supervisor who can <u>function</u> effectively throughout the program.

EXERCISE IN AVOIDING SEXIST PRONOUNS

Use various methods of avoiding the sexist pronouns in the following.

1. By frequently and quickly responding to journals, the instructor can avoid long weekends of journal reading, and she can monitor the progress of each student.

2. If the purpose of the journal is to prepare for class, the instructor might explain that she will call on the student to read from his journal.

3. When an instructor explains the weight of the journal, she can also explain how she will grade the entries.

4. If the instructor wants the student to react to class lectures and respond to readings, she could give him a model entry for his journal.

5. If a student wants to study at another approved university outside Ontario:

(a) he must register as a full-time resident and he must pay his fees at the other university. During his period away from this university, he must maintain his registration here; however, he will be exempted from paying his tuition fees for that period. For the period to be counted towards his residence, the work he performs must be equivalent to that which he would have accomplished over a similar period at this university.

6. Each town reeve applicant must list two persons whom she has asked to submit confidential letters about her ability.

7. A candidate for this award must be a citizen of Canada, or he must have held landed immigrant status for one year prior to his submitting the application.

8. Unsatisfactory performance by the student may cause proceedings to be instituted requiring him to withdraw from his programme.

9. If a student can demonstrate that his transcript is in some way misleading, he may appeal to the Board of Studies to have the error corrected.

10. Assuming a student attempts four or more courses during the year, and his average performance in the courses which he has passed is less than 60 per cent, he will be placed on probation. By the end of his probationary period he must have raised his overall average on all courses which he has passed to at least 60 per cent, or he will be required to withdraw.

11. The customer makes her selection from about 2500 items displayed behind transparent panels so that she can see the products but she cannot remove them. She inserts a small plastic card in a slot and she presses a button to select her item. She then receives the item she has selected, and she puts it in her cart.

12. Having assessed the manner in which his particular industry is likely to expand over the future years, the plant manager or engineer may not experience too much trouble in roughly estimating an optimum layout for the plant which could serve him efficiently for at least ten years into the future. He will then find, however, that there is no way in which the existing production volume of the plant can support the immediate construction cost of his complete new facility. This is because he must obviously initiate the construction process on his current operational budget, while the reason he needs the new facilities is because his operational budget is too low.

ANSWERS

1. and ___ can monitor (subject ellipsis)

2. that students <u>will be asked</u> to read from <u>their</u> journal<u>s</u> (agentless passive, plural)

3. <u>When explaining</u> ... the instructor can also explain how the entries <u>will be graded</u>. (temporal -ing preceding main clause, passive)

4. student<u>s</u> ... readings, <u>it</u> might be a good idea to give <u>them</u> a model entry. (plural, anticipatory it, plural, untriggered associate)

5. (a) <u>the student</u> must register as a full-time resident and pay ___ fees at the other university. During <u>the</u> period away from this university, <u>the student</u> must maintain ___ registration here, but ___ will be exempted from paying tuition fees for that period. For the period to the counted towards ___ residence, that work <u>performed by the student</u> must be equivalent to that which <u>would have been accomplished</u> over a similar period at this university. (full repetition, ellipsis, unarticled plural, definite article, full repetition, unarticled singular, subject ellipsis-passive, unarticled singular, agentive passive with full repetition, agentless passive)

6. <u>who has been asked</u> ... about the <u>applicant's</u> ability. (agentless passive, partial repetition)

7. or ___ have held ... <u>prior to submitting</u> the application (subject-modal ellipsis, temporal -ing)

8. requiring <u>withdrawal</u>. (noun complementation, untriggered associate)

9. Any student who can demonstrate that <u>the</u> transcript ... may appeal (defining relative clause, definite article)

10. A student <u>who</u> has attempted four or more courses during the year and whose average performance in courses <u>passed</u> is less than 60 per cent will be placed on probation. By the end of <u>the</u> probationary period <u>the student's</u> overall average on all courses <u>passed must have been raised</u> to at least 60 per cent, or <u>withdrawal</u> will be required. (defining complex subject with defining relative and triggered associate clauses, defining -ed clause as predicative adjective, definite article, full repetition, defining -ed clause as predicative adjective, agentless passive, nominative noun)

11. makes selection<u>s</u> (<u>or selects</u>) ... so that they <u>can be seen</u> but not <u>removed</u>. After insert<u>ing</u> a small plastic card in a slot and press<u>ing</u> a button, <u>the customer</u> receives an item <u>to put</u> in <u>the</u> cart (unarticled plural (or direct verb), agentless passive, agentless passive, temporal -ings, full repetition, indefinite article, purpose clause, definite article)

12. ... <u>the</u> particular industry ... <u>The entrepreneur</u> will then find ... could <u>operate</u> efficiently ... cost of the complete new facility. This is because <u>the</u> construction process must obviously <u>be initiated</u> on the current operational budget, while the reason the new facilities are needed is because <u>the</u> operational budget is too low. (definite article, intransitive verb, generic noun, definite article, agentless passive, agentless passive, definite article)

REFERENCES

We would like to thank reviewers of this journal and our students for helpful suggestions.

1. Lakoff, Robin. 1973. Language and Woman's Place. *Language in Society* 2:45–50.

2. Bodine, Anne. 1975. Androcentrism in Prescriptive Grammar: Singular "They," Sex-Indefinite "He," and "He or She." *Language in Society* 4:129–46.

3. Stanley, Julia P. 1977. Gender-Marking in American English: Usage and Reference. In *Sexism and Language*. Alleen Pace Nilsen, et al., eds., pp. 43–74. Urbana, IL: National Council of Teachers of English.

4. Martyna, Wendy. 1978. What Does "He" Mean? Use of the Generic Masculine. *Journal of Communication* 28:131–38.

5. Bate, Barbara. 1978. Nonsexist Language Use in Transition. *Journal of Communication* 28:139–49.

6. Purnell, Sandra E. 1978. Politically Speaking, Do Women Exist? *Journal of Communication* 28:150–55.

7. Orasanu, Judith, Mariam K. Slater, and Leonore Loeb Adler. 1979. *Language, Sex and Gender: Does "La Difference" Make a Difference?* New York: New York Academy of Sciences, Vol. 32.

8. Vetterling-Braggin, Mary, ed. 1981. *Sexist Language: A Modern Philosophical Analysis*. Littlefield: Adams.

9. Frank, Francine, and Frank Anshen. 1983. *Language and the Sexes*. Albany: State University of New York Press.

10. Baron, Dennis. 1986. *Grammar and Gender*. New Haven: Yale University Press.

11. Bolinger, Dwight. 1987. Bias in Language: The Case of Sexism. In *Language, Communication and Education*. Barbara M. Mayor and A.K. Pugh, eds., pp. 153–66. London: Croom Helm.

12. Wendlinger, Robert M., and Lucille Matthews. 1973. How to Eliminate Sexist Language from Your Organization's Writing: Some Guidelines for the Manager and Supervisor. In *Affirmative Action for Women: A Practical Guide*. Dorothy Jongeward and Dru Scott, eds. pp. 309–30. Reading, MA: Addison-Wesley.

13. Stiegler, Christine B. 1980. The Art of Nonsexist Communication. How to Personalize Your Communication Techniques. *Management World* 9 (June):13–15;36.

14. Colwill, Nina. 1983. Sexist Language: Sex Role Liberation's Pettiest Issue? *Business Quarterly* 48 (July):6;20.

15. Pickens, Judy E. 1984. Language for All: How to Write and Speak Without Bias. *Management World* 13 (November):34–35.

16. Newsom, Douglas Ann. 1986. Despite Progress, Sexism in Language Persists. *Public Relations Journal* 42 (August):5.

17. APA Task Force on Issues of Sexual Bias in Graduate Education. 1975. Guidelines for Nonsexist Use of Language. *American Psychologist* 30:683 –84.

18. Guidelines for Nonsexist Use of Language in NCTE Publications. 1977. In *Sexism and Language*. Alleen Pace Nilsen, et al., eds., pp. 181–91. Urbana, IL: National Council of Teachers of English.

19. McGraw-Hill Book Company. [1980s]. *Guidelines for Bias-Free Publishing*. Hightstown, NJ: McGraw Hill Book Company.

20. Prentice-Hall College Division Guidelines on Sexism. 1983. In *Communication Systems and Procedures for the Modern Office*. Nathan Krevolin, pp. 439–46. Englewood Cliffs: Prentice-Hall.

21. Graham, Alma. [1980s]. *Words that Make Women Disappear*. Toronto: Ontario Status of Women Council.

22. Treasury Board of Canada. 1982. Elimination of Sexual Stereotyping. *Administrative Policy Manual*. Ch. 484. Ottawa.

23. Conseil du Trésor. 1983. Lignes directrices relatives à la suppression des stéréotypes sexuels. *Manuel de la politique administrative*. Ch. 484. Ottawa.

24. Employment and Immigration Canada/Emploi et Immigration Canada. 1983. *Eliminating Sex-role Stereotyping: Editorial Guidelines for Employment and Immigration Canada Communications 1983/Élimination des stéréotypes sexuels*. Ottawa: Supply and Services Canada/ Approvisionnements et Services Canada.

25. Santé et Bien-Être Social Canada. 1982. *Lignes directrices visant à éliminer les stéréotypes sexuels de la langue et du matériel visuel*. Ottawa: Santé et Bien-Être Social Canada.

26. Health and Welfare Canada. 1983. *Guidelines for the Elimination of Sexual Stereotyping in Language and Visual Material*. Ottawa: Health and Welfare Canada.

27. Sah, Manju, and Catherine Rancy. 1984. *Guidelines for Non-sexist Writing/Vers un language non sexiste*. [Ottawa]: Canadian Advisory Council on the Status of Women/Conseil consultatif canadien de la situation de la femme.

28. Eichler, Margrit, and Jeanne Lapointe. 1985. *On the Treatment of the Sexes in Research/Le traitement objectif des sexes dans la recherche*. Jeanne Lapointe et Margrit Eichler. Ottawa: Social Sciences and Humanities Research Council of Canada/Conseil de recherches en sciences humaines du Canada.

29. Correctional Service Canada/Service correctionnel Canada. 1985. *On Equal Terms: How To Eliminate Sexism in Communications/D'Égal à égale: quelques moyens d'éliminer les éléments sexistes des communications*.

Ottawa: Minister of Supply and Services Canada/Ministre des Approvisionnements et Services.

30. Veterans Affairs Canada/Anciens Combattants. 1986. *Beyond Stereotypes: Communicating Without Bias/L'Écueil des stéréotypes: Comment l'éviter*. Ottawa: Veterans Affairs/Anciens Combattants.

31. Secretariat d'État du Canada. 1983. *Guide du rédacteur de l'administration fédérale*. Ottawa: Approvisionnements et Services Canada.

32. Department of the Secretary of State of Canada. 1985. *The Canadian Style. A Guide to Writing and Editing*. Toronto: Minister of Supply and Services Canada.

33. Messenger, William E., and Jan de Bruyn. 1986. *The Canadian Writer's Handbook*. 2nd ed. Scarborough: Prentice-Hall Canada.

34. Sabin, William A., and Sheila A. O'Neill. 1986. *The Gregg Reference Manual*. 3rd Canadian ed. Toronto: McGraw-Hill Ryerson.

35. Miller, Casey, and Kate Swift. 1980. *The Handbook of Nonsexist Writing*. New York: Barnes & Noble.

36. International Association of Business Communicators. 1982. *Without Bias: A Guidebook for Nondiscriminatory Communication*. 2nd ed. New York: John Wiley & Sons.

37. Sorrels, Bobbye D. 1983. *The Nonsexist Communicator: Solving the Problems of Gender and Awkwardness in Modern English*. Englewood Cliffs: Prentice-Hall.

38. Cline, Carolyn Garrett, and Lynn Masel-Walters. 1983. At Least the Editors are Trying: Women and Sexism in Corporate Publications. *ABCA Bulletin* 46(3):26–30.

39. Jameson, Daphne A. 1982. Reducing Sexually Biased Language in Business Communication. In *Readings in Business Communication*. Robert D. Gieselman, ed., pp. 202–210. 3rd ed. Champaign, IL: Stipes.

40. The Iceperson Cometh (As He or She or They Must to All). 1983. *ABCA Bulletin* 46(3):23–24.

41. Tibbetts, Charlene. 1983. Sex and the Language. *ABCA Bulletin* 46(3):24–26.

42. Paxson, William C. 1985. Nondiscriminatory Writing. In *Strategies for Business and Technical Writing*. Kevin J. Harty, ed., pp. 109–111. 2nd ed. San Diego: Harcourt Brace Jovanovich.

43. Christian, Barbara. 1986. Doing Without the Generic He/Man in Technical Communications. *Journal of Technical Writing and Communication* 16:87–98.

44. Shear, Marie. 1987. Little Cat Feet: Subtle Sexism and the Writer's Craft. *The Bulletin* [of ABC]. 50(1):17–18.

45. Murphy, Herta A., Charles E. Peck, and Sheila A. O'Neill. 1983.

Effective Business Communications. First Canadian ed. Toronto: McGraw-Hill Ryerson.

46. Blicq, Ron S. 1987. *Technically-Write! Communicating in a Technological Era.* Canadian 3rd ed. Scarborough: Prentice-Hall Canada.

47. Employment and Immigration Canada. 1977. *CCDO Manual of Sex-Free Occupational Titles.* Ottawa: Minister of Supply and Services Canada.

48. Farb, Peter. 1978. *Humankind.* London: J. Cape.

49. Stevenson, Janet H. 1979. Who's Hue? An Alternative Generic Pronoun. *Journal of Communication* 2:238–39.

Source: Michael P. Jordan and Jennifer J. Connor, "Avoiding Sexist Pronouns," *Technostyle* 6.3 (1987): 16–38. Reprinted with the permission of the Canadian Association of Teachers of Technical Writing.

GLOSSARY

AMBIGUOUS PASSAGE A passage with at least two possible interpretations.

ANALOGY A comparison in which the compared items are dissimilar, except for some important feature they share.

ANTICIPATORY IT The use of *it* in subject position when the "real" subject has been moved to follow the verb. For example: *It* is generally assumed that this is the case.

BRAINSTORMING Recording all ideas about a topic in the order in which they arise.

CLASSIFICATION Grouping items into categories.

COHESION The linking of clauses and sentences to make a text.

DESCRIPTIVE (INDICATIVE) ABSTRACT An abstract that states the purpose and topics of an article or report, but does not give the substance.

DICTION Word choice.

DOCUMENTATION Identification of sources of statements, graphics, and ideas.

ETYMOLOGY The history and original meaning of a word.

FORECASTING STATEMENT A statement that gives the reader a frame within which to place the material that follows.

GANTT CHART A chart that displays when particular substeps of a project will take place and when they will be completed.

GENRE A category of document, such as letter, memorandum, report, proposal, manual.

GRAMMATICAL PARALLELISM The use of the same grammatical structure for two or more items.

HIERARCHICAL RELATIONSHIP A relationship in which one member is superior to another.

INFORMATIVE ABSTRACT An abstract that summarizes the most important points of an article or report.

IN-HOUSE DOCUMENT A document addressed to a member of the writer's organization.

LAYOUT The placement of print and graphics on the page.

LETTERHEAD Stationery on which the source's name, address, and logo are printed.

MODIFIER An adjective or adverb, or an adjectival, adverbial, participial, or infinitive phrase or clause.

NOMINALIZATION A noun form that is related to a verb or an adjective. For example, *involvement* is a nominalization corresponding to the verb *to involve*.

OUT-OF-HOUSE DOCUMENT A document addressed to someone outside the writer's organization.

PARTICIPIAL PHRASE A phrase that begins with a present participle of a verb (ending in -ing) or a past participle of a verb (usually ending in -ed).

PARTITION The dividing of something into its parts.

PREPOSITIONAL PHRASE A phrase that begins with a preposition (with, in, on, over, by).

QUANTIFIER A word such as all, some, many, most, few or a phrase such as several of that refers to a quantity or portion.

READER-BASED PROSE Prose that is designed to meet the needs of the reader.

RELATIVE CLAUSE A clause that begins with who, which, or that and modifies a noun.

TRANSITION STATEMENT A statement that indicates that one part of a discourse or one topic is finished and another is about to begin.

TREE DIAGRAM A graphic device for displaying hierarchical relationships.

TYPOGRAPHY Sizes and types of print.

VENN DIAGRAM A diagram that shows the relationship between sets.

WRITER-BASED PROSE Prose that meets the needs of the writer.

YOU-ATTITUDE Giving explicit prominence to the point of view of the reader.

SELECTED BIBLIOGRAPHY

HANDBOOKS

Department of the Secretary of State. *The Canadian Style: A Guide to Writing and Editing.* Toronto: Dundurn, 1985.

Hodges, John C., Mary E. Whitten, Judy Brown, and Jane Flick. *Harbrace College Handbook for Canadian Writers.* 3d ed. Toronto: Harcourt Brace Jovanovich, 1990.

Messenger, William E., and Jan de Bruyn. *The Canadian Writer's Handbook.* 2d ed. Scarborough, ON: Prentice-Hall, 1986.

Willis, Hulon, and Enno Klammer. *A Brief Handbook of English.* 3d ed. New York: Harcourt Brace Jovanovich, 1986.

STYLE

Vande Kopple, William. *Clear and Coherent Prose: A Functional Approach.* Glenview, IL: Scott, Foresman, 1989.

Williams, Joseph M. *Style: Ten Lessons in Clarity & Grace.* 3d ed. Glenview, IL: Scott, Foresman, 1989.

GRAPHICS

Lefferts, Robert. *How to Prepare Charts and Graphs for Effective Reports.* New York: Barnes & Noble, 1981.

MacGregor, A.J. *Graphics Simplified: How to Plan and Prepare Effective Charts, Graphs, Illustrations, and Other Visual Aids.* Toronto: University of Toronto Press, 1979.

Scientific Illustration Committee of the CBE, *Illustrating Science: Standards for Publication.* Bethesda, MD: Council of Biology Editors, 1988.

Tufte, Edward R. *The Visual Display of Quantitative Information.* Cheshire, CT: Graphics Press, 1983.

ABSTRACTS

Cremmins, Edward T. *The Art of Abstracting.* Philadelphia: ISI Press, 1982.

PROPOSALS

Locke, Lawrence F., Waneen Wyrick Spirduso, and Stephen J. Silverman. *Proposals that Work: A Guide for Planning Dissertation and Grant Proposals.* Newbury Park, CA: SAGE, 1987.

Stewart, Rodney D., and Ann L. Stewart. *Proposal Preparation.* New York: John Wiley & Sons, 1984.

DESKTOP PUBLISHING

Carney, T.F. *Publishing by Microcomputer: Its Potential and Its Problems.* Cambridge, England: Peter Francis, 1988.

Miles, John. *Design for Desktop Publishing: A Guide to Layout and Typography on the Personal Computer.* San Francisco: Chronicle, 1987.

Shushan, Ronnie, and Don Wright. *Desktop Publishing Design.* Redmond, WA: Microsoft Press, 1989.

SCIENTIFIC ARTICLES

Day, Robert A. *How to Write and Publish a Scientific Paper.* 3d ed. Phoenix, AZ: Oryx, 1988.

Michaelson, Herbert. *How to Write and Publish Engineering Papers and Reports.* Philadelphia, PA: ISI Press, 1986.

INDEX

NOV 13 1995

NOV 13 1997